OTHER FAST FACTS BOOKS

D1246091

Fast Facts About PTSD: A Guide for Nurses and Other Health Care Professionals (*Adams*)

Fast Facts for the NEW NURSE PRACTITIONER: What You Really Need to Know in a Nutshell, 2e (*Aktan*)

Fast Facts for the ER NURSE: Emergency Department Orientation in a Nutshell, 3e (*Buettner*)

Fast Facts About GI AND LIVER DISEASES FOR NURSES: What APRNs Need to Know in a Nutshell (*Chaney*)

Fast Facts for the MEDICAL–SURGICAL NURSE: Clinical Orientation in a Nutshell (*Ciocco*)

Fast Facts on COMBATING NURSE BULLYING, INCIVILITY, AND WORKPLACE VIOLENCE: What Nurses Need to Know in a Nutshell (*Ciocco*)

Fast Facts for the NURSE PRECEPTOR: Keys to Providing a Successful Preceptorship in a Nutshell (*Ciocco*)

Fast Facts for the OPERATING ROOM NURSE: An Orientation and Care Guide in a Nutshell (*Criscitelli*)

Fast Facts for the ANTEPARTUM AND POSTPARTUM NURSE: A Nursing Orientation and Care Guide in a Nutshell (*Davidson*)

Fast Facts for the NEONATAL NURSE: A Nursing Orientation and Care Guide in a Nutshell (*Davidson*)

Fast Facts About PRESSURE ULCER CARE FOR NURSES: How to Prevent, Detect, and Resolve Them in a Nutshell (*Dziedzic*)

Fast Facts for the GERONTOLOGY NURSE: A Nursing Care Guide in a Nutshell (*Eliopoulos*)

Fast Facts for the LONG-TERM CARE NURSE: What Nursing Home and Assisted Living Nurses Need to Know in a Nutshell (*Eliopoulos*)

Fast Facts for the CLINICAL NURSE MANAGER: Managing a Changing Workplace in a Nutshell, 2e (*Fry*)

Fast Facts for EVIDENCE-BASED PRACTICE: Implementing EBP in a Nutshell, 2e (*Godshall*)

Fast Facts for Nurses About HOME INFUSION THERAPY: The Expert's Best Practice Guide in a Nutshell (*Gorski*)

Fast Facts About NURSING AND THE LAW: Law for Nurses in a Nutshell (*Grant, Ballard*)

Fast Facts for the L&D NURSE: Labor & Delivery Orientation in a Nutshell, 2e (*Groll*)

Fast Facts for the RADIOLOGY NURSE: An Orientation and Nursing Care Guide in a Nutshell (*Grossman*)

Fast Facts on ADOLESCENT HEALTH FOR NURSING AND HEALTH PROFESSIONALS: A Care Guide in a Nutshell (*Herrman*)

Fast Facts for the FAITH COMMUNITY NURSE: Implementing FCN/Parish Nursing in a Nutshell (*Hickman*)

Fast Facts for the CARDIAC SURGERY NURSE: Caring for Cardiac Surgery Patients in a Nutshell, 2e (*Hodge*)

Fast Facts About the NURSING PROFESSION: Historical Perspectives in a Nutshell (*Hunt*)

Fast Facts for the CLINICAL NURSING INSTRUCTOR: Clinical Teaching in a Nutshell, 3e (*Kan, Stabler-Haas*)

Fast Facts for the WOUND CARE NURSE: Practical Wound Management in a Nutshell (*Kifer*)

Fast Facts About EKGs FOR NURSES: The Rules of Identifying EKGs in a Nutshell (*Landrum*)

Fast Facts for the CRITICAL CARE NURSE: Critical Care Nursing in a Nutshell (*Landrum*)

Fast Facts for the TRAVEL NURSE: Travel Nursing in a Nutshell (*Landrum*)

Fast Facts for the SCHOOL NURSE: School Nursing in a Nutshell, 2e (*Loschiavo*)

Fast Facts for MANAGING PATIENTS WITH A PSYCHIATRIC DISORDER: What RNs, NPs, and New Psych Nurses Need to Know (*Marshall*)

Fast Facts About CURRICULUM DEVELOPMENT IN NURSING: How to Develop & Evaluate Educational Programs in a Nutshell (*McCoy, Anema*)

Fast Facts for DEMENTIA CARE: What Nurses Need to Know in a Nutshell (*Miller*)

Fast Facts for HEALTH PROMOTION IN NURSING: Promoting Wellness in a Nutshell (*Miller*)

Fast Facts for STROKE CARE NURSING: An Expert Guide in a Nutshell (*Morrison*)

Fast Facts for the MEDICAL OFFICE NURSE: What You Really Need to Know in a Nutshell (*Richmeier*)

Fast Facts for the PEDIATRIC NURSE: An Orientation Guide in a Nutshell (*Rupert, Young*)

Fast Facts About the GYNECOLOGICAL EXAM FOR NURSE PRACTITIONERS: Conducting the GYN Exam in a Nutshell (*Secor, Fantasia*)

Fast Facts for the STUDENT NURSE: Nursing Student Success in a Nutshell (*Stabler-Haas*)

Fast Facts for CAREER SUCCESS IN NURSING: Making the Most of Mentoring in a Nutshell (*Vance*)

Fast Facts for the TRIAGE NURSE: An Orientation and Care Guide in a Nutshell (*Visser, (Montejano, Grossman*)

Fast Facts for DEVELOPING A NURSING ACADEMIC PORTFOLIO: What You Really Need to Know in a Nutshell (*Wittmann-Price*)

Fast Facts for the HOSPICE NURSE: A Concise Guide to End-of-Life Care (*Wright*)

Fast Facts for the CLASSROOM NURSING INSTRUCTOR: Classroom Teaching in a Nutshell (*Yoder-Wise, Kowalski*)

Forthcoming FAST FACTS Books

Fast Facts for the OPERATING ROOM NURSE: An Orientation and Care Guide in a Nutshell, 2e (*Criscitelli*)

Fast Facts for TESTING AND EVALUATION IN NURSING: Teaching Skills in a Nutshell (*Dusaj*)

Fast Facts for the CRITICAL CARE NURSE: Critical Care Nursing in a Nutshell, 2e (*Landrum*)

Fast Facts About CURRICULUM DEVELOPMENT IN NURSING: How to Develop and Evaluate Educational Programs in a Nutshell, 2e (*McCoy, Anema*)

Fast Facts About the GYNECOLOGIC EXAM: A Professional Guide for NPs, PAs, and Midwives, 2e (*Secor, Fantasia*)

FAST FACTS
About **PTSD**

Lisa Y. Adams, PhD, MSc, RN, has a 25-year history of progressive leadership positions in the areas of seniors, mental health, and addictions. She has conducted eight peer-reviewed research studies and has published 22 articles, and is currently working with a professor from Harvard University to publish many more. Dr. Adams is an active volunteer in a variety of organizations in Newfoundland, Canada, and is a member of many professional associations in both Canada and the United States. She is also an award-winning author who has been recognized by the *Journal of American Nursing* for her previously published book, *Workplace Mental Health Manual for Nurse Managers* (Springer Publishing, 2014).

FAST FACTS
About **PTSD**

A Guide for Nurses and Other Health Care Professionals

Lisa Y. Adams, PhD, MSc, RN

SPRINGER PUBLISHING COMPANY
NEW YORK

Springer Publishing Company, LLC
11 West 42nd Street
New York, NY 10036
www.springerpub.com

Acquisitions Editor: Margaret Zuccarini
Senior Production Editor: Kris Parrish
Compositor: Westchester Publishing Services

ISBN: 978-0-8261-7008-8
ebook ISBN: 978-0-8261-7009-5

17 18 19 20 / 5 4 3 2 1

The author and the publisher of this Work have made every effort to use sources believed to be reliable to provide information that is accurate and compatible with the standards generally accepted at the time of publication. Because medical science is continually advancing, our knowledge base continues to expand. Therefore, as new information becomes available, changes in procedures become necessary. We recommend that the reader always consult current research and specific institutional policies before performing any clinical procedure. The author and publisher shall not be liable for any special, consequential, or exemplary damages resulting, in whole or in part, from the readers' use of, or reliance on, the information contained in this book. The publisher has no responsibility for the persistence or accuracy of URLs for external or third-party Internet websites referred to in this publication and does not guarantee that any content on such websites is, or will remain, accurate or appropriate.

Library of Congress Cataloging-in-Publication Data

Names: Adams, Lisa Y., 1968- author.
Title: Fast facts about PTSD : a guide for nurses and other health care professionals / Lisa Y. Adams.
Description: New York, NY : Springer Publishing Company, LLC, [2018] | Includes bibliographical references and index.
Identifiers: LCCN 2017016198 (print) | LCCN 2017018901 (ebook) | ISBN 9780826170095 (ebook) | ISBN 9780826170088 (hard copy : alk. paper)
Subjects: | MESH: Stress Disorders, Post-Traumatic
Classification: LCC RC552.P67 (ebook) | LCC RC552.P67 (print) | NLM WM 172.5 | DDC 616.85/21—dc23
LC record available at https://lccn.loc.gov/2017016198

Printed in the United States of America.

*This book is dedicated to all of those who are suffering
or have suffered with PTSD, particularly frontline emergency responders
and military personnel with combat experience, and also
to the innocent citizens who have suffered at the hands of terrorists
and to those caught in unnecessary wars. The world needs to pay
attention to your suffering and respond with love, compassion,
and hope so that you may rise above the mental anguish and hurt
and grow stronger as people, citizens, and spiritual beings.*

Contents

Preface

Mental health and mental illness are everyone's business and permeate all sectors of society and all people. Although beliefs about mental health vary across cultures, generations, and ages, the reality of posttraumatic stress disorder (PTSD) has emerged as a growing concern in recent years. The definition of *mental health* as employed by the World Health Organization (WHO, 2014, para. 1) is "a state of well-being in which every individual realizes his or her own potential, can cope with the normal stresses of life, can work productively and fruitfully, and is able to make a contribution to her or his community." All components of this definition present the challenges that individuals with PTSD face daily.

One thing that is universally accepted about PTSD is the effort required by health care professionals to care for individuals suffering from different degrees of PTSD. Although many interventions exist for health care professionals to use for their patients with PTSD, it is critical to remember that all individuals respond differently not only to the trauma and stress experienced, but also to the treatment regimens and support that are available to them. Hence, an individualized approach to assessment, diagnosis, and treatment is always a must.

It is hoped that this guide will help the health care clinician better understand the effects of trauma, what the assessment of PTSD should entail, and what interventions are most effective. Recognizing, understanding, and having an increased awareness of PTSD, as well as identifying who it impacts and how it does so, are important if health care clinicians are to work together to implement appropriate interventions and obtain the best possible outcomes for all involved. Although this guide is surely nonexhaustive, it is a great starting point for those working with individuals who are suffering from PTSD.

Lisa Y. Adams

Reference

World Health Organization. (2014). Mental health: A state of well-being. Retrieved from http://www.who.int/features/factfiles/mental_health/en

I

The Beginnings
of PTSD

1

Understanding Stress, Mental Health, and Mental Illness

Both mental health and mental illness are a concern for all age groups of people in society. Beliefs about mental health vary across cultures, generations, and ages. Physical health and mental health have a mutual relationship—a change in one can prompt a change in the other. Hence, when physical or mental health becomes compromised and impacts the other, an individual can find it exceedingly difficult to function without intervention(s). Posttraumatic stress disorder (PTSD), an increasing concern in recent years, is an example of this mutual relationship. PTSD touches many lives, families, workplaces, and societies. Because it is a challenging illness to work with, health care clinicians need to be armed with as much knowledge and expertise as possible to reach the most deeply impacted individuals. Individualizing treatment for patients who suffer from PTSD is a priority; hence, a clinician's knowledge, assessments skills, and competency to intervene are all critical parameters.

In this chapter, you will learn:

■ An understanding of the meaning of mental health and mental illness

(*continued*)

- How stress is significant to one's mental health and a precipitator of mental illness
- Common signs and symptoms of stress
- Common causes or origins of mental illness

STRESS

Stress results from the life we live, the environment around us, the people with whom we interact, and the events that make up our days. It is one of life's paradoxical conditions because we find stress hard to live with and we cannot live without it; hence, it has both positive and negative effects. However, when there is too much stress or an escalated level of stressors, and we are unable to cope with them, stress becomes "ugly."

A stressor is any event, object, occurrence, or situation that an individual perceives as a threat, whether it is an actual or perceived threat. It is the tensions that we face every day where stressors signal our body to adapt to the current environment or to stay and fight them off to protect ourselves or seek flight from them, as if to escape injury/harm or the threat of injury/harm.

However, the benefits of stress often go unnoticed. Were it not for stress, individuals would be unmotivated, unengaged, and less productive, not to mention out of shape and with a "flaccid" brain, so to speak. Although stress is often associated with negativity and viewed as something to avoid, this is not always the case.

Stress can be good; it serves various purposes, such as charging us for productivity, engaging us to perform everyday activities at home and at work, and driving us to succeed in our goals. It keeps our neurons in check and healthy. Furthermore, stress is also responsible for us being able to escape harm or danger. Stress triggers bodily and brain processes that prepare us to fight or flight when faced with a fearful event, danger, or catastrophe. Hence, stress makes possible our survival.

However, when we are unable to bounce back from bad stress with our coping defenses, mechanisms, and brain and body processes, bad stress then turns ugly. Bad stress becomes stuck and we are not able to handle an event or situation; we feel overwhelmed and our body is finding it difficult to adapt. When we begin to lose our focus, concentration, and vision, stress becomes ugly.

Common Signs of Stress

The American Institute of Stress (2017) recognizes 50 common signs of stress:

1. Frequent headaches, jaw clenching, or pain
2. Gritting, grinding of teeth
3. Stuttering or stammering
4. Tremors, trembling of lips and hands
5. Neck ache, back pain, muscle spasms
6. Light headedness, faintness, dizziness
7. Ringing, buzzing, or popping sounds
8. Frequent blushing, sweating
9. Cold or sweaty hands and feet
10. Dry mouth, problems swallowing
11. Frequent colds, infections, herpes sores
12. Rashes, itching, hives, "goose bumps"
13. Unexplained or frequent "allergy" attacks
14. Heartburn, stomach pain, nausea
15. Excess belching, flatulence
16. Constipation, diarrhea, loss of bowel control
17. Difficulty breathing, frequent sighing
18. Sudden attacks of life-threatening panic
19. Chest pain, palpitations, rapid pulse
20. Frequent urination
21. Diminished sexual desire or performance
22. Excess anxiety, worry, guilt, nervousness
23. Increased anger, frustration, hostility
24. Depression, frequent or wild mood swings
25. Increased or decreased appetite
26. Insomnia, nightmares, disturbing dreams
27. Difficulty concentrating, racing thoughts
28. Trouble learning new information
29. Forgetfulness, disorganization, confusion
30. Difficulty in making decisions
31. Feeling overloaded or overwhelmed
32. Frequent crying spells or suicidal thoughts
33. Feelings of loneliness or worthlessness
34. Little interest in appearance, punctuality
35. Nervous habits, fidgeting, feet tapping
36. Increased frustration, irritability, edginess
37. Overreaction to petty annoyances

38. Increased number of minor accidents
39. Obsessive or compulsive behavior
40. Reduced work efficiency or productivity
41. Lies or excuses to cover up poor work
42. Rapid or mumbled speech
43. Excessive defensiveness or suspiciousness
44. Problems in communication and the sharing of information
45. Social withdrawal and isolation
46. Constant tiredness, weakness, fatigue
47. Frequent use of over-the-counter drugs
48. Weight gain or loss without diet
49. Increased smoking, alcohol, or drug use
50. Excessive gambling or impulse buying

Fast Facts

The level of stress one has or experiences has a direct correlation and impact on one's mental health and the development of a mental illness.

ANXIETY

Anxiety is a bodily process that can develop as a result of stress that we are having difficulty handling. As a recognized disorder in the *Diagnostic and Statistical Manual of Mental Disorders*, Fifth Edition (*DSM-5*; American Psychiatric Association, 2013), it can manifest itself in many different ways, each having some common underlying symptomatology. Although there are various anxiety disorders, we highlight two of the most common in this chapter, namely generalized anxiety disorder and panic disorder.

Generalized Anxiety Disorder

Individuals with this disorder have an excessive amount of anxiety and worry that can occur for months and even years. As a result, they deal with multiple stressors at once. Generalized anxiety disorder symptoms include:

- Restlessness or feeling wound up or on edge
- Being easily fatigued

- Difficulty concentrating or having one's mind go blank
- Irritability
- Muscle tension
- Difficulty controlling worry
- Sleep problems (difficulty falling or staying asleep or restless, unsatisfying sleep; National Institute of Mental Health [NIMH], 2016)

Panic Disorder

Individuals suffering from panic disorder feel overwhelmed and dysfunctional. They have sudden and unexpected panic attacks, which are characterized as sudden periods of escalated and intense fear so intense that the individuals feel they are losing or have lost control of themselves. These panic attacks elicit the following symptoms:

- Palpitations, pounding heart, or accelerated heart rate; some individuals even feel like they may be having a heart attack
- Sweating
- Trembling or shaking
- Sensations of shortness of breath, smothering, or choking
- Feeling of impending doom (NIMH, 2016)

MENTAL HEALTH

Mental health is very closely related to stress. According to the World Health Organization (WHO, 2014, para. 1), mental health is defined as "a state of well-being in which every individual realizes his or her own potential, can cope with the normal stresses of life, can work productively and fruitfully, and is able to make a contribution to her or his community." One of the key concepts in the definition of mental health is stress and the fact that normal stressors can be dealt with appropriately. However, it is when these stressors are overwhelming and are unable to be dealt with in a normal manner that we begin to see mental health becoming compromised. There are many early warning signs of mental health becoming compromised, where one or more of the following feelings/emotions and/or behaviors occur:

- Eating or sleeping too much or too little
- Pulling away from people and usual activities
- Having low or no energy

- Feeling numb or like nothing matters
- Having unexplained aches and pains
- Feeling helpless or hopeless
- Smoking, drinking, or using drugs more than usual
- Feeling unusually confused, forgetful, on edge, angry, upset, worried, or scared
- Yelling or fighting with family and friends
- Experiencing severe mood swings that cause problems in relationships
- Having persistent thoughts and memories you cannot get out of your head
- Hearing voices or believing things that are not true
- Thinking of harming yourself or others
- Inability to perform daily tasks, such as taking care of your kids or getting to work or school (U.S. Department of Health and Human Services, 2017)

Fast Facts

When faced with high levels of stress, we need to be able to cope effectively so as to maintain good mental health.

MENTAL ILLNESS

As stated, there is a relationship between mental health and mental illness. A mental illness develops when an individual's mental health becomes compromised for a very prolonged period of time and the body and brain are unable to deal with it or recover. This occurs when one's coping mechanisms and degree of adaptability are unable to meet the demands of stress to the point that one is unable to function normally in everyday life. Essentially, the mind becomes overwhelmed. As defined by Mayo Clinic (2015), "Mental illness refers to a wide range of mental health conditions—disorders that affect your mood, thinking and behavior" (para. 1). We all have mental health concerns from time to time, such as when there is a death of a loved one, but the majority of us are able to bounce back to normal with the help of our defense mechanisms, coping skills, and the presence of other factors that give us strength such as our social support network and our spirituality.

Many of the symptoms associated with mental illness overlap with those we have already experienced from stress, anxiety, or when mental health become compromised. At this point, an individual finds it increasingly difficult to function in everyday living. Some of these symptoms, depending on the mental illness that an individual manifests, are:

- Feeling sad or down
- Confused thinking or reduced ability to concentrate
- Excessive fears or worries, or extreme feelings of guilt
- Extreme mood changes of highs and lows
- Withdrawal from friends and activities
- Significant tiredness, low energy, or problems sleeping
- Detachment from reality (delusions), paranoia, or hallucinations
- Inability to cope with daily problems or stress
- Trouble understanding and relating to situations and to people
- Alcohol or drug abuse
- Major changes in eating habits
- Sex drive changes
- Excessive anger, hostility, or violence
- Suicidal thinking
- Sometimes, symptoms of a mental health disorder appear as physical problems, such as stomach pain, back pain, headache, or other unexplained aches and pains (Mayo Clinic, 2015)

ETIOLOGY OF MENTAL ILLNESS

The etiology of mental illness remains a mystery. In our discussion, it is perhaps best to approach this topic from the perspective that factors such as excessive stress act to increase one's predisposition to the development of mental illness. An individual's predisposition to the development of a mental illness does not often occur from a lone source. In fact, it often arises from many sources. These sources can be internal or external to the individual. Internal causes of mental illness have been researched and found to be closely associated with genetics, chemical/neurotransmitter levels, internal injury/disease processes, and psychological/emotional health.

External causes of mental illness are many, but similar to internal sources, they often do not act alone. External causes include the people with whom we interact and the environment in which we live. Whatever those experiences with events/objects and/or people look like and how they unfold can determine, significantly, one's risk of developing mental illness. At a people level, a difficult colleague, a playground bully, and a manipulative mother can all create escalated levels of stress and weaken one's ability to cope and hence precipitate the onset of a mental illness. At an environmental level, our surroundings and the events or situations, whether natural or man-made, can all weaken our psyche, challenge our coping, and interfere with our ability to adapt. Situations or events at this level may include losing our house or loved one in a hurricane, abusing drugs, receiving a diagnosis of terminal cancer, being in an intensive care unit postoperatively, or working at a stressful frontline job where you see people being harmed or dying on a regular basis.

There are many different etiologies of mental illness depending on individual experiences. Although the exact cause of mental illness has been debated for years, it remains a gray area. When we talk about causes of mental illness, we typically focus on core sources, such as biological, psychological, environmental, and life's lived experiences or some combination thereof.

The following is a list of some of the identified causes of mental illness; it is not an exhaustive list:

- Biological
  - Brain biochemistry and neurotransmitters
  - Brain injury (acquired)
  - Infection
  - Genetics
  - Congenital abnormalities (caused when an expectant mother abuses opioids, for example)
  - Poor nutrition
- Psychological
  - Abuse—emotional, sexual, physical
  - Neglect or dysfunctional parenting/raising
  - Normal but significant life events (loss of a loved one)
- Environmental
  - Disasters (natural or man-made)
  - Violence
  - Accidents (Katz, Cojucar, Beheshti, Nakamura, & Murray, 2012)

In this chapter, you have studied the fundamentals of stress, mental health, and mental disorders. Practicing clinicians, I am certain, have their own views and an even more enriched definition than I have provided. However, for growing and aspiring clinicians, this serves as a beginning to understand the impact of stress, how mental health becomes compromised, and how the existence of anxiety and other mental illnesses can arise as a result of unresolved or overwhelming stress.

References

American Institute of Stress. (2017). Stress effects. Retrieved from http://www.stress.org/stress-effects

American Psychiatric Association. (2013). *Diagnostic and statistical manual of mental disorders* (5th ed.). Arlington, VA: American Psychiatric Publishing.

Katz, L., Cojucar, G., Beheshti, S., Nakamura, E., & Murray, M. (2012). Military sexual trauma during combat: Prevalence, readjustment, and gender differences in those deployed in the conflicts in Iraq and Afghanistan. *Violence and Victims, 27*(4), 487–499.

Mayo Clinic. (2015). Mental illness: Definition. Retrieved from http://www.mayoclinic.org/diseases-conditions/mental-illness/basics/definition/con-20033813

National Institute of Mental Health. (2016). Anxiety disorders. Retrieved from https://www.nimh.nih.gov/health/topics/anxiety-disorders/index.shtml

U.S. Department of Health and Human Services. (2017). What is mental health? Retrieved from https://www.mentalhealth.gov/basics/what-is-mental-health

World Health Organization. (2014). Mental health: A state of well-being. Retrieved from http://www.who.int/features/factfiles/mental_health/en

2

Trauma

We would be remiss in our discussion of posttraumatic stress disorder (PTSD) if we did not include a discussion about trauma. Trauma is the underlying and critical focus that needs to be recognized and understood if health care clinicians are to do due diligence in their care of individuals suffering from PTSD. Although the epidemiology of PTSD varies globally and there exist many causes of PTSD, its presence is a significant societal concern as many people, societies, and communities are impacted. For those for whom trauma arises from more local matters, such as domestic violence, rape, childhood abuse, and so on, the identification of an increased risk for the development of PTSD is of great value given that the symptomatology is not necessarily immediate and/or obvious. The prevention of the effects of trauma occurs at many levels: primary, secondary, and tertiary. Unequivocally, the development of PTSD depends on various parameters of the trauma experienced, inclusive but not exhaustive of severity, intensity, duration of exposure, immediacy, and so forth.

In this chapter, you will learn:

- What trauma is
- How trauma relates to mental health and the potential development of PTSD
- How trauma can be classified
- The importance of fear as it relates to trauma

WHAT IS TRAUMA?

Trauma is a very individualized and personal thing: "What traumatizes one person can be of less significance to others. This variation in people's reactions occurs because of their individual personality, beliefs, personal values, and previous experiences (especially from other traumatic events in their life). It also occurs because each person's experience of the incident is unique. However, in all cases the individual has experienced a threatening event that has caused him/her to respond with intense fear, helplessness, or horror" (Veterans Affairs Canada, 2015, para. 1). According to the Crisis and Trauma Resource Institute (2017), "trauma is a wound that injures us emotionally, psychologically and physiologically. Trauma occurs when a person experiences a threat, including sexual violence, to physical and/or psychological survival of oneself or a close family member or friend" (p. 1). This can be a single, onetime event or repetitious in nature, and is often unexpected and shocking to the individual. It can occur anywhere, any place, and any time, and at one's home, one's work, or in one's community. More commonly, trauma results from exposure to repeated or prolonged stressors (e.g., childhood abuse or neglect, domestic violence, experiences during war) that occur within specific types of relationships (e.g., partner/spousal, parent–child) or other closed contexts (e.g., military unit, school; Toronto Psychology Centre, 2016).

Fast Facts

The impact of trauma on any individual depends on how it is perceived.

TRAUMA, MENTAL HEALTH, AND PTSD

The significance of trauma has gained increasing recognition in recent years as civil unrest, terrorism, war, and military involvement threaten and occur globally. On the local level, events of accidents, neglect, and abuse also occur. Advanced technology and more open communication and information highways enable us to see the outside world and these events more easily and readily, bringing the existence of these traumatic events into our awareness, our homes, our lives, and our minds. For health care professionals, frontline emergency response personnel, and military in combat, who seek to protect or care for people, the effects of trauma have become all too common.

The relationship between trauma and PTSD is important to understand. Hence, it should be carefully defined with clarification how one impacts the other and the ultimate potential outcome for individuals experiencing either. Although trauma is often thought of as physical injuries, it extends far beyond that, particularly affecting our mental well-being.

Trauma is the personal experience of interpersonal violence, including sexual abuse, physical abuse, severe neglect, loss, and/or the witnessing of violence, terrorism, and/or disasters (National Executive Training Institute [NETI], 2005). As you will come to better understand, trauma can impact every aspect of our existence and being.

The magnitude of trauma from a psychological perspective is important for health care providers to acknowledge and understand so that their knowledge, expertise, and required interventions can be successfully translated into practice. Examples of trauma include a natural disaster, physical or sexual abuse, rape, motor vehicle accidents (MVAs), domestic violence, war, and terrorism—more to be discussed later. Furthermore, disasters such as hurricanes, earthquakes, and floods can claim lives, destroy homes or whole communities, and cause serious physical and psychological injuries. The September 11, 2001, terrorist attack in the United States is one significant example. Mass shootings in schools or communities and physical or sexual assaults are other examples. Traumatic events threaten people's sense of physical and psychological safety.

The effects of trauma can be devastating especially when they are out of one's control. According to the Crisis and Trauma Resource Institute (2017), we "each have innate capabilities to respond to such situations and return to a state of equilibrium. However, if the intensity of the situation overwhelms our resilience, often with intense helplessness, shame or terror, and we are not able to re-establish a sense of relative safety, our built-in survival mechanisms remain on high alert continually responding to threat; thus, we become traumatized" (p. 1). The experience of traumatic events exerts a multifold negative impact on every aspect of our lives and society. We may begin to view ourselves and our capabilities negatively, damaging our self-esteem. Negative feelings about ourselves spill over into how we view others and the world. Hence, we become fearful of a world or environment that is unsafe, unpredictable, and/or with a damaged structure. In any event, our bodies become overstimulated and our nervous system hyperaroused, leaving us feeling like we are always on the alert for danger or situations and/or people who are threatening. This state of hyperarousal can create many physiological manifestations such as irritability, short-tempered, headache, hypertension, pain, and gastrointestinal symptoms (such as diarrhea) from an increased peristalsis (Toronto Psychology Centre, 2016).

Trauma early in life includes child abuse, neglect, witnessing violence, and disrupted attachment; later traumatic experiences include violence, accidents, natural disaster, war, sudden unexpected loss, and other life events (Taylor, 2007). Experiences such as these can interfere with a person's sense of safety, self and self-efficacy, as well as the ability to regulate emotions and navigate relationships. People who have experienced trauma commonly feel terror, shame, helplessness, and powerlessness (Poole & Greaves, 2012).

Psychological trauma is an emotionally painful, shocking, stressful, and sometimes life-threatening experience (including witnessing events) that may involve physical injuries, but it also can happen without physical injury. More formally, psychological trauma is defined as "the unique individual experience of an event or enduring conditions, in which the individual's ability to integrate his or her emotional experience is overwhelmed or the individual experiences (subjectively) a threat to life, bodily integrity, or sanity (threats to one's mental health)" (Pearlman & Saakvitne, 1995, p. 60). As the brain is the major organ that stands most vulnerable during psychological trauma, it is often one's perception of the traumatic event that predicts the impact the event may exert. A person needs only to perceive an event to be threatening for his or her nervous system to react fully in a survival manner. Hence, unresolved trauma leaves a person more vulnerable to experience trauma with later events (Crisis and Trauma Resource Institute, 2017). If trauma is left unresolved, the underlying neuropathophysiology of the trauma that later precipitates the development of PTSD is particularly complex.

PATHOPHYSIOLOGY OF TRAUMA

In addition to the external environmental trauma and perceptions of the individual that initiate the possible development of PTSD, the neuropathophysiology of trauma sets the foundation for it. From complex neurophysiological and neurobiological interactions and processes, abnormalities arising from the dysregulation of adrenergic, hypothalamic–pituitary–adrenocortical (HPA), monoaminergic, peptide, glutamatergic, GABAergic, cannabinoid, opioid, and other neurotransmitter and neuroendocrine systems unfold into what we have come to know as PTSD (Friedman & Bernardy, 2016).

The clinical course of trauma and eventual PTSD is driven by pathophysiological changes in the amygdala and hippocampus (Vieweg et al., 2006). The amygdala activation during traumatic exposure ignites a sudden cascade of psychobiological mechanisms that are initially protective but, if sustained, are associated with PTSD (Friedman & Bernardy, 2016). Research has shown that exposure to traumatic stimuli can lead to fear conditioning, with resultant activation of the amygdala and associated structures, such as the hypothalamus, locus ceruleus, periaqueductal gray, and parabrachial nucleus. This activation and the accompanying autonomic neurotransmitter and endocrine activity produce many of the symptoms of PTSD that we see clinically (Gore, 2015). Gore (2015) adds that the orbito-prefrontal cortex and hippocampus also exert an inhibiting effect on this activation. However, in people who develop PTSD, the orbito-prefrontal cortex appears to be "less capable of inhibiting this activation, possibly due to stress-induced atrophy of specific nuclei in this region" (Gore, 2015, "Etiology" para. 3). Although the HPA axis plays a significant role in the stress response, adaptation to stress, and the maintenance of homeostasis (Kudielka & Kirschbaum, 2005), any dysfunction in the HPA axis becomes manifested as numerous psychosomatic and psychiatric disorders (Tsigos & Chrousos, 2002). Furthermore, via the HPA axis when faced with stress the hypothalamus releases increased amounts of the neurotransmitter corticotropin-releasing factor (CRF) and hence cortisol, which together encode the memories of trauma and the effects of anxiety (Bailey, Cordell, Sobin, & Neumeister, 2013; Hubbard, Nakashima, Lee, & Takahashi, 2007).

Fast Facts

Trauma can jeopardize one's good mental health.

TYPES OF TRAUMA

There are a number of dimensions that affect how an individual responds to and copes with trauma. These dimensions include magnitude, complexity, frequency, duration, and whether it occurs from an interpersonal or external source. As trauma and traumatic events are perceived differently by each individual experiencing it, this underlying premise helps to determine, explain, and predict an individual's response. These dimensions can be seen in the descriptions of the following four types of trauma.

Single incident or shock trauma is related to an unexpected and overwhelming event, such as an accident, natural disaster, a single episode of abuse or assault, sudden loss, or witnessing violence. Shock trauma occurs when a person has a shock reaction to a traumatic event. It usually involves high levels of activation from the nervous system as the person reacts from deep, primitive instincts. Often the event(s) is/are very sudden and/or extremely severe but not always. For example, medical procedures can be planned and still have a traumatic effect. Traumatic loss is another distinct form of shock trauma. Examples here include surgeries, dental procedures, MVAs, falls, plane crashes (or near misses), natural disasters such as earthquakes, flood, fires, and hurricanes, stillbirth, miscarriages, sudden infant death syndrome (SIDS), tragic death of any loved one, and terminal illness diagnosis (Crisis and Trauma Resource Institute, 2017).

Complex/repetitive or relational trauma is related to ongoing abuse, domestic violence, war, or ongoing betrayal, often involving being trapped emotionally and/or physically. Generally, it is an experience of threat from another person that adds a layer of violation and disruption. The impact is especially complicated if the source of the threat is someone in a position of trust or supposed to be in the safe realm for the individual. Examples here include war, terrorism, genocide, political conflicts, bullying, violence, robbery, physical or sexual assault, domestic violence, and abuse in the family (Crisis and Trauma Resource Institute, 2017).

Both sudden traumatic events and repeated or prolonged traumatic exposure may lead to the development of PTSD. However, when the trauma is perpetrated by another human being, particularly if inflicted intentionally, there is a greater likelihood of developing PTSD. Additionally, cumulative interpersonal trauma, such as child abuse, can result in more severe and pervasive symptoms and problems; it is here that it becomes complex trauma (Toronto Psychology Centre, 2016).

Developmental trauma results from exposure to early ongoing or repetitive trauma (as infants, children, and youth) involving neglect, abandonment, physical abuse or assault, sexual abuse or assault, emotional abuse, witnessing violence or death, and/or coercion or betrayal. This often occurs within the child's caregiving system and interferes with healthy attachment and development. In particular, the optimal development of the child's nervous system is interrupted. Furthermore, experiences of developmental trauma can make a person more vulnerable to later experiences of trauma (Crisis and Trauma Resource Institute, 2017).

Intergenerational trauma or historical trauma, as it is sometimes called, describes the psychological or emotional wounds that can be experienced by people who have endured significant trauma. These wounds span over generations and life times and are often inflicted by subjugating and dominant populations. Families and survivors of genocides such as the Holocaust, slavery, war, colonialism, the Civil Rights Movement, and groups of people or subpopulations such as the Native and Aboriginal people who have been demeaned and ostracized for years by Western civilizations would experience and pass on those lived experiences to future generations (Bombay, Matheson, & Anisman, 2009).

Coping and adaptation patterns developed in response to trauma are passed from one generation to the next. As Castelloe (2012) describes, legacies, rituals, stories, and practices, either consciously or unconsciously, passed down from elders to children, maintain the flow of trauma, anxiety, and behavioral adaptations to what was once traumatically unthinkable, avoided, unforgivable, and fearful. Bombay et al. (2009) add that the transmission of traumatic negativity produces long-lasting ramifications on people's overall well-being, appraisal processes, coping styles, lifestyles, life's choices, parental behaviors, one's sense of controllability, predictability, and ambiguity, as well as behavioral and neuronal reactivity, and may also have long-lasting repercussions on physical and psychological health and hence increases one's predisposition to the development of mental illnesses, such as depression, anxiety, PTSD, and substance abuse disorder.

As we have noted, trauma comes in many forms and has no boundaries or exemptions for how and whom it may impact. Whether it arises internally or externally, or under one's control or not, it is still the uniqueness of all of us, as humans, that determines how we respond to it.

UNDERSTANDING FEAR

Fear is the accompanying emotion that is expressed with trauma. Psychologically, fear can be an emotion and/or feeling. Initially manifested as a feeling and one that we react to, we develop fear as a subjective feeling that creates a sense of uneasiness, discomfort, and/or an unconscious perception of a real or perceived threat or danger. Once this feeling of fear to an object or event becomes a conscious reality and is internalized, it then manifests itself as an emotion (Roy, 2010).

The experience of fear for individuals suffering from PTSD is quite different from what is normally experienced. According to new research, the brain of someone with PTSD abnormally processes and generalizes nonthreatening objects or events as if they were in fact related to the original trauma source (Nauert, 2017). In a study from the Duke University School of Medicine and the Durham VA Medical Center, it was found that areas of the brain function differently among people with PTSD. The abnormal brain processing caused them to generalize nonthreatening events as if they were the original trauma. Hence, "this generalization process leads to a proliferation of symptoms over time as patients generalize to a variety of new triggers" (Morey, as cited in Preidt, 2015, para. 9). Furthermore, as Park (2012) reminds us to consider, "it's not individual traumatic events that have the most impact, but the cumulative effect of a lifetime's worth of stress that might cause the most dramatic changes in brain volume" (para. 2).

References

Bailey, C. R., Cordell, E., Sobin, S. M., & Neumeister, A. (2013). Recent progress in understanding the pathophysiology of post-traumatic stress disorder: Implications for targeted pharmacological treatment. *CNS Drugs*, *27*(3), 221–232. doi:10.1007/s40263-013-0051-4

Bombay, A., Matheson, K., & Anisman, H. (2009). Convergence of multiple processes among First Nations peoples in Canada. *International Journal of Indigenous Health*, *5*(3), 6–47.

Castelloe, M. (2012). How trauma is carried across generations. Retrieved from https://www.psychologytoday.com/blog/the-me-in-we/201205/how-trauma-is-carried-across-generations

Crisis & Trauma Resource Institute. (2017). Understanding trauma. Retrieved from http://ca.ctrinstitute.com/wp-content/uploads/2017/03/Understanding-Trauma.pdf

Friedman, M. J., & Bernardy, N. C. (2016). Considering future pharmacotherapy for PTSD. *Neuroscience Letters*, *S0304-3940*(16), 30900-4. doi:10.1016/j.neulet.2016.11.048

Gore, T. A. (2015). Posttraumatic stress disorder. In I. Ahmed, *Medscape*. Retrieved from http://emedicine.medscape.com/article/288154-overview

Hubbard, D. T., Nakashima, B. R., Lee, I., & Takahashi, L. K. (2007). Activation of basolateral amygdala corticotropin-releasing factor 1 receptors modulates the consolidation of contextual fear. *Neuroscience*, *150*(4), 818–828.

Kudielka, B. M., & Kirschbaum, C. (2005). Sex differences in HPA axis responses to stress: A review. *Biological Psychology*, *69*(1), 113–132.

National Executive Training Institute. (2005). *Training curriculum for reduction of seclusion and restraint. Draft curriculum manual*. Alexandria, VA: National Association of State Mental Health Program Directors, National Technical Assistance Center for State Mental Health Planning.

Nauert, R. (2017). PTSD patients have different brain response to fear. Retrieved from http://psychcentral.com/news/2015/12/16/ptsd-patients-have-different-brain-response-to-fear/96304.html

Park, A. (2012). Study: Stress shrinks the brain and lowers our ability to cope with adversity. Retrieved from http://healthland.time.com/2012/01/09/study-stress-shrinks-the-brain-and-lowers-our-ability-to-cope-with-adversity/#ixzz25MXqR2Xc

Pearlman, L. A., & Saakvitne, K. W. (1995). *Trauma and the therapist*. New York, NY: Norton.

Poole, N., & Greaves, L. (Ed.) (2012). *Becoming trauma informed*. Toronto, ON, Canada: Centre for Addiction and Mental Health.

Preidt, B. (2015). Study maps areas of brain linked to PTSD. Retrieved from https://consumer.healthday.com/mental-health-information-25/post-traumatic-stress-disorder-news-773/study-maps-areas-of-brain-linked-to-ptsd-706184.htm

Roy, S. (2013). The psychology of fear. Retrieved from http://www.wakingtimes.com/2013/10/31/psychology-of-fear

Taylor, S. (2007). Post-traumatic stress disorder: Choosing the treatment that is right for you. *Visions*, *3*(3), 23–24.

Toronto Psychology Centre. (2016). Trauma and abuse. Retrieved from http://torontopsychologycentre.com/areas-of-focus/trauma-and-abuse

Tsigos, C., & Chrousos, G. P. (2002). Hypothalamic-pituitary-adrenal axis, neuroendocrine factors and stress. *Journal of Psychosomatic Research*, *53*(4), 865–871.

Veterans Affairs Canada. (2015). Post-traumatic stress disorder (PTSD) and war-related stress. Retrieved from http://www.veterans.gc.ca/eng/services/health/mental-health/publications/ptsd-warstress#Item3-2

Vieweg, W. V. R., Julius, D. A., Fernandez, A., Beatty-Brooks, M., Hettema, J. M., & Pandurangi, A. K. (2016). Postraumatic stress disorder: Clinical features, pathophysiology and treatment. *American Journal of Medicine*, *119*(5), 383–390.

II

The Impact of PTSD

3

PTSD 101

When in danger, it is natural for a human being to feel afraid. This fear triggers many split-second changes in the body to prepare to defend against the danger or to avoid it. This "fight-or-flight" response is a healthy reaction meant to protect a person from harm. But in posttraumatic stress disorder (PTSD), this reaction is changed or damaged and an individual experiences an altered reaction instead. When people have or develop PTSD, they feel stressed or frightened even when they are no longer in danger.

Although PTSD was first brought to public attention through media in relation to war veterans and the rising occurrence of suicide, it can result from a variety of traumatic incidents, such as mugging, rape, torture, being kidnapped or held captive, child abuse, car accidents, train wrecks, plane crashes, bombings, or natural disasters such as floods or earthquakes (National Institute of Mental Health [NIMH], 2015).

In this chapter, you will learn:

- What PTSD is and its epidemiology
- What some of the theories behind PTSD are
- How to assess, screen, diagnose, and treat PTSD
- The presenting symptomatology of PTSD

PTSD is defined as a mental health condition that is triggered by a terrifying event—from either experiencing it or witnessing it (Mayo Clinic, 2016a). PTSD results from an acutely stressful event, exposure to horror, or being confronted by trauma and can have possibly lifelong effects. PTSD represents a pathological expression of the human stress response (Pitman et al., 2012) abnormalities in brain function associated with fear and reward circuitry (Rasmusson & Shalev, 2014). Gore (2015) add that it is a pathological anxiety that usually occurs after an individual experiences or witnesses severe trauma that constitutes a threat to the physical integrity or life of the individual or of another person.

Generally, if the person meets all of the following criteria, he or she has PTSD:

1. Has experienced a potentially traumatic event at least a month ago
2. Has at least one reexperiencing symptom and one avoidance symptom and one hyperarousal symptom
3. Has difficulties in day-to-day functioning

However, the real complete definition of what fits the criteria to be diagnosed with PTSD is that outlined by the *Diagnostic and Statistical Manual of Mental Disorders*, Fifth Edition (*DSM-5*; American Psychiatric Association, 2013), to be covered later.

HISTORY OF PTSD

The history of PTSD, as we know it today, has been brief. Because of its close association with mental illnesses that present with some similar symptomatology, it has perhaps been buried by society as a taboo issue. Although it was never formally called PTSD, it should be considered that people in prehistoric times likely suffered from the effects of trauma. Friedman (2013) suggests that the fear elicited when facing dinosaurs and saber tooth tigers would have resulted in PTSD-like symptomatology.

The actual diagnosis of PTSD has only been in existence for about 4 decades, when it was formally entered into the *Diagnostic and Statistical Manual of Mental Disorders*, Third Edition (*DSM-III*; American Psychiatric Association, 1980) with diagnostic criteria. At that time, PTSD was considered to be in a category in which "a traumatic event was conceptualized as a catastrophic stressor that was outside the range of usual human experience" (Friedman, 2013, p. 548). Its basis was built solely on the fact that it was caused by outside traumatic events and/or catastrophes that were clearly differentiated from the normal stressors of life, such as divorce, death of a loved one, failure, rejection, serious illness, and financial hardship.

THEORETICAL UNDERPINNINGS OF PTSD

Many of the theories presented to describe and help understand PTSD are primarily based on psychology. Some such theories include the dual representation theory of PTSD, emotional processing theory, and Ehlers and Clark's (2000) cognitive theory. Although the theories help clinicians and patients better understand the development and symptoms of PTSD, the interventions and approach to each remain general and consistent.

Dual Representation Theory of PTSD

The dual representation theory of PTSD was proposed by Brewin, Dalgliesh, and Joseph (1996). According to this theory, many of the features and details of some traumatic event—the sounds, smells, and sights, for example—are initially retained in a system called situationally accessible memory, somewhat akin to episodic memory. When individuals reflect upon this information consciously, attempting to understand or to integrate these features and details, the ensuing insights are retained in another system instead, called verbally accessible memory, somewhat akin to semantic memory. When cues or stimuli in the environment that are associated with this traumatic event are encountered, they will tend to activate or prime the contents of this memory system. Hence, individuals will then experience intrusive images and flashbacks, which are classic signs of PTSD. Accordingly, dissociation immediately after some traumatic event should predict subsequent PTSD (Moss, 2016).

Emotional Processing Theory

The emotional processing theory emerged out of a form of treatment for PTSD that utilized exposure. In general, it provides the fundamental response to anxiety disorders (Foa & Kozak, 1986). According to this theory, fear is activated through associative networks that include information about the feared stimulus, escape or avoidance responses to the feared stimulus, and the meaning of the fear (e.g., threat or danger).

Emotional processing theory proposes that exposure can alter the relationships between the fear stimulus and these networks (McLean & Foa, 2011). For this to happen, the network must first be activated, and then new information must be encoded that is incompatible with what is in the fear network. This is accomplished through habituation. Staying in contact with the feared stimulus occurs until anxiety is reduced. At this point, the encoding of new information that is incompatible with the fear stimulus is permitted (e.g., it is not dangerous). It is believed that "fear becomes problematic when it is intense to a degree that it gets in the way of functioning, or when it persists even when there are no clear indications of danger" (McLean & Foa, 2011, p. 1151). This creates the emergence of maladaptive or pathological fear structures. However, it is asserted that chronic avoidance (e.g., escape behavior, avoidance, dissociation), which often occurs following trauma, leaves maladaptive schemas in place, as, because individuals do not remain in a situation long enough for new learning to occur, these maladaptive behaviors are difficult to change (Portland Psychotherapy, 2017).

Ehlers and Clark's Cognitive Theory

The PTSD theory proposed by Ehlers and Clark focuses on the cognitive symptomatology that is seen once an individual begins to manifest PTSD. They suggest that "PTSD becomes persistent when individuals process the trauma in a way that leads to a sense of serious, current threat" (Ehlers & Clark, 2000, p. 319). They add that this sense of threat arises as a result of two processes that are rooted in an individual's cognition. First, an individual exercises "excessively negative appraisals of the trauma and/or its sequelae" (p. 319) and second, as a result of this, there is a "disturbance of autobiographical memory characterised by poor elaboration and contextualisation, strong associative memory and strong perceptual priming" (p. 319). As a result, any attempt to change either of these is prevented by a "series of problematic behavioural and cognitive strategies" (p. 319).

Fast Facts

PTSD is a mental illness that can often go unnoticed and undetected.

PREVALENCE

Prevalence is the actual number of cases with the disease, either during a period of time (period prevalence) or at a particular date in time (point prevalence). Using the *DSM-5* criteria, the internationally renowned classification system of diseases, PTSD is common. In a large, representative sample in the United States, the estimated lifetime prevalence of PTSD was 7.8%, with females (10.4%) having much higher rates than did males (5.0%; Kessler et al., 2005). Women often have a greater prevalence of PTSD compared to men because they are more often the victims of domestic violence, abuse, and rape (WebMD, 2017).

Estimates for 12-month prevalence differed across countries, which ranged between 1.3% in Australia (Creamer, Burgess, & McFarlane, 2001) and 3.6% in the United States (Narrow, Raw, Robins, & Reiger, 2002). The disorder has also been found to be common in later life, but perhaps primarily at subsyndromal PTSD levels (van Zelst, de Beurs, Beekman, Deeq, & van Dyck, 2003).

At present, 7.7 million Americans aged 18 and older have PTSD (Anxiety and Depression Association of America, 2015). It is estimated that about 7.8 million Americans will experience PTSD at some point in their lives (WebMD, 2017). Furthermore, 67% of people exposed to mass violence have been shown to develop PTSD, a higher rate than those of people exposed to natural disasters or other types of traumatic events (Anxiety and Depression Association of America, 2015).

INCIDENCE

Incidence, or the rate of new (or newly diagnosed) cases of the disease, is generally reported as the number of new cases occurring within a period of time (e.g., per month, per year). To make it more meaningful, the incidence rate is often reported as a fraction of the population at risk of developing the disease (e.g., per 100,000 or per million population). As was found for the prevalence rate, the risk of developing PTSD after a traumatic event was much higher for women (20.4%) than for men (8.1%; Breslau, Davis, Andreski, Peterson, & Schultz, 1997; Kessler et al., 2005). For younger urban populations as well, a higher risk at 23.6% has been reported, with women (30.2%) still having a much higher risk than men (13%; Breslau et al., 1997).

Estimates of the incidence of PTSD are more frequently reported after various natural and other disasters. In various studies of the effects of road traffic accidents (not resulting in an overnight hospital stay), rates of 25% to 30% are reported. The study of 200 young survivors of the sinking of the cruise ship *Jupiter* (Yule et al., 2000) reported an incidence of PTSD of 51%. Most cases manifested within the first few weeks, with delayed onset being rare. Other disorders such as anxiety and depression were common as well. Studies of the mental health of child refugees from war-torn countries find the incidence to be close to 67%. Therefore, significantly increased demands may be made at all levels of primary and secondary child and adolescent mental health services following traumatic events (National Institute for Health and Care Excellence [NICE], 2005, p. 105).

THE ETIOLOGY OF PTSD

There are various causes of PTSD. Knowing and understanding the causes of PTSD help health care providers better identify and care for individuals who may be at risk of developing PTSD. One can develop PTSD when one goes through, witnesses, or learns about an event involving actual or threatened death and/or serious injury or sexual violation (Mayo Clinic, 2016a). Although physical, biological, psychological, environmental, and spiritual sources can all either precipitate and/or exacerbate the initiation and development of PTSD, it is important to remember that the extent to which an individual develops or experiences PTSD is often dependent on the duration and intensity of the traumatic experience, as was previously discussed.

PTSD can occur at any age, including childhood. Although anyone can develop PTSD at any age, it is important to remember that not everyone who lives through a dangerous event develops PTSD. In fact, most people will not develop the disorder, such as war veterans and survivors of physical and sexual assault, abuse, accidents, disasters, and many other serious events. However, women are more likely to develop PTSD than men, and there is some evidence that susceptibility to the disorder may run in families.

PTSD can also occur as a result of a variety of circumstances and/or experiences with some being more traumatic than others. Some people get PTSD after a friend or family member experiences danger or is harmed. The sudden, unexpected death of a loved one can also cause PTSD (NIMH, 2015).

SYMPTOMATOLOGY OF PTSD

PTSD can impact all age groups from children, to adolescents, to adults, and to older adults. There are some common underlying features associated with PTSD that are found across all ages. It is important, however, to remain cognizant of the fact that symptoms may not occur immediately post-event, and could in fact be quite delayed in onset, occurring months or even years after the event occurred. These symptoms generally include "anxiety, depression, anger, insomnia, numbing, and medically unexplained complaints" (World Health Organization [WHO] and United Nations High Commissioner of Refugees, 2013, p. 12).

If the event occurred less than a month ago, assess for symptoms of acute stress with onset after the event. These symptoms may include insomnia, avoidance, reexperiencing, heightened current threat, any disturbing emotions or thoughts, changes in behavior that trouble the person or others around them (e.g., aggressiveness, social isolation/withdrawal, and risk-taking behavior, especially in adolescents), regressive behaviors including bedwetting (in children), and medically unexplained physical complaints including hyperventilation and dissociative disorders of movement and sensation (e.g., paralysis, inability to speak or see; WHO, 2013, p. 8). In adolescents with PTSD, "risk-taking behaviour is a common feature. Alcohol and drug use problems are common in adults and adolescents with PTSD" (WHO and United Nations High Commissioner of Refugees, 2013, p. 12).

It is also important to remember that PTSD symptoms can vary in intensity over time. A person may have more PTSD symptoms when under stress in general, or when encountering reminders of the traumatic experiences. For example, a veteran may hear a car backfire and relive combat experiences. Or an assault victim may see a report on the news about a sexual assault and feel overcome by memories of his or her own assault (Mayo Clinic, 2016b). It is believed, however, that the intensity of these symptoms will decrease over time during recovery.

Fast Facts

Although many theories underpin PTSD, the presenting symptomatology remains the same.

CATEGORIES OF SYMPTOMS

In addition to the common symptomatology that occurs with PTSD, symptoms may be categorized into one of three groups: reexperiencing of symptoms, avoidance symptoms, and hyperarousal symptoms (NIMH, 2015).

The *reexperiencing of symptoms* is what occurs when someone is first experiencing PTSD. These symptoms can often occur as flashbacks or reliving the trauma over and over again where the person experiences physical symptoms, such as a racing heart and sweating. Bad dreams and frightening thoughts can also symbolize that a person has reexperiencing symptoms. A flashback is an episode where the person believes and acts for a moment as though he or she is back at the time of the event, living through it again. People with flashbacks lose touch with reality, usually for a few seconds or minutes (NIMH, 2015).

Intrusive memories also occur. An intrusive memory is unwanted, usually vivid and causes intense fear or horror (WHO, 2013). Symptoms in this category can significantly impact one's life and daily routines. They can start from the person's own thoughts and feelings. Words, objects, or situations that are reminders of the event can also trigger reexperiencing of the event, such as images, sounds (e.g., sound of a gun), and smells (e.g., odor of assailant). Slight differences may occur in children, where symptoms of reexperiencing may also be displayed through frightening dreams without clear content, night terrors, or trauma-specific reenactments in repetitive play or drawings (WHO, 2013).

The second category of symptoms for PTSD is the *avoidance symptoms*. Symptoms or behaviors in this category may be manifested by individuals as staying away or trying to avoid thinking or talking about places, events, objects, thoughts, and memories that are reminders of the experience, as well as feeling emotionally numb, feeling strong guilt, depression, or worry, losing interest in activities that were enjoyable in the past, and having trouble remembering the dangerous event. Things that remind a person of the traumatic event can trigger avoidance symptoms. These symptoms may cause a person to change his or her personal routine. Although people usually use these strategies as a way to avoid reexperiencing symptoms that cause them significant distress, paradoxically, such avoidance strategies tend to increase the occurrence of reexperiencing symptoms (WHO, 2013).

The third and final category of PTSD symptomatology is that of *hyperarousal*. Symptoms under this category include being easily startled, feeling "tense" or "on edge," having difficulty sleeping, and/or having angry outbursts for no obvious reason (WHO, 2013). For example, affected persons may still feel a sense of impending doom and that they are in acute danger. This experience of heightened current threat or perceived threat can make the person hypervigilant and prone to experiencing exaggerated startle responses. Although hypervigilance means an exaggerated concern and alertness to danger and

BOX 3.1 NEGATIVE CHANGES IN MOOD AND THINKING WITH PTSD

- Negative feelings about yourself or other people
- Inability to experience positive emotions
- Feeling emotionally numb
- Lack of interest in activities you once enjoyed
- Hopelessness about the future
- Memory problems, including not remembering important aspects of the traumatic event
- Difficulty maintaining close relationships

being increasingly watchful in public places, an exaggerated startle response means simply being easily startled such as with unexpected sudden movements or loud noises. These symptoms are usually constant, instead of being triggered by things that remind one of the traumatic event (WHO, 2013). Furthermore, they can make the person feel stressed and angry and may make daily tasks, such as eating or concentrating, difficult.

Mayo Clinic (2016b) believes that there is a fourth category of symptoms that brings negative changes in thinking and mood, as described in Box 3.1. The symptomatology of PTSD is important to know and understand as a clinician for it provides the impetus for a complete screening and assessment.

SCREENING/ASSESSMENT

History taking and a full health history are critical to a diagnosis of PTSD. The assessment of PTSD and any related concerns is the cornerstone of effective treatment and practice. A health care professional or nurse uses a systematic, dynamic way to collect and analyze data about a patient, the first step in delivering care. Assessment includes not only physiological factors, but also psychological, sociocultural, spiritual, economic, and lifestyle factors.

Assessment of PTSD should value early detection and recognition and be completed in a manner that is integrated, prudent, thorough, and well informed. The goal of assessment should be to develop an individualized treatment and support plan that includes goals based on the strengths and need areas of the individual. Mental health and addictions clinicians should be consistent in their approach and be open to using a trauma lens to assess for external influences, such as severe trauma that may have precipitated PTSD.

As outlined by Foa and Yadin (2011), a comprehensive assessment of PTSD evaluates all of the diagnostic criteria, assesses associated features and comorbid disorders, and establishes a differential diagnosis. Although some of these tasks can be accomplished with self-report measures, most are best accomplished with a structured interview. This enables the attending clinician to assess both the verbal and nonverbal responses of the individual. Furthermore, clinical interviews provide opportunities to ask follow-up questions, to clarify items and responses, and to use clinical judgment in making the final ratings. However, it is first necessary to establish that an individual has been exposed to an extreme stressor that satisfies the *DSM-5* definition of trauma, as described in the *DSM-5*'s criterion A. The patient must have directly experienced the event, witnessed it, or learned about it indirectly; the event must have been life-threatening, involved serious injury, or threatened physical integrity; and it must have triggered an intense emotional response of fear, horror, or helplessness.

Not every traumatized person develops full-blown or even minor PTSD. Symptoms usually begin within 3 months of the incident but occasionally emerge years afterward. They must last more than a month to be considered PTSD. The course of the illness varies. Some people recover within 6 months, whereas others have symptoms that last much longer. In some people, the condition becomes chronic. Symptoms often make it hard to go about daily life, go to school or work, be with friends, and take care of important tasks (NIMH, 2015).

There are many standards of practice to follow when completing an assessment of an individual for suspected PTSD. The information that the health care professional is seeking to collect can be very sensitive in nature, so honest, respectful, and sincere communication strategies are encouraged. Some of these standards of practice to remain cognizant of follow.

Mental health and addictions clinicians should recognize that:

- The accurate and timely assessment process should help promote an increased quality of life and be supportive to patient's life choices and decisions.
- Intake/screening and assessment are very different and assessment takes several sessions to complete.

- Comprehensive assessments shall be ongoing and continuous, since information may change as the individual's situation stabilizes and as trust develops in the therapeutic relationship.
- The assessment process should motivate the individual to continue in the treatment and support process.
- Assessment is supported as a process of engagement, information exchange, and decision making to determine the appropriate course of action for the patient.
- An integrated assessment shall be completed for all individuals with PTSD concerns. This integrated assessment ensures that mental health and substance use concerns/issues are assessed in the context of each other. It consists of gathering key information and engaging in a process with the individual that enables a practitioner to:
  - Establish (or rule out) the presence or absence of the disorder
  - Help determine the individual's readiness for change
  - Begin the development of an appropriate treatment relationship (Substance Abuse and Mental Health Services Administration [SAMHSA], 2017)
  - Establish a baseline of signs, symptoms, and behaviors that can be used to monitor progress over time (SAMHSA, 2017)
  - Build a therapeutic alliance with the patient
  - Identify the severity of symptoms
  - Collect a thorough history of the patient
  - Discuss the impact of PTSD and concerns in other life areas
  - Support or deal with crisis management and stabilization
  - Use brief PTSD questions to help complete a biopsychosocial assessment
  - Obtain mental health treatment history and monitor responses to reduction in PTSD symptoms
  - Establish risk of suicide, intake history, and observation

Effective treatment of PTSD can only take place if the disorder is recognized. In some cases (e.g., following a major disaster), specific arrangements to screen people at risk may be considered. For the vast majority of people with PTSD, opportunities for recognition and identification come as part of routine health care interventions, for example, following an assault or an accident for which physical treatment is required, or when a person discloses domestic violence or a history of childhood sexual abuse. Identification of PTSD in children presents particular problems, but these problems can be improved if children are asked directly about their experiences (NICE, 2005, p. 124).

SCREENING FOR PTSD

In practice, PTSD screening is only likely to be done when someone is felt to be at higher than usual risk of suffering from the disorder. Common reasons for this are known involvement in a major traumatic event, being from a higher risk group (e.g., refugees, asylum seekers, accident victims, military/ex-military, emergency services personnel, the bereaved, police, firefighters, prison officers, and journalists), or the presence of some symptoms of PTSD, as was clearly outlined and discussed in Chapter 2.

Most screening instruments focus on the detection of early psychological distress shortly after the traumatic event rather than the other factors associated with PTSD discussed earlier. Screening individuals in anticipation of later onset of PTSD has not been a topic of research; however, such ability would be significant in identifying individuals who might benefit from evidence-based early interventions before the PTSD truly manifests. At present, most health care professionals and/or nurses rely on the screening approach used for acute stress disorder (ASD) that often occurs within 1 month of the traumatic event. As reported by NICE (2005), unfortunately the results of the currently available research on predictive screening are disappointing and that no accurate way of screening for the later development of PTSD has been identified (p. 99).

Various screening tools for PTSD have been identified and are used across the globe (see Box 3.2). These may be of potential use in screening programs following major traumatic events and in primary and secondary care, when individuals with PTSD first present to someone other than a mental health professional, such as a primary care worker or an emergency unit worker.

Traditionally, PTSD had been diagnosed with tools such as the Clinician-Administered PTSD Scale (CAPS) or the PTSD Symptom Checklist (PCL; Luftman et al., 2016; Prins et al., 2016). Although these are very useful diagnostic tools for PTSD, a faster five-question screening tool, the Primary Care PTSD Screen (PC-PTSD), was developed to be used as an initial screening device (Prins et al., 2016). This tool has been validated against both the CAPS and the PCL as a reliable screening tool in primary care clinics, and it is now the primary screening tool for PTSD in the U.S. Department of Veterans Affairs health care system (Prins et al., 2016).

BOX 3.2 PTSD SCREENING TOOLS

- The Impact of Event Scale (IES) contains 15 questions about intrusion and avoidance relative to a specified event, which are answered on a 4-point scale.

- The PTSD Checklist—Civilian (PCL–C) version contains the 17 *Diagnostic and Statistical Manual of Mental Disorders, Fourth Edition* (*DSM-IV*; American Psychiatric Association, 1994) PTSD symptoms, which are rated on a scale ranging from 1 (not at all) to 5 (extremely).

- The Posttraumatic Stress Symptom Scale—Self-Report (PSS–SR) version and Posttraumatic Diagnostic Scale (PDS). Developed from the 17 *Diagnostic and Statistical Manual of Mental Disorders*, Third Edition, Revised (*DSM-III-R*; American Psychiatric Association, 1987) PTSD symptoms to the *DSM-IV* ones rated on a 4-point scale. The PDS includes 12 preliminary items inquiring about the occurrence of specific traumatic experiences and a further nine questions assessing impairment.

- The Davidson Trauma Scale (DTS) consists of 17 items corresponding to each of the *DSM-IV* symptoms scored for both frequency and severity during the previous week on scales of 0 to 4.

- The SPAN test comprises the "startle," "physiological upset on reminders," "anger," and "numbness" questions derived from the DTS, scored for both frequency and severity during the previous week on scales of 0 to 4.

- The Self-Rating Scale for Posttraumatic Stress Disorder (SRS–PTSD) contains 17 items corresponding to the *DSM-III-R* symptoms of PTSD using a 3-point scale.

- The Brief DSMPTSD–III–R and DSMPTSD–IV (BPTSD–6; Fullerton, 2000) are based on the IES and the Symptom Checklist-90-R (SCL–90–R) as core instruments, supplemented by 12 PTSD-specific items scored on a 4-point scale. Fullerton (2000) reported on the use of these 12 items alone in screening for PTSD.

- The Screen for Posttraumatic Stress Symptoms (SPTSS) is not tied to a single traumatic event and covers the 17 *DSM-IV* items using an 11-point scale.

(*continued*)

BOX 3.2 PTSD SCREENING TOOLS (*CONTINUED*)

- The Posttraumatic Stress Disorder Questionnaire (PTSD–Q) has the 17 *DSM-IV* symptoms and uses a 7-point scale.
- The Penn Inventory has questions with options of four sentences, modeled on the Beck Depression Inventory, which measure the presence or absence of PTSD symptoms as well as their degree, frequency, or intensity.
- The Trauma Screening Questionnaire (TSQ) consists of the 10 reexperiencing and arousal items from the PSS–SR, modified to provide only two response options. Respondents indicate whether or not they have experienced each symptom at least twice in the past week.
- The Disaster-Related Psychological Screening Test (DRPST) consists of seven items (three reexperiencing symptoms, three arousal symptoms, and one arousal symptom answered present or absent) derived from the 17 PTSD symptoms and nine symptoms of major depression.
- The Self-Rating Inventory for Posttraumatic Stress Disorder (SRIP) consists of 22 items based on *DSM-IV* symptoms using a 4-point intensity scale.

The five main screening questions of the PC-PTSD are as follows:

- In your experience as a civilian provider, have you ever had an emergency-related experience that was so frightening, horrible, or upsetting?
- Have had nightmares about it and thought about it when you did not want to?
- Tried hard not to think about it or went out of your way to avoid situations that reminded you of it?
- Were constantly on guard, watchful, or easily startled?
- Felt numb or detached from others, activities, or your surroundings?

The CAPS screening tool also assesses for the dissociative subtype of PTSD and hence includes items relating to feelings or experiences of depersonalization ("Have there been times when you felt as if you were outside of your body, watching yourself as if you were another person?")

and derealization ("Have there been times when things going on around you seemed unreal or very strange and unfamiliar?"; Lanius, Brand, Vermetten, Frewen, & Spiegel, 2012). Other assessment tools to assess dissociative-type PTSD are self-report rating scales that assess dissociative symptomatology. These include the Dissociative Experiences Scale, the Multiscale Dissociation Inventory, the Traumatic Dissociation Scale, and the Stanford Acute Stress Reaction Questionnaire.

In practice, the questionnaires that appear to have the greatest potential for routine use in primary care are the Trauma Screening Questionnaire (TSQ) and the SPAN, although both have their limitations. The TSQ has 10 questions requiring yes/no answers, which, for example, may be considered too many in a busy primary care setting. The SPAN has only four questions, but the nature of the SPAN symptoms (e.g., numbing) is not so straightforward, and the response scales (0 to 4 ratings for both frequency and severity) and scoring are more complicated than is the case for the TSQ.

Another instrument that performs well is the Impact of Event Scale (IES). Many individuals are familiar with this scale and, like the TSQ, this scale has the advantage of being validated on independent samples within 1 year of a traumatic event (NICE, 2005, p. 101).

DIAGNOSIS

Making the diagnosis of PTSD is no easy task. As in other mental health disorders, the *DSM-5* is used to categorize the diagnosis of PTSD with increased precision and accuracy. The *DSM-5* provides the most recent and up-to-date information and research available on PTSD. Generally, the diagnostic criteria for PTSD include "(a) a history of exposure to a traumatic event that meets specific stipulations and symptoms from each of four symptom clusters: (b) intrusion, (c) avoidance, (d) negative alterations in cognitions and mood, and (e) alterations in arousal and reactivity" (American Psychiatric Association, 2013). The sixth criterion concerns duration of symptoms; the seventh assesses functioning; and the eighth clarifies symptoms as not attributable to a substance or co-occurring medical condition.

Most clinicians recommend following the *DSM* when making a diagnosis of PTSD. Although the underlying criteria for its presence have evolved over time, the most current version of the *DSM*, the *DSM-5*, is advisable to use for making a diagnosis of PTSD.

Full copyrighted criteria are available from the American Psychiatric Association (2013). All of the criteria listed in the *DSM-5* are required for the diagnosis of PTSD. These diagnostic criteria are as follows:

Criterion A: Stressor (One Required)

The person was exposed to death, threatened death, actual or threatened serious injury, or actual or threatened sexual violence, in the following way(s):

- Direct exposure
- Witnessing the trauma
- Indirectly, by learning that a close relative or close friend was exposed to trauma. If the event involved actual or threatened death, it must have been violent or accidental
- Learning that a relative or close friend was exposed to a trauma
- Indirect exposure to aversive details of the trauma, usually in the course of professional duties (e.g., first responders, medics) or by learning that a close relative or close friend was exposed to trauma. If the event involved actual or threatened death, it must have been violent or accidental
- Repeated or extreme indirect exposure to aversive details of the event(s), usually in the course of professional duties (e.g., first responders, collecting body parts; professionals repeatedly exposed to details of child abuse). This does not include indirect nonprofessional exposure through electronic media, television, movies, or pictures

Criterion B: Intrusion Symptoms (One Required)

The traumatic event is persistently reexperienced in the following way(s):

- Intrusive thoughts
- Emotional distress after exposure to traumatic reminders
- Physical reactivity after exposure to traumatic reminders
- Recurrent, involuntary, and intrusive memories. Note: Children older than six may express this symptom in repetitive play
- Traumatic nightmares. Note: Children may have frightening dreams without content related to the trauma(s)
- Dissociative reactions (e.g., flashbacks), which may occur on a continuum from brief episodes to complete loss of consciousness. Note: Children may reenact the event in play

- Intense or prolonged distress after exposure to traumatic reminders
- Marked physiologic reactivity after exposure to trauma-related stimuli

Criterion C: Avoidance (One Required)

Persistent effortful avoidance of distressing trauma-related stimuli after the traumatic event, in the following way(s):

- Trauma-related thoughts or feelings
- Trauma-related external reminders (e.g., people, places, conversations, activities, objects, or situations)

Criterion D: Negative Alterations in Cognitions and Mood (Two Required)

Negative thoughts or feelings that began or worsened after the traumatic event can present as follows:

- Inability to recall key features of the trauma (usually dissociative amnesia; not due to head injury, alcohol, or drugs)
- Negative affect
- Feeling isolated
- Difficulty experiencing positive affect
- Persistent (and often distorted) negative beliefs and expectations about oneself or the world (e.g., "I am bad," "The world is completely dangerous")
- Persistent distorted blame of self or others for causing the traumatic event or for resulting consequences
- Persistent negative trauma-related emotions (e.g., fear, horror, anger, guilt, or shame)
- Markedly diminished interest in (pretraumatic) significant activities
- Feeling isolated or alienated from others (e.g., detachment or estrangement)
- Constricted affect: persistent inability to experience positive emotions

Criterion E: Alterations in Arousal and Reactivity (Two Required)

Trauma-related arousal and reactivity that began or worsened after the trauma, in the following way(s):

- Irritability or aggression
- Risky, reckless, or self-destructive behavior
- Hypervigilance
- Heightened startle reaction
- Difficulty concentrating
- Difficulty sleeping

Criterion F: Duration

Persistence of symptoms (in Criteria B, C, D, and E) for more than 1 month.

Criterion G: Functional Significance (Required)

Significant symptom-related distress or functional impairment (e.g., social, occupational).

Criterion H: Exclusion (Required)

Symptoms are not due to medication, substance use, or other illnesses.

In addition to meeting the diagnostic criteria for PTSD, an individual can experience high levels of either of the following.

There are two specifications of PTSD recognized by the *DSM-5*. In addition to meeting the diagnostic criteria for PTSD, an individual experiences high levels of either of the following. Lanius et al. (2012) suggest "states of depersonalization and derealization provide striking examples of how consciousness can be altered to accommodate overwhelming experience that allows the person to continue functioning under fierce conditions" (p. 706):

1. *Depersonalization:* The experience of being an outside observer of or detached from oneself (e.g., feeling as if "this is not happening to me" or one were in a dream). This "out-of-body" or depersonalization experience during which individuals often see themselves observing their own body from above has the capacity to create the perception that "this is not happening to me" and is typically accompanied by an attenuation of the emotional experience.

2. *Derealization:* The experience of unreality, distance, or distortion (e.g., "things are not real"). States of derealization occur when individuals experience "things are not real; it is just a dream," create the perception that "this is not really happening to me," and are often associated with the experience of decreased emotional intensity (Lanius et al., 2012).

As compared to individuals with PTSD alone, patients with a diagnosis of the dissociative subtype of PTSD also showed the following (Lanius et al., 2012):

■ Repeated traumatization and early adverse experience prior to onset of PTSD
■ Increased psychiatric comorbidity, in particular specific phobia and borderline and avoidant personality disorders among women, but not men
■ Increased functional impairment
■ Increased suicidality (including suicidal ideation, plans, and attempts)

Specify If: With Delayed Expression

Full diagnosis is not met until at least 6 months after the trauma(s), although onset of symptoms may occur immediately.

Fast Facts

Clinicians need to familiarize themselves with PTSD in order to assess, screen, diagnose, and treat it. The differential diagnosis of PTSD will help with this.

DIFFERENTIAL DIAGNOSIS

Because PTSD exhibits similar symptomatology when compared to other anxiety disorders, it is important as a clinician to be able to differentiate PTSD from other comparable illnesses so that an appropriate treatment regimen can be started.

Acute stress disorder (ASD) is a mental health disorder that is most often confused with PTSD. First, symptoms of ASD must occur within 1 month of a traumatic event. Second, this symptomatology characteristic of ASD should not last any longer than 1 month. Should these symptoms occur for longer than 1 month, a clinician can begin to suspect PTSD instead (Cohen, 2016; The Ranch, 2014). In addition, PTSD can also be diagnosed in people who never experienced the effects of ASD (The Ranch, 2014).

For *anxiety* in general, PTSD does have some differences. For example, the person who has experienced a traumatic event will typically exhibit avoidance, irritability, and/or anxiety that is somehow directly associated with the traumatic event encountered. Furthermore, PTSD persons will seek to avoid any reference to or event that in some way is associated with the trauma experienced, so much so that they begin to manifest significant alterations in their thinking and/or mood (Cohen, 2016).

A *phobia* also has similar symptomatology to PTSD. Although both disorders have trigger events, the trigger in PTSD will produce anxiety symptomatology. However, the trigger in the case of a phobia does not induce anxiety-type symptomatology (Cohen, 2016).

Obsessive-compulsive disorder (OCD) is very much like PTSD in many ways. However, the type of thoughts experienced with each is what differs. Unlike PTSD where thoughts are always connected to a past traumatic event or witness thereof, those experienced by someone with OCD do not relate to past trauma (Cohen, 2016).

Adjustment disorder possesses many similarities to PTSD because both trigger anxiety as a result of being exposed to a stressor. However, in the case of adjustment disorder, the stressor is not necessarily severe as it is in PTSD and does not have to be "outside" the normal human experience (Cohen, 2016).

EVALUATION

In evaluating the outcomes of clinical interventions and/or treatment regimens implemented for patients suffering from PTSD, the holistic human being needs to be considered. As physical and mental health go hand in hand, it is important to look for even the most subtle signs of improvement or recovery. Furthermore, remaining cognizant that recovery is not going to happen overnight or within a short period of time is critical; small steps of improvement are the expected norm.

ICD-10 CODING SYSTEM

There is no one specific *International Classification of Diseases* (*ICD-10*) code for PTSD; however, there are a total of three codes to reflect its existence as a diagnosis. PTSD falls under the general heading of "Reaction to severe stress, and adjustment disorders." Hence, for billing purposes, one of the three codes below must be provided.

- F43.1 Posttraumatic stress disorder (PTSD)
    - F43.10 Posttraumatic stress disorder, unspecified
    - F43.11 Posttraumatic stress disorder, acute
    - F43.12 Posttraumatic stress disorder, chronic

Fast Facts

The complexity of PTSD makes the *DSM-5* diagnostic criteria even more important.

References

American Psychiatric Association. (1980). *Diagnostic and statistical manual of mental disorders* (3rd ed.). Washington, DC: Author.

American Psychiatric Association. (1987). *Diagnostic and statistical manual of mental disorders* (3rd ed., revised). Washington, DC: Author.

American Psychiatric Association. (1994). *Diagnostic and statistical manual of mental disorders* (4th ed.). Washington, DC: Author.

American Psychiatric Association. (2013). *Diagnostic and statistical manual of mental disorders* (5th ed.). Arlington, VA: American Psychiatric Publishing.

Anxiety and Depression Association of America. (2016). Posttraumatic stress disorder (PTSD). Retrieved from https://www.adaa.org/understanding-anxiety/posttraumatic-stress-disorder-ptsd

Breslau, N., Davis, G. C., Andreski, P., Peterson, E. L., & Schultz, L. R. (1997). Sex differences in posttraumatic stress disorder. *Archives of General Psychiatry*, *54*, 1044–1048.

Brewin, C. R., Dalgliesh, T., & Joseph, S. (1996). A dual representation theory of posttraumatic stress disorder. *Psychological Review*, *103*, 670–686.

Cohen, H. (2016). Differential diagnosis of PTSD symptoms. Retrieved from https://psychcentral.com/lib/differential-diagnosis-of-ptsd

Creamer, M., Burgess, P., & McFarlane, A. C. (2001). Post-traumatic stress disorder: Findings from the Australian National Survey of Mental Health and Well-being. *Psychological Medicine*, *31*, 1237–1247.

Ehlers, A., & Clark, D. M. (2000). A cognitive model of posttraumatic stress disorder. *Behavior Research and Therapy*, *38*(2000), 319–345.

Foa, E. B., & Kozak, M. J. (1986). Emotional processing of fear: Exposure to corrective information. *Psychological Bulletin*, *99*, 20–35.

Foa, E. B., & Yadin, E. (2011). Assessment and diagnosis of posttraumatic stress disorder. Retrieved from http://www.psychiatrictimes.com/ptsd/assessment -and-diagnosis-posttraumatic-stress-disorder#sthash.D2NXI6Vo.dpuf

Friedman, M. J. (2013). Finalizing PTSD in *DSM-5*: Getting here from there and where to go next. *Journal of Traumatic Stress*, *26*(5), 548–556. doi:10 .1002/jts.21840

Fullerton, C. S. (2000). Measurement of posttraumatic stress disorder in community samples. *Nordic Journal of Psychiatry*, *54*(1), 5–12. doi:10.1080/ 080394800427519

Gore, T. A. (2015). Posttraumatic stress disorder. In I. Ahmed, *Medscape*. Retrieved from http://emedicine.medscape.com/article/288154-overview

Kessler, R. C., Berglund, P. A., Demler, O., Jin, R., Merikangas, K. R., & Walters, E. E. (2005). Lifetime prevalence and age-of-onset distributions of DSM-IV disorders in the National Comorbidity Survey Replication. *Archives of General Psychiatry*, *62*, 593–602.

Lanius, R. A., Brand, B., Vermetten, E., Frewen, P. A., & Spiegel, D. (2012). The dissociative subtype of posttraumatic stress disorder: Rationale, clinical and neurobiological evidence, and implications. *Depression and Anxiety*, *29*, 701–708. doi:10.1002/da.21889

Luftman, K., Aydelotte, J., Rix, K., Ali, S., Houck, K., Coopwood, T. B., . . . Davis, M. (2017). PTSD in those who care for the injured. *Injury*, *48*(2), 293–296. doi:10.1016/j.injury.2016.11.001

Mayo Clinic. (2016a). Post-traumatic stress disorder (PTSD): Causes. Retrieved from http://www.mayoclinic.org/diseases-conditions/post -traumatic-stress-disorder/basics/causes/con-20022540

Mayo Clinic. (2016b). Post traumatic stress disorder (PTSD): Symptoms. Retrieved from http://www.mayoclinic.org/diseases-conditions/post-trau matic-stress-disorder/basics/symptoms/con-20022540

McLean, C. P., & Foa, E. B. (2011). Prolonged exposure therapy for post-traumatic stress disorder: A review of evidence and dissemination. *Expert Reviews Neurother*, *11*(8), 1151–1163.

Moss, S. (2016). Dual representation theory of PTSD. Retrieved from http:// www.sicotests.com/psyarticle.asp?id=305

Narrow, W. E., Rae, D. S., Robins, L. N., & Reiger, D. A. (2002). Revised prevalence estimates of mental disorders in the United States: Using a clinical significance criterion to reconcile 2 surveys' estimates. *Archives of General Psychiatry*, *59*, 115–123.

National Institute for Health and Care Excellence. (2005). Post-traumatic stress disorder: The management of PTSD in adults and children in primary and secondary care. Retrieved from https://www.nice.org.uk/guidance/cg26/evidence/full-guideline-including-appendices-113-pdf-193442221

National Institute of Mental Health. (2015). Post-traumatic stress disorder (PTSD). Retrieved from https://www.nimh.nih.gov/health/publications/helping-children-and-adolescents-cope-with-violence-and-disasters-community-members/index.shtml

Pitman, R. K., Rasmusson, A. M., Koenen, K. C., Shin, L. M., Orr, S. P., Gilbertson, M. W., . . . Liberzon, I. (2012). Biological studies of post-traumatic stress disorder. *Natural Review of Neuroscience*, *13*(11), 769–787.

Portland Psychotherapy. (2017). An overview of emotional processing theory. Retrieved from http://portlandpsychotherapytraining.com/2011/11/07/an-overview-of-emotional-processing-theory

Prins, A., Bovin, M. J., Smolenski, D. J., Mark, B. P., Kimerling, R., Jenkins-Guarnieri, M. A., . . . Tiet, Q. Q. (2016). The Primary Care PTSD Screen for DSM-5 (PC-PTSD-5): Development and evaluation within a veteran primary care sample. *Journal of General Internal Medicine*, *31*, 1206–1211. doi:10.1007/s11606-016-3703-5

Rasmusson, A. M., & Shalev, A. (2014). Integrating the neuroendocrinology, neurochemistry and neuroimmunology of PTSD to date and the challenges ahead. In M. J. Friedman, T. M. Keane, & P. A. Resick (Eds.), *Handbook of PTSD: Science and practice* (2nd ed., pp. 275–299). New York, NY: Guilford Press.

Substance Abuse and Mental Health Services Administration. (2017). Post-traumatic stress disorder (PTSD). Retrieved from https://www.samhsa.gov/treatment/mental-disorders/post-traumatic-stress-disorder

The Ranch. (2014). Why do some people develop delayed PTSD? Retrieved from https://www.recoveryranch.com/articles/mental-health-articles/why-do-some-people-develop-delayed-ptsd

van Zelst, W. H., de Beurs, E., Beekman, A. T., Deeq, D. J., & van Dyck, R. (2003). Prevalence and risk factors of posttraumatic stress disorder in older adults. *Psychotherapy and Psychosomatics*, *72*, 333–342.

WebMD. (2017). Posttraumatic stress disorder. Retrieved from http://www.webmd.com/mental-health/post-traumatic-stress-disorder?page=2

World Health Organization. (2013). *Guidelines for the Management of Conditions Specifically Related to Stress*. Geneva, Switzerland: Author. Retrieved from http://apps.who.int/iris/bitstream/10665/85119/1/9789241505406_eng.pdf

World Health Organization and United Nations High Commissioner for Refugees. (2013). Assessment and management of conditions specifically related to stress: mhGAP intervention guide module (version 1.0). Retrieved from http://apps.who.int/iris/bitstream/10665/85623/1/9789241505932_eng.pdf

Yule, W., Bolton, D., Udwin, O., Boyle, S., O'Ryan, D., & Nurrish, J. (2000). The long-term psychological effects of a disaster experienced in adolescence. I: The incidence and course of PTSD. *Journal of Child Psychology and Psychiatry*, *41*, 503–511.

4

Who Suffers or Is at Risk?

The susceptibility of an individual for developing posttraumatic stress disorder (PTSD) varies across the spectra of age, gender, generation, workplace, and so forth. There are no hard and fast rules as to the type and number of persons who will develop PTSD. However, we do know that those who are at the greatest risk are often repeatedly exposed to trauma and/or violence without any social support, coping skills, and so forth. For example, although paramedics are often exposed repeatedly to trauma and bear witness to a great deal of suffering on the front lines, very few paramedics actually develop PTSD due to their thorough training, skill set, support, and so on (Streb, Haller, & Michael, 2014).

In this chapter, you will learn:

- The different predisposing factors that increase one's risk of developing PTSD
- The different professions that are at increased risk
- How people in the military are at increased risk of developing PTSD
- The different kinds of traumatic experiences lived and how one's risk to developing PTSD increases

WORK RELATED

People work for a variety of reasons. Unequivocally, work serves many purposes for people, including self-satisfaction, income generation, sense of identity, and a communal sense of purpose (Adams, 2015). Most individuals spend about 30% of their lives at work, so it certainly plays a significant role in the lives that we all live. For health care clinicians, first responders, and military personnel who are working to save a patient, a family member, a comrade, a community, or a country during war, the accompanying violence, traumatic scenes/images witnessed, and death or destruction of humanity can take a toll physically, mentally, and psychologically.

Health Care and Emergency Response Personnel

In a book that targets PTSD and how to optimally care for patients suffering from PTSD, we would be remiss if we didn't speak about how the health care professional can also suffer from the effects of PTSD. Whether you are a physician, nurse, or paramedic, you are at an increased risk of developing PTSD merely from the role you fulfill and the nature of your job/career. By helping others who are suffering from PTSD, one's mental, physical, and emotional resources and defenses are at risk of becoming compromised.

When clinicians' stress is at high level and their mental health is deteriorating, patient care can suffer. For example, a nurse's stress level in the emergency department is considered quite high and very often correlated with decreasing patient safety (Carayon & Gurses, 2005; Elfering, Semmer, & Grebner, 2006). Emergency nurses are especially vulnerable to posttraumatic stress reactions due to repetitive exposure to work-related traumatic incidents. For them, the most traumatic event is the death or serious injury of a child/adolescent, which not only affects them personally but also impacts the quality care they provide to their patients (Adriaesnnens, de Gucht, & Maes, 2012).

Compassion fatigue and burnout are a couple of outcomes health care clinicians can experience as a result of trauma and the continuously giving of themselves to patient care. Burnout or cumulative stress is the state of physical, emotional, and mental exhaustion caused by a depletion of a person's ability to cope with his or her environment (Maslach, 1982). In the United States, there is an identified burnout epidemic occurring among physicians (Drummond, 2015). In health care professionals, it is associated with increased turnover, employee absenteeism, poor coworker support, depersonalization, decreased performance, decreased patient satisfaction, and difficulty in recruiting and retaining clinicians (Sundin, Hochwälder, & Lisspers, 2011; Vahey, Aiken, Sloane, Clarke, & Vargas, 2004). Increased malpractice suits, drug abuse, and suicide rates are all recognized outcomes from physician burnout (Drummond, 2015).

As suggested by Mark and Smith (2012), increasing job demands are associated with higher levels of mental health problems such as anxiety and depression. Job burnout is symbolized by three main characteristics (Smith, Segal, & Segal, 2013):

- Exhaustion (e.g., the depletion or draining of mental resources)
- Cynicism (e.g., indifference or a distant attitude toward one's job)
- Lack of professional efficacy (e.g., the tendency to evaluate one's work performance negatively, resulting in feelings of insufficiency and poor job-related self-esteem)

To set the record straight, just because burnout can occur among clinicians does not mean that you as a clinician will develop it. There are various factors that can predispose an individual to an increased risk of developing burnout. But because burnout can sneak upon you unexpectedly, it is good to spot the clues before it goes too far. (Mayo Clinic, 2013):

- You literally dread Mondays coming (if you are an 8–4 worker) and/or the beginning of your series of shifts. You are using up a lot of energy worrying about this day.
- You just cannot seem to get the energy or motivation to engage in some sort of social activity.
- You often have a drink or two after you get home from work and fall asleep in front of the television.
- You feel like you are getting in a rut, all days begin to look alike, there is too much work to do in so little time, and you do not feel appreciated for what work you do.
- You have become cynical, critical, impatient, and irritable.
- You feel disillusioned and dissatisfied with your job (Mayo Clinic, 2013).

If you are experiencing more than a few of these signs, it may be time to take a break, seek support and career counseling, or talk to your manager about making some changes to your job. Seeking medical advice from your doctor or someone from the employee assistance program in your organization is highly encouraged. Due to the nature of burnout and the fact that it is often job related and intense, it is best to recognize the warning signs before they occur.

As health care professionals and emergency response (ER) personnel fulfill the requirements of protecting individuals, they are deemed very giving and caring professions. As a result of immense giving of themselves, these professionals can suffer from a common condition known as compassion fatigue. The occurrence of compassion fatigue further begins to increase the vulnerabilities of their mental processes. However, clinicians tend to endure more ingrained consequences of stress merely from the role they play in society with their caring, altruistic, and nurturing sense of self.

Compassion fatigue is the combination of secondary traumatic stress and burnout experienced by helping professionals and other care providers (Figley, 1995; Stamm, 1995). Secondary traumatic stress has been defined as "the stress resulting from helping or wanting to help a traumatized or suffering person" (Figley, 1995, p. 10). It is experienced by trauma health care professionals as they provide care for others, and it correlates highly with burnout (Vahey et al., 2004). It arises from repeated exposure to traumatic events, as is the case with the ongoing care of patients with cancer. A caregiver's empathy level with traumatized individuals is hypothesized to play a significant role in the transmission of traumatic stress from patient to nurse (Figley, 1995). The more empathetic the clinician, the greater the risk for developing compassion fatigue. It is prevalent among health care providers and ranges from 16% to 39% in nurses, with burnout ranging from 8% to 38% (Hooper, Craig, Janvrin, Wetsel, & Reimels, 2010; Potter et al., 2013; P. M. Robins, Meltzer, & Zelikovsky, 2009). Compassion fatigue leaves the health care clinician with sleepless nights, nightmares, increased risk of substance abuse, and increased risk for medication errors (Perry, Toffner, Merrick, & Dalton, 2011; Stamm, 2002).

Firefighters, police officers, and peace officers are often on the front lines when trauma or violence emerges. They have witnessed many a grotesque scene from homicides, suicides, accidents, and instances of domestic violence, and have helped to intervene for both the dying and the survivors. Although any person may experience a critical incident, conventional wisdom says that members of law enforcement, firefighting units, and emergency medical services are at great risk for PTSD. However, less than 5% of emergency services personnel will develop long-term PTSD symptomatology (Pulley, 2005; this percentage increases when responders endure the death of a coworker in the line of duty). This rate is only slightly higher than the general population average of 3% to 4% (Pulley, 2005), which indicates that despite the remarkably high levels of exposure to trauma, emergency workers are resilient, and people who join the field may self-select for emotional resilience.

According to Veterans Affairs Canada (2017), 30% of Royal Canadian Mounted Police disability pensioners suffered mental health conditions such as depression and anxiety disorders. Depression is the leading cause of workplace disability and is more prevalent than PTSD in police and military organizations, although the two conditions often occur together.

Whether it is a one-time acute traumatic event or repetitious traumatic events, there is a risk for the development of PTSD for a paramedic, who is typically the first person on the scene of an accident. However, as discussed previously, it is important to recognize that not every traumatized person develops full-blown or even minor PTSD (NIOSH, 2008).

For paramedic trainees in particular, the incidence of PTSD symptomatology was alarming. Robbers and Jenkins (2005) found that workers on the scene of the September 11, 2001, terrorism attacks on the United States are still experiencing high levels of PTSD. As suggested by Fjeldheim et al. (2014), almost 20% of paramedic trainees were beginning to manifest signs of PTSD, after 90% of them had witnessed traumatic events during training. Interestingly, length of exposure at the attack site is related to increased levels of PTSD (Addiction Search, 2017). Luftman et al. (2016) found in their survey of 546 health care workers that all disciplines were at risk of developing PTSD. However, those on the actual scene of trauma had the greatest risk of developing PTSD. Of those surveyed and working outside of the hospital, the flight paramedics (50%) and paramedics (44%) were at the highest risk. In hospital, the emergency department resident (29%) and the emergency department nurse (27%) were at the greatest risk.

War Veterans and Active Military Personnel

The impact of war on an individual's mental health and the increased predisposition for the development of PTSD and other mental illness has been threaded throughout research since its initial observation post–World War I where many returning soldiers were noticed to be "shell-shocked" (Kelly, 2015). Approximately 30% of men and women who have spent time in a war-zone experience PTSD (Gore, 2015).

For soldiers returning from combat, other mental disorders, in addition to PTSD, may be precipitated or worsened by exposure to combat; these include depression (Thaipisuttikul, Ittasakul, Waleeprakhon, Wisajun, & Jullagate, 2014), anxiety, psychosis, and substance abuse (Reeves, Parker, & Konkle-Parker, 2005). According to Blore, Sim, Forbes, Creamer, and Kelsall (2015), Gulf War veterans had more than twice the odds of experiencing depression and dysthymia or chronic dysphoria compared to nondeployed military personnel. Thomas et al. (2010) also found that rates of depression in returning combat soldiers were as high as 31%. Hence, clinicians and policy makers need to be aware of this increased risk when managing veterans' health.

Traumatic stress disorder has been designated as one of the signature wounds of the Iraq/Afghanistan war (Yarvis, 2011). Hence, military personnel exposed to war-zone trauma, in general, are at an increased risk for developing PTSD. Those at the greatest risk are those exposed to the highest levels of war-zone stress, those wounded in action, those incarcerated as prisoners of war, and those who manifest acute war-zone reactions, such as combat stress reaction (CSR). In addition to problems directly attributable to PTSD symptoms, individuals with this disorder frequently suffer from other comorbid psychiatric disorders, such as depression, other anxiety disorders, and alcohol or substance abuse/dependence. The resulting constellation of psychiatric symptoms frequently impairs marital, vocational, and social functioning. The likelihood of developing chronic PTSD depends on premilitary and postmilitary factors in addition to features of the trauma itself. Premilitary factors include negative environmental factors in childhood, economic deprivation, family psychiatric history, age of entry into the military, premilitary educational attainment, and personality characteristics. Postmilitary factors include social support and the veteran's coping skills.

Among American military personnel, there are three populations at risk for unique problems that may amplify the psychological impact of war-zone stress. They are women whose war-zone experiences may be complicated by sexual assault and harassment; non-White ethnic minority individuals whose premilitary, postmilitary, and military experience is affected by the many manifestations of racism; and those with war-related physical disabilities, whose PTSD and medical problems often exacerbate each other. The longitudinal course of PTSD is quite variable. Some trauma survivors may achieve complete recovery, whereas others may develop a persistent mental disorder in which they are severely and chronically incapacitated. Other patterns include delayed, chronic, and intermittent PTSD. Theoretically, primary preventive measures might include prevention of war or screening out vulnerable military recruits. In practice, primary preventive measures have included psychoeducational and inoculation approaches. Secondary preventive measures have been attempted through critical incident stress debriefing administered according to the principles of proximity, immediacy, expectancy, and simplicity. Tertiary preventive measures have included psychotherapy, pharmacotherapy, dual-diagnosis approaches, peer counseling, and inpatient treatment. Few treatments have been rigorously evaluated. There are both theoretical reasons and empirical findings to suggest that military veterans with PTSD are at greater risk for more physical health problems, poorer health status, and more medical service usage. Much more research is needed on this matter. Despite the potential adverse impact of war-zone exposure on mental and physical health, there is also evidence that trauma can sometimes have salutary effects on personality and overall function (Freidman, Schnurr, & McDonagh-Coyle, 1994).

Veterans of the military conflicts in Iraq and Afghanistan may have been exposed to significant psychological stressors, resulting in mental and emotional disorders. However, the duration in combat plays a significant role—the greater amount of time spent in combat, the greater the effect and risk for PTSD. This was discovered following Operation Iraqi Freedom and Operation Enduring Freedom (Afghanistan), where soldiers of the Iraqi Freedom conflict had greater combat exposure (Gore, 2015). Treatment of PTSD often requires both psychological and pharmacological interventions (Reeves et al., 2005). As expressed by Baker (2014), the conflicts in the Middle East and the resulting trauma and its impact continue to haunt many in both expressed and hidden manners. One military study, in particular, found that 38.5% of those with suicidal ideations developed a plan and 34% of them with a plan made an attempt on their lives within the following year (Nock et al., 2014). Even 50 years later, World War II veterans reported a reactivation of PTSD symptomatology in later life, which was precipitated by other stressors such as physical ill health, loneliness, and even retirement (Macleod, 1994).

Assessment and Screening in War Veterans

The insidious nature of PTSD symptoms is most evident in war veterans. As many initial PTSD symptoms are easily masked and missed especially by older male veterans, specific and direct questioning is necessary, particularly given that the telling of the story from memory is especially difficult (Macleod, 1994).

During a hospital stay or a visit to a primary health care provider, a veteran or family member may confide in the health care provider about worrisome symptoms that suggest PTSD. Many PTSD sufferers adopt avoidance behaviors, which deters them from seeking help and contributes to underdetection of the disorder. However, PTSD is often accompanied by such mental and physical conditions as depression, anxiety, substance abuse, headache, stomach ache, and chronic pain. When veterans seek care for these problems, the health care provider should stay alert for and address traumatic stress symptoms, elicit the patient's trauma history, screen for PTSD, recommend referrals, and follow-up as appropriate.

By using an interdisciplinary approach, health care providers are more likely to recognize and successfully address the physical, mental, and emotional effects of PTSD in veterans.

If the patient has a positive PTSD screen:

- Identify your concern for the patient and emphasize the need for follow-up screening for suicidal ideation
- Refer the patient to an appropriate clinician for a complete psychological evaluation and treatment recommendations
- Arrange for follow-up assessment and health teaching (Rossignol & Chandler, 2010)

Although Charles, Harrison, and Britt (2014) suggest that the highest rate of PTSD occurs in veterans between 18 and 54 years of age, all age groups should be carefully evaluated by general practitioners when managing veterans' health as the impact of PTSD may be delayed for months or even years.

Fast Facts

PTSD impacts everyone regardless of age, gender, location, and profession.

INTRINSIC AND/OR PERSONAL VIOLENCE AND TURMOIL

The causes of personal violence and turmoil come in many forms, which include biologic/genetics, rape and/or sexual assault, domestic violence, child abuse, childhood bullying, and the diagnosis of a terminal and/or critical illness.

Biological/Genetic Predisposition

The biological and genetic implications of developing PTSD have been discussed. Although many suggest that it can occur because of hereditary endowment in the form of personality characteristics (Mayo Clinic, 2015) or as an increased disposition for the development of other mental illnesses such as anxiety and depression (Mayo Clinic, 2015), with one's own or one's family history of mental illness increasing the risk of developing PTSD (Anxiety and Depression Association of America, 2015; National Institute of Mental Health [NIMH], 2014), much discussion on genetics is currently ongoing. At present, many scientists are focusing on genes that play a role in creating fear memories. Understanding how fear memories are created may help to refine or find new interventions for reducing the symptoms of PTSD.

The existence of previous mental health disorders plays a role in predisposing one to the development of PTSD. In one study, Nock et al. (2014) found that approximately 30% of military suicide attempts were associated with pre-enlistment mental disorders; hence, it creates the need for early screening and intervention strategies for this particular group of military.

Biologically, there are many measures that can determine the risk with which one can be predisposed or susceptible to the development of PTSD after being involved in, learning about, or witnessing a traumatic event. The brain is what regulates the chemicals and hormones released as the body responds to stress (Mayo Clinic, 2015). Studying parts of the brain involved in dealing with fear and stress helps researchers better understand possible causes of PTSD. One such brain structure is the amygdala, known for its role in emotion, learning, and memory. The amygdala appears to be active in fear acquisition, or learning to fear an event (such as touching a hot stove), as well as in the early stages of fear extinction, or learning not to fear (NIMH, 2016). Storing extinction memories and dampening the original fear response appear to involve the prefrontal cortex (PFC) area of the brain, involved in tasks such as decision making, problem solving, and judgment. Therefore, our brain not only learns and stores the feared event, but also triggers how we should best respond given past experiences. Certain areas of the PFC play slightly different roles. For example, when it deems a source of stress controllable, the medial PFC suppresses the amygdala, an alarm center deep in the brainstem, and controls the stress response. The ventromedial PFC helps sustain long-term extinction of fearful memories, and the size of this brain area may affect its ability to do so (NIMH, 2014). Hence, individual differences in these genes or brain areas may only set the stage for PTSD without causing symptoms.

Furthermore, stathmin, a protein needed to form fear memories, is also believed to play a significant role. In one study, mice that did not make stathmin were less likely than normal mice to "freeze," a natural, protective response to danger, after being exposed to a fearful experience. They also showed less innate fear by exploring open spaces more willingly than normal mice (NIMH, 2016). Gastrin-releasing peptide (GRP), a signaling chemical in the brain released during emotional events, seems to help control the fear response, and lack of GRP may lead to the creation of greater and more lasting memories of fear as what often occurs in PTSD (NIMH, 2016). Moreover, a version of the 5-HTTLPR gene, which controls levels of serotonin—a brain chemical related to mood—appears to fuel the fear response (NIMH, 2014). Hence, like in many other mental illnesses, it is likely that many genes with small effects are at work in PTSD.

Diagnosed With a Critical Illness

For a young developing child, whose life and experiences lie ahead, the diagnosis of a critical or terminal illness brings his or her dreams and aspirations to a sudden halt. Similarly, for adults as well, when all is going as planned and life is good, an unexpected diagnosis tends to negate their happy, healthy life. The news of a critical and/or terminal illness can produce detrimental consequences for children and adults.

For many, the diagnosis occurs in childhood and the impact of such trauma arises later into adolescence and young adulthood (Langeveld, Grootenhuis, Voûte, & de Haan, 2004; Lee & Santacroce, 2007). The study by Lee and Santacroce (2007), done in the state of California, found that 13% of childhood cancer survivors who had results indicative of PTSD were often living alone and had no form of health insurance, which perhaps precipitated previous stressors. The authors emphasize the importance of screening all children who have experienced childhood cancer so that prompt and early intervention and diagnosis can begin. Langeveld et al. (2004) add that although the percentage of adults who had survived childhood cancer only experienced PTSD symptoms at a similar rate as that of the general population, it was most often correlated with female gender, low education level, and being unemployed. However, as Caldera, Palma, Penayo, and Kullgren (2001) point out, it is often the more educated patients who are seeking out help for PTSD. Yet again, clinically, this reinforces the importance of early detection and intervention in such subpopulations.

For adults as well, the symptomatology of PTSD following a critical or terminal diagnosis is quite real. Breast cancer, for example, is known to be accompanied by one of the strongest forms of chemotherapy. Even 20 years later, women who have endured a diagnosis and treatment of breast cancer experience distressing symptomatology, comparable to that of PTSD (Kornblith & Ligibel, 2003). The female gender is considered a higher risk category (Mayou, Ehlers, & Bryant, 2002; Van Loey Maas, Faber, & Taal, 2003). Women are twice as likely to develop PTSD as men, and children can also develop it (Anxiety and Depression Association of America, 2015). Men tend to experience more traumatic events than women, but women experience higher impact events (i.e., those that are more likely to lead to PTSD; Kessler, Sonnega, Bromet, Hughes, & Nelson, 1995; M. B. Stein, Walker, Hazen, & Forde, 1997). Furthermore, women are more likely to develop PTSD in response to a traumatic event than men; this enhanced risk is not explained by differences in the type of traumatic event (Kessler et al., 1995).

Let us not forget the loved ones left behind because of a terminal illness. Those who are left grieving also succumb to the effects of trauma and possibly PTSD, after such a sudden loss of a friend or loved one. As suggested by Kristensen, Elklit, Karstoft, and Palic (2014), 1 month after the loss of a loved one, 30% of people had PTSD-type symptoms, which decreased only slightly to 22% after 6 months.

Rape/Sexual Assault Victims

Rape is perhaps one of the most traumatic experiences someone can experience. Particularly for women, rape is the form of trauma most commonly related to PTSD (Kessler et al., 1995). It is up front and personal, a violent and traumatic coercive event against someone involuntarily and against his or her will. In the case of rape or sexual assault, the physical wounds can heal but the emotional scars of fear from the unwanted violent intrusion of one's body can live on in one's mind for a long time.

Sexual assault comes in many forms. For example, an individual can be the victim of unwanted touching, grabbing, oral sex, anal sex, sexual penetration with an object, and/or sexual intercourse. Furthermore, "the force used by the aggressor can be either physical or nonphysical" (U.S. Department of Veterans Affairs, 2015, para. 4).

Following are examples of how people are forced or coerced into having unwanted sex; they may be:

- Taken advantage of by someone who has some form of authority over them (e.g., doctor, teacher, boss)
- Bribed or manipulated into sexual activity against their will
- Unable to give their consent because they are under the influence of alcohol or drugs
- Threatened with harm or that people that they care about will be hurt
- Physically forced or violently assaulted (U.S. Department of Veterans Affairs, 2015, "What Is Sexual Assault?")

For individuals, whether male or female, this is not an easy story to recollect. They may share their story as if the event happened to someone else, yet they are very aware that it happened to them but there is just numbness or no feeling. However, the flashbacks make it very real for them, particularly around the anniversary date it occurred (NIMH, 2014).

The severity of trauma by rape/sexual assault is well founded. Möller, Bäckström, Söndergaard, & Helström (2014), for example, found that dissociation often occurred because of rape/sexual assault (we highlighted dissociation earlier in the diagnostic criteria of PTSD). In their study, although 39% of all sexually assaulted women interviewed had developed PTSD at the 6-month assessment, and 47% suffered from moderate or severe depression, the risk of developing PTSD was compounded by a combination of victim vulnerability and the extent of the dramatic nature of the current assault. Similar studies in Africa, where unfortunately rape is all too common, found that 87% of the women raped suffered from severe PTSD symptomatology, particularly when the woman was unmarried, unemployed, and lacked social support (Mgoqi-Mbalo, Zhang, & Ntuli, 2017). Not only did rape/sexual assault put these women at risk for PTSD, but it also increased their propensity to developing depression (Mgoqi-Mbalo et al., 2017; Möller et al., 2014), substance abuse (Vujanovic, Bonn-Miller, & Petry, 2016), and anxiety disorders (McMillan & Asmundson, 2016).

Domestic Violence

Domestic violence remains a growing concern regardless of the society in which one lives. The history of criminalization of domestic violence is an astonishing one.

In 1910, the U.S. Supreme Court ruled that a wife had no cause for action on an assault and battery charge against her husband because it "would open the doors of the courts to accusations of all sorts of one spouse against the other and bring into public notice complaints for assault, slander and libel" (Women Safe, 2011). Even up to 1977, California announced, in its Penal Code, that "wives charging husbands with criminal assault and battery must suffer more injuries than commonly needed for charges of battery" (Women Safe, 2011). The current 2017 announcement by Russia to do the same (Hanrahan, 2017) leaves many women wrought with worry. For the women of Russia, this translates into husbands being able to injure their wives without legal consequences as long as the women do not require hospital treatment—all under the belief that the state should not interfere with family life.

Intimate partner violence (IPV) is a recurring theme in the discussion of PTSD. It is significant from two perspectives: the individual who has lived at the violent hands of his or her spouse and develops PTSD because of that life, the individual with PTSD who is violent toward his or her family.

First, the individual who lives with a violent spouse/partner is at risk for developing PTSD. The repeated violence, derogatory statements, and put-downs, as well as the constant fear of not knowing what tomorrow will bring, all set the stage for the development of PTSD in the victim. According to the U.S. Department of Veterans Affairs (2015), IPV refers specifically to violence and aggression between intimate partners. IPV can include physical, sexual, or psychological abuse or stalking. Acts of IPV range in how often they occur or how violent they are. It can happen to women or men who have intimate relationships with women, men, or both. It can happen irrespective of age, income, race, ethnicity, culture, religion, or disability. IPV includes, but is not limited to, the following:

- *Physical violence:* Hitting, pushing, grabbing, biting, choking/strangulating, shaking, slapping, kicking, hair pulling, or restraining
- *Sexual violence:* Attempted or actual sexual contact when the partner does not want to or is unable to consent (e.g., when affected by alcohol or illness)
- *Threats of physical or sexual abuse:* Ways to cause fear through words, looks, actions, or weapons

- *Psychological or emotional abuse:* Name-calling, humiliating, putting one down, keeping one from friends and family, bullying, or controlling where one goes or what one wears
- *Stalking:* Following, harassing, or unwanted contacts, which make one feel afraid

According to various researchers, PTSD as a result of having lived a life with violence, fear, and hurt at the hands of a spouse is a reality for many. Kemp, Green, Hovanitz, and Rawlings (1995) found that 81% of battered women and almost 63% of the women experiencing solely verbal abuse met diagnostic criteria for PTSD. Although women are more often the victim than men (Astin, Lawrence, & Foy, 1993; Kemp, Green, Hovanitz, & Rawlings, 1995), treating such a population becomes a significant challenge, especially when women choose to remain with their abusive partner, as often occurs (Astin et al., 1993; Schlee, Heyman, & O'Leary, 1998).

On the flip side is the individual who suffers from PTSD and behaves in ways that are violent and aggressive toward his or her partner/spouse. All too often, intimate partner conflict is a common finding when one of the partners has been deployed on military tours. According to Miller et al. (2013), PTSD was associated with more frequent displays of hostility and psychological abuse and fewer expressions of acceptance and humor in both veterans and their partners. What often results in families where one of the individuals is a war veteran suffering from PTSD is increased relationship discord, poor relationship adjustment, and elevated psychological and physical aggression toward partners. Rabenhorst et al. (2013) have uncovered the increased frequency of spousal abuse after partners have returned from duty. In the study by Gupta et al. (2014), almost 73% of women experienced crisis-level violence at the hands of their military spouses.

Child Abuse Victims

Young children learn primarily from their immediate environment; what is experienced and learned from that environment, be it good or bad, has a long-lasting impact on children. Child abuse, molestation, neglect, and/or abandonment, particularly when from individuals who are trusted by children such as a parent, relative, or neighbor, are highly negative and even traumatic experiences for children to endure. Hence, as such children grow into adolescents and then adults, unfortunately many of those negative experiences of fear, isolation, pain, feeling devalued and unloved, and worthless come along with them. According to the U.S. Department of Health and Human Services' statistics, in 2006, almost 1 million (905,000) children had been maltreated, with 16% of them having been physically abused and the remainder having been neglected or sexually abused (Babbel, 2011). But the impact of child abuse and neglect does not end here for the individual.

In the immediacy of the event while the victim is still a child, the horrific and developmental effects do not go unnoticed. Children who are sexually abused present with a host of psychological difficulties, including dissociation and PTSD symptoms. Furthermore, negative repercussions associated with sexual abuse may interfere with children's ability to interact competently with their peers, and might put them at risk for later peer victimization (Hébert, Lavoie, & Blais, 2014).

Various sequelae of child abuse and neglect follow the individual into adulthood. Because it occurred during significant times of growth and development, the impact of such negative events and the responses it invoked thus all become incorporated into the demeanor and even the personality of the individual. Hence, many forms of childhood neglect and abuse become linked to various mental health and/or psychological problems that later become manifested in adulthood. Some of these mental health and/or psychological problems include PTSD (Bendall, Alvarez-Jimenez, Hulbert, McGorry, & Jackson, 2012).

Bendall, Alvarez-Jimenez, Hulbert, McGorry, & Jackson (2012) add that the trauma experienced in childhood significantly increased the risk of PTSD in adulthood at rates of 47% (95% confidence interval [CI] 31%–64%) for nonpsychotic PTSD symptoms, 64% (95% CI 48%–80%) for childhood trauma, and 39% (95% CI 23%–55%) for childhood trauma-related, clinical-level PTSD symptoms.

In the words of Lubit and Pataki (2016), traumatic events on children have far-reaching effects beyond the scope of just the physically felt abuse received. The child not only has fewer emotional, psychological, and intellectual resources in place to cope with such stressful events, but at a time when development of the brain and body is critical, the magnitude of the stress from abuse can alter the development pathway and hence position a child behind his or her peers and the normal developmental milestones.

As a result of child abuse, the development of PTSD is a reality for some. The development of PTSD becomes apparent in many mental, emotional, and psychological ways, including:

- Children behave in a nervous or anxious manner
- They have bad dreams

- They may act out certain aspects of the abuse in their play and drawings
- They may lose skills once developed and acquired and begin to act in a manner that seems younger than they actually are, such as by sucking their thumb and wetting their bed
- They show out of place or inappropriate sexual behaviors not expected of a child their age, such as acting and dressing in a seductive manner
- Acting out (especially boys)—have behavior problems, are cruel to others, and run away
- Acting in—become withdrawn from everyone, show signs of depression, and talk about or try to commit suicide
- Confused—for sexual abuse in particular, not knowing how someone they trusted could do this to them
- Attention seeking—children may learn that the only way to get people's attention or love is to give up something sexual or their own self-respect
- Self-blame—blaming themselves for the abuse; maybe they had said or done something to signal to the adult that they wanted it or that maybe there was something wrong with them and they were singled out for that reason
- Sexual disorientation—if the abuser is gay, children may wonder if that means they are now "gay"
- Emotion
  - Emotion regulation difficulties such as too much or too little emotion, limited awareness of feelings, difficulty with self-soothing
  - Chronic feelings of fear, anger, shame, sadness, helplessness, hopelessness
  - Impulsive or self-destructive behaviors related to difficulties managing emotions (addictions, self-harm, disordered eating)
- Mind/self-concept
  - Sense of self as bad, inadequate, weak, powerless, worthless, undeserving
  - Self-critical and self-blaming; hypersensitivity to criticism and rejection
  - Identity problems (e.g., not feeling whole, lacking a clear, stable sense of self, inner sense of confusion, frequent changes in career, life goals, and so on)
  - Alterations in attention and memory (e.g., dissociation, difficulty focusing)

- Relationships
  - Problems with trust and intimacy in relationships (e.g., jealousy, difficulties committing to relationships, difficulty being vulnerable)
  - Difficulties with self-assertion and setting limits in relationships
  - Sense of isolation and alienation (e.g., difficulties connecting to others)
- Body
  - Frequent physical health problems (e.g., chronic pain, irritable bowel syndrome, headaches, hypertension, sexual pain, and dysfunction)
  - Hypersensitivity to physical contact, sounds, and other stimuli
  - Sleep problems (Lubit & Pataki, 2016; Toronto Psychology Centre, 2016; U.S. Department of Veterans Affairs, 2015)

What happens as a result of childhood abuse is often referred to as a complex form of trauma. Complex trauma refers to repeated interpersonal trauma, often occurring in childhood. This type of trauma includes sexual and physical abuse as well as emotional abuse and neglect. Emotional abuse can include verbal attacks, incidents of humiliating or threatening behavior, and witnessing violence against loved ones; whereas emotional neglect involves a failure to provide a child's basic emotional needs, such as love, attention, understanding, affection, support, and protection (Toronto Psychology Centre, 2016).

These forms of abuse are particularly damaging to the development of a child; they have a profound impact and impinge on brain development and features of personality and expression, and can often involve harm and/or betrayal with close relationships that are supposed to be trustworthy, nurturing, and protective. As a result, these experiences compromise normal self-development, self-esteem, self-confidence, and basic trust in primary relationships and precipitate the development of other mental illnesses and addictions as well (Toronto Psychology Centre, 2016).

Childhood Bullying

Much like the impact of child abuse, sexual assault, and neglect, childhood bullying can leave scars that significantly increase the susceptibility of a child to develop PTSD (Hébert, Lavoie, & Blais, 2014). Although the physical scars heal, the psychological and emotional scars exert long-lasting effects.

Physical, emotional, and psychological scars of play and socializing gone wrong continue to haunt children into later adolescence and even adulthood. In a study by Turner, Finkelhor, Shattuck, Hamby, and Mitchell (2014), almost half (48.4%) of the children interviewed experienced at least one episode of peer traumatization in 1 year. In what they called a "power imbalance," children who were victimized by their peers showed significantly higher levels of fear, missing school, and trauma symptomatology.

Cyberbullying is another venue often used to intimidate, embarrass, and humiliate other children. Preidt (2016) suggest that while bullying among children it is often underdiagnosed and hence undertreated, those presenting to an emergency department often have symptoms correlated with PTSD symptomatology as related to community violence, physical peer violence, and cyberbullying and occurred so at a rate of more than 23%.

Previous traumatic events experienced by children seemed to increase their risk of being bullied. Using a subpopulation of children who were previously sexually abused, Hébert, Langevin, and Daigneault (2016) found that these children later reported being picked on (60%), verbally victimized (51%), and physically victimized (35%), which tripled the risk to which these children later presented with PTSD and dissociation symptomatology.

EXTERNAL UNCONTROLLABLE INFLUENCES

Natural Disasters

Whether it is an earthquake (Kun, Han, Chen, & Yao, 2009), flooding (Kos, 2017), hurricane (Caldera et al., 2001), or tsunami, the experience of trauma causes PTSD to impact up to 45% of people involved (Bromet et al., 2016; Kun, Chen, et al., 2009). Studies of severe natural disasters (e.g., Armenian earthquake, mudslides in Mexico, Hurricane Andrew in the United States) show that 50% or more of those affected suffer from clinically significant distress or psychopathology (National Center for PTSD, 2016). Although Caldera et al. (2001) suggest that natural disasters most often occur in low-income countries, and while Mother Nature knows no boundaries, they found that illiterates, females, and those with previous mental health problems need to be prioritized for early postdisaster intervention. As suggested by Kun, Han, et al. (2009), it is not just the disaster itself, but also the fallout from it, such as the destruction of one's home (Kun, Han, et al., 2009) or the forced displacement from one's home (Bromet et al., 2016), that creates a great deal of stress pushing one toward the limits of PTSD. Bromet et al. (2016) add that factors such as severity of exposure, history of prior stress exposure, and preexisting mental disorders also increase the risk of PTSD.

Refugees/Immigrants

The year 2015 to 2016 saw perhaps the largest catastrophe for refugees seeking safety and security through political asylum. It seemed like every day was an eventful and fatal one off the shores of Europe, particularly in the year 2016. Via the Internet, people in the comfort of their own homes got up close and personal and saw what individuals would endure to escape violence, war, and war crimes in their home countries. Hence, it got the world's attention. In the first 8 months of 2016, the world witnessed 3,176 refugee deaths, compared to the 2,754 who died during that time in 2015 (Baral, 2016). The bodies of young children being washed upon the shores of Europe was a sight no one can even begin to imagine.

The types of violence encountered in war-torn countries varied. For example, according to Chu, Keller, and Rasmussen (2013), personal forms of violence from rape/sexual assault were significantly associated with worse PTSD outcomes, as were postmigration factors such as measures of financial and legal insecurity. Forms of torture, imprisonment, bombings, executions, and witnessing others commit suicide as well had devastating effects on the psyche (Ferrada-Noli, Asberg, Ormstad, Lundin, & Sundbom, 1998a).

The effects of such trauma encountered by refugees and immigrants set them up, not only for PTSD where it occurred in 76% of the people studied, but for other psychiatric comorbidities and suicide as well (Ferrada-Noli, Asberg, Ormstad, Lundin, & Sundbom, 1998b).

Motor Vehicle Accidents

When you hear about a motor vehicle accident (MVA) occurring, you rarely hear about the follow-up for how and if an individual recovered, unless, of course, he or she died because of the accident. Trauma experienced in MVAs represents a significant precipitant of why PTSD develops (Beck & Coffey, 2007; Buckley, 2016; Koch, 2002; D. J. Stein et al., 2016). In the United States, MVAs accounted for the most frequently experienced traumatic event by males (25%) and the second most frequent traumatic event experienced by females (13%; Buckley, 2016). High-commuter volume and personal travel attribute to a high traffic flow and hence the potential for MVAs to occur with 1% of the U.S. population experiencing MVAs per year. Although the majority do not develop mental health issues (D. J. Stein et al., 2016), many do, the most common of which includes depression, PTSD, and anxiety with an average of 60% of survivors seeking treatment for PTSD-type symptomatology. Trauma from MVAs produces quite a different picture from other trauma because of the pain from physical injuries incurred during the accident (Koch, 2002).

One aspect of MVA-related PTSD that is different from PTSD caused by other traumas is the increased likelihood of being injured or developing a chronic pain condition as a result of the trauma. As a result, many people who have been in an MVA present first to their primary care physicians for treatment and do not consider psychological treatment for some time. Unfortunately, studies have shown that of the people who develop PTSD and do not seek psychological treatment, approximately half continue to have symptoms for more than 6 months or a year. Therefore, it is important to identify the symptoms early on and seek appropriate psychological treatment (Buckley, 2016; D. J. Stein et al., 2016). However, like other forms of trauma, the pretrauma condition of an individual plays a significant role if PTSD develops or not. For example, pre-MVA factors such as coping skills, mental health status, and level of social support all impact on how trauma is perceived and dealt with. Severity of the accident, degree of injury experienced, and any loss of life also play a significant role.

Witness to Trauma

Living a good-quality life after either witnessing or being involved at close proximity to a traumatic event is one of life's greatest challenges. For those living in war-torn regions or areas of much civil unrest, this impact is magnified even more so as friends, neighbors, and loved ones are subjected to the harshest of conditions, a road of emotional turmoil and grave losses. These sentinel events for individuals can be short lived or lengthy and ongoing over a longer duration of time, hence taking a significant toll on not just the people, friends, or loved ones but families and communities as well.

The unsettledness of war as well as the trauma of seeing life annihilated right before one's eyes is a vision that is not so easily forgotten. The ambiguity that war brings as loved ones and friends go missing or die is particularly stressful. The forced disappearance of persons, particularly during wartime or crisis unrest, occurs worldwide and affects not only individuals but their families and communities as well (Blauuw & Lahteenmaki, 2002). Ambiguous loss resembles trauma, because a person is unable to resolve the situation that causes pain, confusion, shock, distress, and often immobilization (Boss, 2006; S. Robins, 2010). Baraković, Avdibegović, and Sinanović (2014) add that women, in particular those with missing family members during war, showed significantly more severe PTSD symptoms. Klaric, Klaric, Stevanovic, Grkovic, and Jonovska (2007) add that "long-term exposure to war and postwar stressors caused serious psychological consequences in civilian women, with PTSD being only one of the disorders in the wide spectrum of posttraumatic reactions. Postwar stressors did not influence the prevalence of PTSD but they did contribute to the intensity and number of posttraumatic symptoms" (p. 175).

Today, the remnants of past wars continue to tighten their grasp on the mental health of many. Still years after the wars of Bosnia and Herzegovina, in the treatment of psychotraumatized persons "in the organizing of health care system schema in postwar Bosnia and Herzegovina, meaningful obstacles are still presented on the both, social and political level, despite mental health service reform performed in Bosnia-Herzegovina. The stigmatization of mental health issues is an important problem in treatment of traumatized individuals especially among war veterans. The lack a single center for psychtrauma in postwar BH shows absence of political will in BH to resolve the problem of war veterans with trauma related psychological disorders" (Avdibegović, Hasanović, Selimbasić, Pajević, & Sinanović, 2008, p. 475).

Fast Facts

Professions that involve the care and protection of vulnerable populations are often at an increased risk for developing PTSD.

References

Adams, L. (2015). *Workplace mental health for nurse managers*. New York, NY: Springer Publishing.

Addiction Search. (2017). Substance abuse among health care professionals. Retrieved from http://www.addictionsearch.com/treatment_articles/article/substance-abuse-among-healthcareprofessionals_49.html

Adriaenssens, J., de Gucht, V., & Maes, S. (2012). The impact of traumatic events on emergency room nurses: Findings from a questionnaire survey. *International Journal of Nursing Studies*, *49*(11), 1411–1422. doi:10.1016/j.ijnurstu.2012.07.003

Anxiety and Depression Association of America. (2016). Symptoms of PTSD. Retrieved from https://www.adaa.org/understanding-anxiety/posttraumatic-stress-disorder-ptsd/symptoms

Astin, M. C., Lawrence, K. J., & Foy, D. W. (1993). Posttraumatic stress disorder among battered women: Risk and resiliency factors. *Violence and Victims*, *8*(1), 17–28.

Avdibegović, E., Hasanović, M., Selimbašić, Z., Pajević, I., & Sinavović, O. (2008). Mental health care of psychotraumatized persons in post-war Bosnia and Herzegovina—experiences from Tuzla Canton. *Psychiatrica Danubina*, *20*(4), 474–484.

Babbel, C. (2011). The lingering trauma of child abuse. *Psychology Today*. Retrieved from https://www.psychologytoday.com/blog/somatic-psychology/201104/the-lingering-trauma-child-abuse

Baker, M. S. (2014). Casualties of the Global War on Terror and their future impact on health care and society: A looming public health crisis. *Military Medicine*, *179*(4), 348–355. doi:10.7205/MILMED-D-13-00471

Baraković, D., Avdibegović, E., & Sinanović, O. (2014). Postraumatic stress disorder in women with war missing family members. *Psychiatria Danubina*, *26*(4), 340–346.

Baral, S. (2016). Refugee crisis 2016 in Europe: Death toll and migrant arrival increases, statistics show. Retrieved from http://www.ibtimes.com/refugee-crisis-2016-europe-death-toll-migrant-arrival-increases-statistics-show-2399933

Beck, G., & Coffey, F. S. (2007). Assessment and treatment of PTSD after a motor vehicle collision: Empirical findings and clinical observations. *Professional Psychological Research*, *38*(6), 629–639.

Bendall, S., Alvarez-Jimenez, M., Hulbert, C. A., McGorry, P. D., & Jackson, H. J. (2012). Childhood trauma increases the risk of post-traumatic stress disorder in response to first-episode psychosis. *Australian and New Zealand Journal of Psychiatry*, *46*(1), 35–39. doi:10.1177/0004867411430871

Blauuw, M., & Lahteenmaki, V. (2002). "Denial and silence" or "acknowledgement and disclosure." *International Review of the Red Cross*, *84*, 767–783.

Blore, J. D., Sim, M. R., Forbes, A. B., Creamer, M. C., & Kelsall, H. L. (2015). Depression in Gulf War veterans: A systematic review and meta-analysis. *Psychological Medicine*, *2*, 1–16.

Boss, P. (2006). *Loss, trauma, and resilience: Therapeutic work with ambiguous loss*. London, UK: W. W. Norton.

Breslau, N., Davis, G. C., & Andreski, P. (1991). Traumatic events and post-traumatic stress disorder in an urban population of young adults. *Archives of General Psychiatry*, *48*, 216–222.

Bromet, E. J., Hobbs, M. J., Clouston, S. A. P., Gonzalez, A., Kotov, R., & Luft, B. J. (2016). *DSM-IV* post-traumatic stress disorder among World Trade Center responders 11–13 years after the disaster of 11 September 2001 (9/11). *Psychological Medicine, 46*(4), 771–783.

Buckley, M. (2016). Traumatic stress and motor vehicle accidents. Retrieved from http://www.ptsd.va.gov/professional/trauma/other/traumatic-stress -vehicle- accidents.asp

Caldera, T., Palma, L., Penayo, U., & Kullgren, G. (2001). Psychological impact of the hurricane Mitch in Nicaragua in a one-year perspective. *Social Psychiatry and Psychiatric Epidemiology, 36*(3), 108–114.

Carayon, P., & Gurses, A. P. (2005). A human factors engineering conceptual framework of nursing workload and patient safety in intensive care units. *Intensive Critical Care Nursing, 21*(5), 284–301.

Charles, J., Harrison, C., & Britt, H. (2014). Post-traumatic stress disorder in veterans. *Australian Family Physician, 43*(11), 753.

Chu, T., Keller, A., & Rasmussen, A. (2013). Effects of post-migration factors on PTSD outcomes among immigrant survivors of political violence. *Journal of Immigrant and Minority Health, 15*(5), 890–897.

Drummond, D. (2015). Physician burnout: Its origin, symptoms, and five main causes. *Family Practice Management, 22*(5), 42–47.

Elfering, N. K., Semmer, S., & Grebner, D. (2006). Work stress and patient safety: Observer-rated work stressors as predictors of characteristics of safety-related events reported by young nurses, *Ergonomics, 49*, 457–469.

Ferrada-Noli, M., Asberg, M., Ormstad, K., Lundin, T., & Sundbom, E. (1998a). Suicidal behavior after severe trauma. Part 1: PTSD diagnoses, psychiatric comorbidity and assessments of suicidal behavior. *Journal of Traumatic Stress, 11*(1), 103–112.

Ferrada-Noli, M., Asberg, M., Ormstad, K., Lundin, T., & Sundbom, E. (1998b). Suicidal behavior after severe trauma. Part 2: PTSD diagnoses, psychiatric comorbidity and assessments of suicidal behavior. *Journal of Traumatic Stress, 11*(1), 113–124.

Figley, C. R. (1995). Compassion fatigue as secondary traumatic stress disorder: An overview. In C. R. Figley (Ed.), *Compassion fatigue: Coping with secondary traumatic stress disorder in those who treat the traumatized* (pp. 1–20). New York, NY: Brunner/Mazel.

Fjeldheim, C. B., Nöthling, J., Pretorius, K., Basson, M., Ganasen, K., Heneke, R., . . . Seed, S. (2014). Trauma exposure, posttraumatic stress disorder and the effect of explanatory variables in paramedic trainees. *BMC Emergency Medicine, 14*(11). doi:10.1186/1471-227X-14-11

Gore, A. T. (2015). Posttraumatic stress disorder. In I. Ahmed, *Medscape.* Retrieved from http://emedicine.medscape.com/article/288154-overview

Gupta, J., Falb, K. L., Carliner, H., Hossain, M., Kpebo, D., & Annan, J. (2014). Associations between exposure to intimate partner violence, armed conflict, and probable PTSD among women in rural Cote d'Ivoire. *PLOS ONE, 9*(5), e96300.

Hanrahan, M. (2017). Anger in Russia as bill aims to decriminalize some domestic violence. Retrieved from http://www.nbcnews.com/news/world/anger-russia-bill-aims-decriminalize-some-domestic-violence-n710421

Hébert, M., Lavoie, F., & Blais, M. (2014). Posttraumatic stress disorder/PTSD in adolescent victims of sexual abuse: Resilience and social support as protection factors. *Ciência and Saúde Coletiva*, *19*(3), 685–694.

Hébert, M., Langevin, R., & Daigneault, I. (2016). The association between peer victimization, PTSD, and dissociation in child victims of sexual abuse. *Journal of Affective Disorders*, *193*, 227–232.

Hooper, C., Craig, J., Janvrin, D. R., Wetsel, M. A., & Reimels, E. (2010). Compassion satisfaction, burnout, and compassion fatigue among emergency nurses compared with nurses in other selected inpatient specialties. *Journal of Emergency Nursing*, *36*, 420–427. doi:10.1016/j.jen.2009.11.02

Kelly, B. D. (2015). Shell shock in Ireland: The Richmond War Hospital. *History of Psychiatry*, *26*(1), 50–63.

Kemp, A., Green, B. L., Hovanitz, C., & Rawlings, E. I. (1995). Incidence and correlates of posttraumatic stress disorder in battered women. *Journal of Interpersonal Violence*, *10*, 43–55.

Kessler, R. C., Sonnega, A., Bromet, E., Hughes, M., & Nelson, C. B. (1995). Posttraumatic stress disorder in the National Comorbidity Survey. *Archives of General Psychiatry*, *52*(12), 1048–1060.

Klaric, M., Klaric, B., Stevanovic, A., Grkovic, J., & Jonovska, S. (2007). Psychological consequences of war trauma and postwar social stressors in women in Bosnia and Herzegovina. *Croatian Medical Journal*, *48*(2), 167–176.

Koch, W. J. (2002). Post-traumatic stress disorder and pain following motor vehicle collisions. *British Columbia Medical Journal*, *44*(6), 298–302.

Kornblith, A. B., & Ligibel, J. (2003). Psychosocial and sexual functioning of survivors of breast cancer. *Seminars in Oncology*, *30*(6), 799–813.

Kos, A. (2017). Queensland floods: Researchers analyse ongoing health effects of traumatic 2011 flooding. Retrieved from http://www.abc.net.au/news/2017-01-15/researchers-analyse-ongoing-health-effects-2011-qld-floods/8182914

Kristensen, T. E., Elklit, A., Karstoft, K.-I., & Palic, S. (2014). Predicting chronic posttraumatic stress disorder in bereaved relatives: A 6-month follow-up study. *American Journal of Hospice and Palliative Medicine*, *31*(4), 396–405. doi:10.1177/1049909113490066

Kun, P., Chen, X., Han, S., Gong, X., Chen, M., & Zhang, W. (2009). Prevalence of post-traumatic stress disorder in Sichuan Province, China after the 2008 Wenchuan earthquake. *Public Health*, *123*(11), 703–707.

Kun, P., Han, S., Chen, X., & Yao, L. (2009). Prevalence and risk factors for posttraumatic stress disorder: A cross-sectional study among survivors of the Wenchuan 2008 earthquake in China. *Depression and Anxiety*, *26*(12), 1134–1140. doi:10.1002/da.20612

Langeveld, N. E., Grootenhuis, M. A., Voûte, P. A., & de Haan, R. J. (2004). Posttraumatic stress symptoms in adult survivors of childhood cancer. *Pediatric Blood and Cancer*, *42*(7), 604–610.

Lee, Y. L., & Santacroce, S. J. (2007). Posttraumatic stress in long-term young adult survivors of childhood cancer: A questionnaire survey. *International Journal of Nursing Studies, 44*(8), 1406–1417.

Lubit, R. H., & Pataki, C. (2016). Posttraumatic stress disorder in children. Retrieved from http://emedicine.medscape.com/article/918844-overview

Luftman, K., Aydelotte, J., Rix, K., Ali, S., Houck, K., Coopwood, T. B., . . . Davis, M. (2017). PTSD in those who care for the injured. *Injury, 48*(2), 293–296. doi:10.1016/j.injury.2016.11.001

Macleod, A. D. (1994). The reactivation of post-traumatic stress disorder in later life. *Australian and New Zealand Journal of Psychiatry, 28*(4), 625–634.

Mark, G., & Smith, A. P. (2012). Occupational stress, job characteristics, coping, and the mental health of nurses. *British Journal of Health Psychology, 17*(3), 505–521. doi:10.1111/j.2044-8287.2011.02051.x

Maslach, C. (1982). *Burnout: The cost of caring.* Englewood Cliffs, NJ: Spectrum.

Mayo Clinic. (2013). Job burnout: How to spot it and take action. Retrieved from http://www.mayoclinic.com/health/burnout/WL00062

Mayo Clinic. (2015). Post-traumatic stress disorder (PTSD): Causes. Retrieved from http://www.mayoclinic.org/diseases-conditions/post-traumatic -stress-disorder/basics/causes/con-20022540

Mayou, R. A., Ehlers, A., & Bryant, B. (2002). Posttraumatic stress disorder after motor vehicle accidents: 3-year follow-up of a prospective longitudinal study. *Behaviour Research and Therapy, 40*(6), 665–675. doi:10.1016/ S0005-7967(01)00069-9

McMillan, K. A., & Asmundson, G. J. (2016). PTSD, social anxiety disorder, and trauma: An examination of the influence of trauma type on comorbidity using a nationally representative sample. *Psychiatry Research, 246,* 561–567. doi:10.1016/j.psychres.2016.10.036

Mgoqi-Mbalo, N., Zhang, M., & Ntuli, S. (2017). Risk factors for PTSD and depression in female survivors of rape. *Psychological Trauma: Theory, Research, Practice and Policy, 9*(3), 301–308. doi:10.1037/tra0000228

Miller, M. W., Wolf, E. J., Reardon, A. F., Harrington, K. M., Ryabchenko, K., Castillo, D., . . . Heyman, R. E. (2013). PTSD and conflict behavior between veterans and their intimate partners. *Journal of Anxiety Disorders, 27*(2), 240–251. doi:10.1016/j.janxdis.2013.02.005

Möller, A. T., Bäckström, T., Söndergaard, H. P., & Helström, L. (2014). Identifying risk factors for PTSD in women seeking medical help after rape. *PLOS ONE.* Retrieved from http://journals.plos.org/plosone/article?id= 10.1371/journal.pone.0111136

National Center for PTSD. (2016). Disasters. Retrieved from https://www .ptsd.va.gov/PTSD/public/types/disasters/index.asp

National Institute of Mental Health. (2014). Post-traumatic stress disorder (PTSD). Retrieved from https://www.nimh.nih.gov/health/publications/ helping-children-and-adolescents-cope-with-violence-and-disasters -community-members/index.shtml

National Institute of Mental Health. (2016). Post-traumatic stress disorder. Retrieved from https://www.nimh.nih.gov/health/publications/post-trau matic-stress-disorder-basics/index.shtml

National Institute for Occupational Safety and Health. (2008). What are the potential adverse health effects of occupational stress? Retrieved from http://www.cdc.gov/niosh/docs/2008-136/pdfs/2008-136.pdf

Nock, M. K., Stein, M. B., Herringa, S. G., Ursano, R. J., Colpe, L. J., Fullerton, C. S., . . . Kessler, R. C. (2014). Prevalence and correlates of suicidal behavior among soldiers: Results from the Army Study to Assess Risk and Resilience in Service members (Army STARRS). *JAMA Psychiatry*, *71*(5), 514–522. doi:10.1001/jamapsychiatry.2014.30

Perry, B., Toffner, G., Merrick, T., & Dalton, J. (2011). An exploration of the experience of compassion fatigue in clinical oncology nurses. *Canadian Oncology Nursing Journal*, *21*, 91–105.

Preidt, B. (2016). Cyberbullying, violence linked to PTSD in teens. Retrieved from https://consumer.healthday.com/kids-health-information-23/ado lescents-and-teen-health-news-719/cyberbullying-violence-linked-to -ptsd-in-teens-708236.html

Potter, P., Deshields, T., Berger, J. A., Clarke, M., Olsen, S., & Chen, L. (2013). Evaluation of a compassion fatigue resiliency program for oncology nurses. *Oncology Nursing Forum*, *40*(2), 180–187. doi:10.1188/13.ONF.180-187

Pulley, S. A. (2005). Critical Incident Stress Management. Retrieved from https://web.archive.org/web/20060811232118/http:/www.emedicine.com/ emerg/topic826.htm

Rabenhorst, M. M., McCarthy, R. J., Thomsen, C. J., Milner, J. S., Travis, W. J., Foster, R. E., & Copeland, C. W. (2013). Spouse abuse among United States Air Force personnel who deployed in support of Operation Iraqi Freedom/ Operation Enduring Freedom. *Journal of Family Psychology*, *27*(5), 754–761.

Reeves, R. R., Parker, J. D., & Konkle-Parker, D. J. (2005). War-related mental health problems of today's veterans: New clinical awareness. *Journal of Psychosocial Nursing and Mental Health Services*, *43*(7), 18–28.

Robbers, M. L. P., & Jenkins, J. M. (2005). Symptomatology of post-traumatic stress disorder among first responders to the Pentagon on 9/11: A pre-liminary analysis of Arlington County Police First Responders. *Police Practice and Research*, *6*, 235–249.

Robins, P. M., Meltzer, L., & Zelikovsky, N. (2009). The experience of second-ary traumatic stress upon care providers working within a children's hos-pital. *Journal of Pediatric Nursing*, *24*, 270–279.

Robins, S. (2010). Ambiguous loss in a non-Western context: Families of the disappeared in post-conflict Nepal. *Family Relations*, *59*, 253–268.

Rossignol, M., & Chandler, H. K. (2010). Recognizing posttraumatic stress disorder in military veterans. *American Nurse Today*, *5*(2), Retrieved from http://www.americannursetoday.com/recognizing-posttraumatic -stress-disorder-in-military-veterans

Schlee, K. A., Heyman, R. E., & O'Leary, K. D. (1998). Group treatment for spouse abuse: Are women with PTSD appropriate participants? *Journal of Family Violence, 13*(1), 1–20.

Smith, M., Segal, J., & Segal, R. (2013). Preventing burnout. Retrieved from http://www.helpguide.org/mental/burnout_signs_symptoms.htm

Stamm, B. H. (Ed.). (1995). *Secondary traumatic stress: Self-care issues for clinicians, researchers, and educators.* Lutherville, MD: Sidran Press.

Stamm, B. H. (2002). Measuring compassion satisfaction as well as fatigue: Developmental history of the compassion satisfaction and fatigue test. In C. R. Figley (Ed.), *Treating compassion fatigue* (pp. 107–119). New York, NY: Brunner-Routledge.

Stein, M. B., Walker, J. R., Hazen, A. L., & Forde, D. R. (1997). Full and partial posttraumatic stress disorder: Findings from a community survey. *American Journal of Psychiatry, 154,* 1114–1119.

Stein, D. J., Karam, E. G., Shahly, V., Hill, E. D., King, A., & Petukhova, M. (2016). Post-traumatic stress disorder associated with life-threatening motor vehicle collisions in the WHO World Mental Health Surveys. *BMC Psychiatry, 16,* 257. doi:10.1186/s12888-016-0957-8

Streb, M., Haller, P., & Michael, T. (2014). PTSD in paramedics: Resilience and sense of coherence. *Behavioral and Cognitive Psychotherapy, 42*(4), 452–463.

Sundin, L., Hochwälder, J., & Lisspers, J. (2011). A longitudinal examination of generic and occupational specific job demands and work-related social support associated with burnout among nurses in Sweden. *Work, 38,* 389–400. doi:10.3233/WOR-2011-1142

Thaipisuttikul, P., Ittasakul, P., Waleeprakhon, P., Wisajun, P., & Jullagate, S. (2014). Psychiatric comorbidities in patients with major depressive disorder. *Neuropsychiatric Disease and Treatment, 10,* 2097–2103.

Thomas, J. L., Wilk, J. E., Riviere, L. A., McGurk, D., Castro, C. A., & Hoge, C. W. (2010). Prevalence of mental health problems and functional impairment among active component and National Guard soldiers 3 and 12 months following combat in Iraq. *Archives of General Psychiatry, 67*(6), 614–623.

Toronto Psychology Centre. (2016). Trauma and abuse. Retrieved from http://torontopsychologycentre.com/areas-of-focus/trauma-and-abuse

Turner, H. A., Finkelhor, D., Shattuck, A., Hamby, S., & Mitchell, K. (2014). Beyond bullying: Aggravating elements of peer victimization episodes. *School Psychology Quarterly.* Advance online publication. doi:10.1037/spq0000058

U.S. Department of Veterans Affairs. (2015). Sexual assault against females. Retrieved from http://www.ptsd.va.gov/public/PTSD-overview/women/sexual-assault-females.asp

Vahey, D. C., Aiken, L. H., Sloane, D. M., Clarke, S. P., & Vargas, D. (2004). Nurse burnout and patient satisfaction. *Medical Care, 42*(Suppl. 2), II57–II66. doi:10.1097/01.mlr.0000109126.50398.5a

Van Loey, N. E. E., Maas, C. J. M., Faber, A. W., & Taal, L. A. (2003). Predictors of chronic posttraumatic stress symptoms following burn injury: Results of a longitudinal study. *Journal of Traumatic Stress, 16*, 361–369.

Van Zelst, W. H., de Beurs, E., Beekman, A. T., Deeg, D. J., & van Dyck, R. (2003). Prevalence and risk factors of post-traumatic stress disorder in older adults. *Psychotherapy and Psychosomatics, 72*, 333–342.

Veterans Affairs Canada. (2017). Learn about PTSD. Retrieved from http://www.veterans.gc.ca/eng/services/health/mental-health/publications/learn-ptsd

Vujanovic, A. A., Bonn-Miller, M. O., & Petry, N. M. (2016). Co-occurring posttraumatic stress and substance use: Emerging research on correlates, mechanisms, and treatments—Introduction to the special issue. *Psychology of Addictive Behaviors, 30*(7), 713–719.

Women Safe. (2011). Overview of historical laws that supported domestic violence. Retrieved from http://www.womensafe.net/home/index.php/domesticviolence/29-overview-of-historical-laws-that-supported-domestic-violence

Yarvis, J. S. (2011). A civilian social worker's guide to the treatment of war-induced PTSD. *Social Work in Health Care, 50*(1), 51–72. doi:10.1080/00981389.2010.518856

5

The Impact of Traumatic Events

Reactions (responses) to trauma can be immediate or delayed. Many reactions can be triggered by persons, places, or things associated with the trauma. Some reactions may appear totally unrelated to the event, person, or object at hand. However, it is important to remember that these are "normal" reactions to "abnormal" events. The experience of even one traumatic event can have devastating consequences for the individual involved. However, trauma can affect individuals in various ways, targeting their physical, psychological/emotional, neurological, social, and spiritual health.

In both the short term and long term, the impact of stress is invasive. Throughout alternating between short bursts of painful memories and periods of avoidance and numbing, the sense of feeling keyed-up persists. The traumatized person has experienced an event that potentially threatened his or her life, or the life of someone else, so the mind and body stay on alert to make sure not to miss any sign that such an event may recur in future. It is safer to get it wrong by overestimating a potential threat than to risk the possibility of missing any future threat. The persistent activation of this threat detection system, however, leaves the traumatized person feeling nervous or on edge much of the time. In addition, the threat detection system is so sensitive that it constantly goes off when there is no danger, in a way that interferes with the person's capacity to live a normal and happy life. A similar explanation exists with regard to anger. Anger was useful in battle or other situations of threat. It hypes us up and promotes our survival—it may often be an adaptive way to respond to a life-threatening situation and certainly better than being immobilized with fear. Again, however, it is no longer useful for our survival once the danger has passed. In fact, as we all know, it starts to cause serious problems in our day-to-day lives.

In this chapter, you will learn:

- The various forms of symptomatology that can impact individuals suffering from posttraumatic stress disorder (PTSD)
- How PTSD affects every aspect of one's life
- How PTSD can manifest itself as suicide

PHYSICAL EFFECTS

Initially, there is not a lot of physical symptomatology to notice, as much of it occurs in the brain. However, in the presence of a threat or trauma, one can be witnessed trying to physically run away from the perceived danger source. Within the body, the full response to stress occurs under the fight-or-flight mechanism. Therefore, what will typically happen is the shutting down of unnecessary bodily processes. As blood is shunted to the brain, muscles, and heart where it is needed most to escape from fight, its supply to the gastrointestinal tract, other organs, and the skin will be stalled.

Depending on the duration of this immediate phase, organs and other important bodily processes may become jeopardized. For example, the occurrence of sepsis following physical trauma results from the multifocal initiation of inflammatory processes. Not only do white blood cells migrate rapidly to the injured area, but the release of proteins also occurs, particularly the HMGB1 protein that can cause a full-body septic inflammation, which is often life-threatening (Toledo, 2012).

Essentially, the body endures the traumatic event(s) that created not only undue stress, physically and psychologically, but also precipitated many other physiological and possibly pathological responses that continue to subject the body to even more stress. But the immediate impact of PTSD does not stop here.

NEUROLOGICAL–BIOLOGICAL EFFECTS

One of the main impacts left by PTSD is neurologically based. Reactions to trauma vary from person to person, from minor disruptions in an individual's life to debilitating responses. Across the continuum, people may experience anxiety, terror, shock, shame, emotional numbness, disconnection, intrusive thoughts, helplessness, and powerlessness. An important variable is the age at which the trauma occurs. For children, early trauma can have especially negative consequences, impacting the development of the brain and normal developmental progression. Memory is often affected—people may not remember parts of what happened, but at the same time may be overwhelmed by sporadic memories that return in flashbacks. Nightmares, depression, irritability, and jumpiness are common. All of these responses can interfere with an individual's sense of safety, self, and self-efficacy, as well as the ability to regulate emotions and navigate relationships.

Cognition has also been a target of trauma. Immediately after trauma, an individual can lose his or her sense of reality, and feel confused and disoriented to the surrounding because of stimulus overload. An inability to focus and concentrate, difficulty in completing complicated tasks that require critical thinking, and memory losses have all been identified as a result of trauma. Kevin Tracey, a neurosurgeon at the Feinstein Institute for Medical Research, suggests that declining cognition occurs and does so as a result of a specific protein, the HMGB1 protein, that emerges during the onset of inflammation and sepsis that causes cognitive dysfunction (Toledo, 2012).

PSYCHOLOGICAL EFFECTS

Psychologically, many factors contribute to the development of mental illness. These range from neglect to abuse, creating low self-esteem and confidence. For example, a child subjected to psychological trauma such as emotional abuse, physical abuse, and/or sexual abuse (Katz, Cojucar, Beheshti, Nakamura, & Murray 2012) has increased susceptibility to the development of a mental illness. Neglect (Katz et al., 2012), the early loss of a parent (Katz et al., 2012), poor ability to relate to others (Katz et al., 2012), feelings of inadequacy, anxiety, low self-esteem, low confidence, anger, and loneliness can all predispose a person to the development of a mental illness (Katz et al., 2012).

Psychological trauma can be overwhelming in an emotional, cognitive, and physical sense (Box 5.1). People who have been traumatized may alternate between feeling empty or "numb" and being flooded by intense feelings of fear, anger, shame, and other emotions (Toronto Psychology Centre, 2016).

BOX 5.1 PSYCHOLOGICAL–EMOTIONAL RESPONSES TO TRAUMA (LEVIN, 2011)

- Shock and disbelief
- Fear and/or anxiety
- Grief, disorientation, denial
- Hyper alertness or hypervigilance
- Irritability, restlessness, outbursts of anger or rage
- Emotional swings—like crying and then laughing
- Worrying or ruminating—intrusive thoughts of the trauma
- Nightmares
- Flashbacks—feeling like the trauma is happening now
- Feelings of helplessness, panic, feeling out of control
- Increased need to control everyday experiences
- Minimizing the experience
- Attempts to avoid anything associated with trauma
- Tendency to isolate oneself
- Feelings of detachment
- Concern over burdening others with problems
- Emotional numbing or restricted range of feelings
- Difficulty trusting and/or feelings of betrayal
- Difficulty concentrating or remembering
- Feelings of self-blame and/or survivor guilt
- Shame
- Diminished interest in everyday activities or depression
- Unpleasant past memories resurfacing
- Suicidal thoughts
- Loss of a sense of order or fairness in the world
- Expectation of doom and fear of the future
- Anger toward religion or belief system
- Loss of beliefs
- Desire for revenge

Source: Levin (2011).

SOCIAL EFFECTS

The experience of PTSD can have immediate effects on people socially. An individual can be so scared, disillusioned, and confused that he or she becomes withdrawn from others. Trauma survivors who have PTSD may have trouble with their close family relationships or friendships. Their symptoms can cause problems with trust, closeness, communication, and problem solving, which may affect the way trauma survivors act with others. In turn, the way a loved one responds to them affects the trauma survivors. A circular pattern may develop that could harm relationships (Anxiety and Depression Association of America, 2016). As found by Baker (2014) the impact of PTSD in witnessing a great deal of family violence suggests the effects of the violence will linger for years and impact across generations because of the stress on families and children.

PSYCHIATRIC EFFECTS

The physiological adaptations that some people develop in response to trauma and to perceived ongoing threats produce an underlying state of "dysregulation"—difficulty controlling or regulating emotional reactions or behaviors. This dysregulation of the brain and body systems perpetuates mental, emotional, and physical distress (B. C. Ministry of Health, 2016). The majority of people with PTSD meet the diagnostic criteria for other psychiatric disorders (Cohen, 2016; Resnick, Kilpatrick, Dansky, Saunders, & Best, 1993). In the immediate short term, what is typically seen are anxiety disorders, such as panic attacks and acute stress disorders. It is often the acute stress disorders that progress to become a full diagnosis of PTSD. Within a short time frame, individuals begin to manifest other mental illnesses, such as depression, agoraphobia, obsessive-compulsive disorder, and/or social phobias and somatization disorders.

Fast Facts

Although the immediate impact of PTSD is often acute, it can represent more long-term effects if not dealt with effectively and in a timely manner.

SUICIDE

Like PTSD, the act or attempt of suicide can cross all forms of trauma, populations, and age groups. Whether the trauma is a result of a natural disaster (Caldera, Palma, Penayo, & Kullgren, 2001), childhood abuse (Cohen, 2016), childhood bullying (Centers for Disease Control and Prevention, 2014), or combat duty (Shane & Kime, 2016), suicide is perhaps one of the greatest fears for someone who is suffering from PTSD. When individuals with PTSD find themselves on the verge of being suicidal and taunted repeatedly with thoughts of suicide, they feel they have nowhere left to turn. For the involved family and/or loved ones, the act of suicide is heart-wrenching. It often leaves friends and families wondering why, maybe they could have done more to help, and so forth. They feel lost, empty, dumbfounded, and shocked. But no words can really describe how those left behind feel. Media around the world bombardus with headlines of how soldiers, justice personnel, emergency services workers, and many other victims of trauma have attempted to commit or successfully committed suicide.

Perhaps the most well-known trauma that has fed such news reports in recent years is that of combat personnel and soldiers returning from duty, only to be faced with the inability to cope with what they had experienced overseas or elsewhere (Castro & Kintzle, 2014). According to Brunet and Monson (2014), it should come as no surprise that several people who died by suicide were former Canadian Armed Forces personnel—a more than twofold increase in dying by suicide compared to the general population. However, this twofold increase in death by suicide as a result of PTSD occurred irrespective of whether the PTSD was developed as part of a military deployment or otherwise. Furthermore, they also found that most people who reported suicidal ideations did not attempt suicide. In a recent study concerning a large military sample, 38.5% of individuals expressing suicidal ideations developed a plan and 34% with a plan made an attempt on their life within the following year. A study by Conner et al. (2014), although adjusting for other mental illnesses, revealed that PTSD was not a risk for suicide overall but once PTSD was linked to a major depression disorder, the risk of suicide increased substantially (Brunet & Monson, 2014). Such a finding is supported elsewhere, where the co-occurrence of PTSD with major depression disorder enhances the risk for suicidal behavior (Oquendo et al., 2005).

Although suicide rates among middle-aged nurses in the United States have declined in recent years (Anderson, Kochanek, & Murphy, 1995), the suicide rate among middle-aged female nurses has increased

(Hawton & Vislisel, 1999). According to Feskanich et al. (2002), a severe level of stress at home or at work was associated with an increased risk of suicide for female nurses. Forty-four percent of the women reported the same stress level at home and at work. Incidence rates for suicide were highest among those who reported severe (24.8 per 100,000) or minimal (13.3 per 100,000) levels of stress both at home and at work, with increased risks in the minimal and severe categories for both home and work stress. Even after adjusting for smoking, coffee consumption, alcohol intake, and marital status, risks remained high. The reason for this increase is believed to result from increased occupational stress levels and easier access to drugs (Feskanich et al., 2002). They further suspect that "the increased risk of suicide among the women who reported minimal stress at home or at work may reflect denial or it may be associated with other risks for suicide, such as social isolation and depression" (Feskanich et al., 2002, p. 95). In a literature review by Hawton and Vislisel (1999), it was found that "there is evidence from several countries that female nurses are at increased risk of suicide." Although there is very little information about the specific causes of suicide, smoking and consumption of caffeine are significant risk factors.

Even among refugees, suicide became a troubling reality for many. The atrocities experienced by refugees from the war-torn countries resulted in 79% of them developing PTSD, with a significant proportion (79%) reporting a high incidence of suicidal thoughts and attempts (Ferrada-Noli, Asberg, Ormstad, Lundin, & Sundbom, 1998a). From this study, more specifically, 40% made suicide attempts, 29% developed detailed suicide plans, and 31% had recurrent suicidal thoughts (Ferrada-Noli, Asberg, Ormstad, Lundin, & Sundbom, 1998b).

Because homicide and/or suicide are the worst possible outcomes for someone suffering from PTSD, it is important to discuss how to diagnose and prevent it.

SUICIDE ASSESSMENT AND RISK

Assessment for the risk of suicide among individuals suffering from PTSD is a priority intervention. A health care clinician needs to be scrupulous in his or her assessment of suicide risk because many of the signs of impending suicide attempts are subtle and discreet.

Many of these warning signs are not overly alarming individually, but collectively they become very concerning. The warning signs of a possible suicide or suicide attempt are described in Box 5.2.

BOX 5.2   WARNING SIGNS OF SUICIDE

- Loss of interest in things the person used to care about
- Irritability and edginess increases
- Giving things away
- Visiting or calling people and saying "Goodbye"
- Methodically making amends, settling quarrels
- Withdrawal and isolation from friends and family
- Sudden decline in functioning at school or work
- Suddenly happier, right after a long, deep depression
- Change in appearance—hygiene, and so forth
- Increased risk-taking behavior (e.g., use of drugs, reckless driving)
- Talking about feeling hopeless, helpless, or worthless
- Hoarding of pills, hiding of weapons
- Talking about suicide and/or what it would be like to die (preoccupied with death)
- Self-injury
- Threatening suicide

Indirect statements
- "What's the use of going on."
- "My parents would be happier if I'd never been born."
- "I just can't take it anymore."

Direct statements
- "Sometimes I just feel like killing myself"
- "If I killed myself, then people would be sorry"
- "You won't have to worry about me much longer"

In my own clinical experience working with patients who are potentially suicidal, I've come to expect the "unexpected." A patient who was admitted with a diagnosis of major depressive disorder had a hospital inpatient stay for about 5 weeks. Her mood and affect seemed to improve somewhat, and she was ultimately approved for a day pass to leave the hospital for a period of time. She returned to the hospital unit that evening; her mood was elated, her affect bright, and she was excited and optimistic with big plans for her future.

Later that evening, she decided to go outside to smoke a cigarette, which was not an uncommon request for her, as she was an avid smoker. She never came back, but was instead found dead in a local body of water. What happened? While out on her day pass, she ultimately decided that her life and the people and events in her life were not improved, which perhaps reinforced for her that she was going to commit suicide. Furthermore, while out on the day pass, unbeknownst to the hospital clinicians, she had gotten her affairs in order. This is just one example of a real situation that can occur when someone has decided to commit suicide. When clinicians see a much happier and brighter affect and mood in their patient, it should not be taken at face value but instead further investigated and the patient should be monitored very closely.

SEVERITY OF RISK OF SUICIDE

Once the possibility of suicide is established, the severity of risk must then be assessed. Questions often asked in the suicide assessment to determine severity or degree of risk are described in Box 5.3.

BOX 5.3 DEGREE/SEVERITY OF SUICIDE RISK

- Does the person have a plan?
- If yes, what is the plan and does the person have access to items necessary for this plan?
- How often does the person think about suicide?
- How badly does the person wish to end his or her life?
- Has the person felt suicidal in the past, or is this the first time?
- Has the person ever attempted suicide before? When?
- Is the person using drugs or alcohol—does he or she have access?
- Will the person be home alone?
- Does the person take medications for mental health concerns—has he or she been taking them?

WHO IS MOST LIKELY TO COMMIT SUICIDE?

Suicide is most prevalent in certain populations in society. Although rates are generally highest in teenagers, adolescents, and the elderly, White elderly men older than 65 have the highest rate of suicide. In addition to this finding, the risk of suicide appears to be highest in the following subpopulations of people (Goldberg, 2016):

- Older people who have lost a spouse through death or divorce
- People who have attempted suicide in the past
- People with a family history of suicide
- People with a friend or coworker who committed suicide
- People with a history of physical, emotional, or sexual abuse
- People who are unmarried, unskilled, or unemployed
- People with long-term pain or a disabling or terminal illness
- People who are prone to violent or impulsive behavior
- People who have recently been released from psychiatric hospitalization (this often is a very frightening period of transition)
- People in certain professions, such as police officers and health clinicians who work with terminally ill patients, emergency response (ER) personnel, and military who are on the front lines of disaster, trauma, and warfare
- People who have either been part of or witnessed trauma, violence, and/or disasters
- Those with substance abuse disorders and/or behaviors

Fast Facts

The act of suicide by an individual who has PTSD represents that he or she feels that there has nowhere left to turn.

References

Anderson, R. N., Kochanek, K. D., & Murphy, S. L. (1995). Report of final mortality statistics. *National Center for Health Statistics Monthly Vital Statistics Report*, 45(11 Suppl. 2), 1–80.

Anxiety and Depression Association of America. (2016). Symptoms of PTSD. Retrieved from https://www.adaa.org/understanding-anxiety/posttraumatic-stress-disorder-ptsd/symptoms

B. C. Ministry of Health. (2016). Post-traumatic stress disorder. Retrieved from https://www.healthlinkbc.ca/health-topics/hw184188

Baker, M. S. (2014). Casualties of the Global War on Terror and their future impact on health care and society: A looming public health crisis. *Military Medicine, 179*(4), 348–355. doi:10.7205/MILMED-D-13-00471

Brunet, A., & Monson, E. (2014). Suicide risk among active and retired Canadian soldiers: The role of posttraumatic stress disorder. *Canadian Journal of Psychiatry, 59*(9), 457–459.

Caldera, T., Palma, L., Penayo, U., & Kullgren, G. (2001). Psychological impact of Hurricane Mitch in Nicaragua in a one-year perspective. *Social Psychiatry and Psychiatric Epidemiology, 36*(3), 108–114.

Castro, C. A., & Kintzle, S. (2014). Suicides in the military: The post-modern combat veteran and the Hemingway effect. *Current Psychiatry Reports, 16*(8), 460.

Centers for Disease Control and Prevention. (2014). The relationship between bullying and suicide: What we know and what it means for schools. Retrieved from https://www.cdc.gov/violenceprevention/pdf/bullying -suicide-translation-final-a.pdf

Cohen, H. (2016). Associated conditions of PTSD. Retrieved from https://psy chcentral.com/lib/associated-conditions-of-ptsd

Conner, K. R., Bossarte, R. M., He, H., Arora, J., Lu, N., Tu, X. M., & Katz, I. R. (2014). Posttraumatic stress disorder and suicide in 5.9 million individuals receiving care in the Veterans Health Administration health system. *Journal of Affective Disorders, 166*, 1–5. doi:10.1016/j.jad .2014.04.067

Ferrada-Noli, M., Asberg, M., Ormstad, K., Lundin, T., & Sundbom, E. (1998a). Suicidal behavior after severe trauma. Part 1: PTSD diagnoses, psychiatric comorbidity and assessments of suicidal behavior. *Journal of Traumatic Stress, 11*(1), 103–112.

Ferrada-Noli, M., Asberg, M., Ormstad, K., Lundin, T., & Sundbom, E. (1998b). Suicidal behavior after severe trauma. Part 2: PTSD diagnoses, psychiatric comorbidity and assessments of suicidal behavior. *Journal of Traumatic Stress, 11*(1), 113–124.

Feskanich, D., Hastrup, J. L., Marshall, J. R., Colditz, G. A., Stampfer, M. J., Willett, W. C., & Kawachi I. (2002). Stress and suicide in the nurses' health study. *Journal of Epidemiology and Community Health, 56*(2), 95–98.

Goldberg, B. (2016). Who is most likely to commit suicide? Retrieved from http://www.webmd.com/mental-health/recognizing-suicidal-behavior#2-3

Hawton, K., & Vislisel, L. (1999). Suicide in nurses. *Suicide Life Threat Behaviors, 29*, 86–95.

Katz, L., Cojucar, G., Beheshti, S., Nakamura, E., & Murray, M. (2012). Military sexual trauma during combat: Prevalence, readjustment, and gender differences in those deployed in the conflicts in Iraq and Afghanistan. *Violence and Victims, 27*(4), 487–499.

Levin, P. (2011). Common responses to trauma and coping strategies. Retrieved from http://www.trauma-pages.com/s/t-facts.php

Oquendo, M., Brent, D. A., Birmaher, B., Greenhill, L., Kolko, D., Stanley, B., . . . & Mann, J. J. (2005). Posttraumatic stress disorder comorbid with major depression: Factors mediating the association with suicidal behavior. *American Journal of Psychiatry, 162*(3), 560–566.

Resnick, H. S., Kilpatrick, D. G., Dansky, B. S., Saunders, B. E., & Best, C. L. (1993). Prevalence of civilian trauma and posttraumatic stress disorder in a representative national sample of women. *Journal of Consulting Clinical Psychology, 61*(6), 984–991.

Shane, L., & Kime, P. (2016). New VA study finds 20 veterans commit suicide each day. Retrieved from http://www.militarytimes.com/story/veterans/2016/07/07/va-suicide-20-daily-research/86788332

Thaipisuttikul, P., Ittasakul, P., Waleeprakhon, P., Wisajun, P., & Jullagate, S. (2014). Psychiatric comorbidities in patients with major depressive disorder. *Neuropsychiatric Disease and Treatment, 10*, 2097–2103.

Toledo, C. (2012). Life after traumatic injury: How the body responds. Retrieved from https://publications.nigms.nih.gov/insidelifescience/life-after-traumatic-injury.html

Toronto Psychology Centre. (2016). Trauma and abuse. Retrieved from http://torontopsychologycentre.com/areas-of-focus/trauma-and-abuse

6

The Long-Term Impact of PTSD

Reactions to trauma and the impact from it do not necessarily begin immediately after trauma. We have already discussed some of the more immediate symptoms, so we now focus our attention on the delayed symptoms of posttraumatic stress disorder (PTSD). Sometimes, symptoms may not appear until years after the event. These symptoms cause significant problems in social or work situations and in relationships (Mayo Clinic, 2016a). Particularly with the high levels of distress associated with memories of severe trauma, such thoughts and feelings tend to be pushed away into the subconscious mind in an effort to protect the person from the distress. The result is that although the memory may go away for a period of time, the need for it to be dealt with has not been addressed and the memory keeps coming back. The movement backward and forward from intrusive thoughts and feelings about the trauma to avoidance and numbing can continue almost indefinitely unless the cycle is addressed in some way.

In addition to the delayed effects of the experienced trauma, some individuals live with the disadvantage of continued trauma that endures a prolonged period of time. As devastating as single-blow traumas are, the traumatic experiences that result in the most serious mental health problems are prolonged and repeated, sometimes extending over years of a person's life (Terr, 1991). People respond differently to trauma based on the lived experiences they have already endured, as well as the severity, duration, and personal closeness of the trauma. Although there are some common underlying themes or characteristics in how people respond to trauma, one of the biggest outcomes is whether or not people develop PTSD as a result of the traumatic event/experience. However, when trauma is prolonged and engulfs an individual every day, it magnifies the challenge for recovery even more so.

Traumatic stress reactions are, therefore, sensible and adaptive both as part of survival during the trauma and in attempts to come to terms with the trauma afterward. Once we recognize where these symptoms come from, it is easier to understand the typical traumatic stress reactions. "The difficult part is letting go of aspects of these reactions that have ceased to provide benefit and are primarily interfering with the traumatized person's quality of life" (Veterans Affairs Canada, 2015, "Why Do Traumatic Stress Symptoms Develop?," para. 3).

In this chapter, you will learn:

- How PTSD creates a long-lasting and sometimes lifetime impact on an individual
- How, like the short-term impact, the long-term impact of PTSD engulfs every aspect of one's life and living
- How psychiatric comorbidities often go hand in hand with PTSD
- How one's quality of life is significantly disrupted by PTSD—so much so that functioning at normal everyday activities is challenging

NEUROLOGICAL IMPACT—THE BRAIN

The brain is the center of perception, cognitive processing, mental thought processes, and behaviors that become manifested as a result. Research data from various studies of functional neuroanatomy and neurochemistry indicate various dysfunctions in certain areas of the brain in individuals who suffer from chronic PTSD. These abnormalities cause the evolution of symptoms of PTSD, deterioration of cognitive functions, and, hence, decreased quality of life of the survivors. The intensity of these symptoms is in direct correlation with the degree of dysfunction in the central nervous system (Bravo-Mehmedbasic, Kucukalic, Kulenovic, & Sulijc, 2010).

In the study led by Loganovsky and Zdanevich (2013) investigating the effects of the Chernobyl disaster and the impact of radiation, it was found that PTSD following radiation emergency is characterized by comorbidity of psychopathology, neurocognitive deficit, and cerebrovascular pathology with an additional increased risk of cerebral atherosclerosis and stroke. The cerebral basis of this PTSD results from the abnormal communication between the pyramidal cells of the neocortex and the hippocampus, and deep brain structures. Changes in bioelectrical brain activity were also found in this study.

SOCIAL IMPACT

The impact of PTSD has far-reaching societal effects. Successful social relations always help to control and buffer against the stress we experience in life. However, social relationships that people build, or the lack thereof, is another fallout for how we face stress that can jeopardize our mental health. Experiencing stress and mental health concerns for prolonged periods of time can actually cause us to distance ourselves from some of our friends. We spend so much of our time absorbed and/or worried about what is happening in our lives, our perceptions become significantly narrowed, and we cannot see the larger picture of how our friends can actually help us during these difficult, mentally challenging times. As suggested by Davis, Lind, and Sorensen (2013), individuals who rely on supportive social networks as a coping mechanism have lower levels of depersonalization. Unequivocally, when social support is lacking, it exacerbates our perception of stress and the onset of mental health concerns even more and is often positively correlated with emotional exhaustion, burnout, and depersonalization (Davis et al., 2013). One's stressed mental health can also result in work–family conflict (Geiger-Brown & Lipscomb, 2010).

PHYSICAL HEALTH

Physical health and mental health always go hand in hand; one affects the other when compromised. Physical health is affected in many ways by traumatic events. Trauma survivors may experience chronic pain, gynecological difficulties, gastrointestinal problems, asthma, heart palpitations, headaches, and musculoskeletal difficulties. Chronic danger and anticipation of violence stress the immune system and can lead to an increased susceptibility to autoimmune disorders, such as chronic fatigue and other illnesses (Poole, 2014). For war veterans in particular, Vasterling et al. (2008) uncovered that postdeployment PTSD severity was associated with changes in somatic health-related functioning and hence impacted individuals' health-related daily functioning. Jakupcak, Luterek, Hunt, Conybeare, and McFall (2008) add that even when accounting for demographic factors, combat and chemical exposure, and health risk behaviors, PTSD symptom severity was significantly associated with poorer health functioning.

When people experience PTSD stress, their threshold of bodily defenses and functions are compromised (Box 6.1). This includes their physical health that is cardiac, cardiovascular, immunity, or gastrointestinal in nature. Hence, heart diseases (NIOSH, 2008; Scott et al., 2013), infections (Scott et al., 2013), sleep difficulties (NIOSH, 2008), autoimmune diseases (Scott et al., 2013), headaches (NIOSH, 2008), impaired gastrointestinal function (Geiger-Brown & Lipscomb, 2010; NIOSH, 2008), and musculoskeletal problems (Geiger-Brown & Lipscomb, 2010) can all occur. When this stress becomes chronic, such as that experienced by many subjected to warfare and childhood abuse, the concern magnifies (Scott et al., 2013).

Hoge, Terhakopian, Castro, Messer, and Engel (2007) suggest that even years after the war and/or combat has occurred, associations between combat-related PTSD and physical health problems persist, which reveals that PTSD was significantly associated with lower ratings of general health, more sick call visits, more missed workdays, more physical symptoms, and high somatic symptom severity, even after controlling for being wounded or injured. Evidence illustrating the increased incidence of persons experiencing cardiovascular disease, respiratory disease, and other physical illness following traumatic events has also been found (Scott et al., 2013), as was stroke (Chen et al., 2015).

BOX 6.1 PHYSICAL RESPONSES TO TRAUMA

- Aches and pains such as headaches, backaches, and stomach aches
- Sudden sweating and/or heart palpitations (fluttering)
- Changes in sleep patterns, appetite, interest in sex
- Constipation or diarrhea
- Easily startled by noises or unexpected touch
- More susceptible to colds and illnesses
- Increased use of alcohol or drugs and/or overeating

Source: Levin (2011).

Three key events occur in the long-term fallout of PTSD. Although these events may occur early in the trauma experience, the body's physiological makeup and processes can delay the effects for each of the organs, genes, system defenses, and cognition. For example, following a severe traumatic event or repetition of such events, organ function can decline. In a disorder that became known as the multiple organ dysfunction syndrome (MODS) in the aftermath of trauma, various organs become deprived of the oxygen supply as the body goes into shock as a result of the trauma. The advent of MODS can occur either very early or later in the recovery from the trauma. In any event, organs deteriorate at various rates. For example, the lungs and kidneys begin to decline first, and are followed shortly thereafter by the liver and intestines (Toledo, 2012).

One's genetic makeup can also become compromised as a result of trauma. Our genes drive our immunity and bodily defenses. However, following trauma, genes behave quite differently than expected. Regardless of whether patients were known to heal quickly or slowly, the same genetic mutations occurred following trauma (Xiao et al., 2011). This finding is perhaps closely linked to the inflammatory response that occurs immediately following trauma.

PSYCHIATRIC COMORBIDITIES

The occurrence of mental illnesses after trauma is common. Trauma can be life changing, especially for those who have faced multiple traumatic events, repeated experiences of abuse, or prolonged exposure to abuse. Furthermore, with the onset of PTSD, individuals often resort to ineffective coping strategies such as substance abuse and drinking alcohol to help them through such troubled times and symptoms. Hence, what often results are psychiatric comorbidities (Baker, 2014; Sareen, 2014).

Many mental illnesses can occur over the long term and over a lifetime for individuals because of the stress and PTSD symptomatology they develop. As the body and brain undergo a dysregulation in response to trauma (Poole, 2014), the involved cognitive processes and responses to external stimuli create ongoing and perpetual behavioral changes and perceptions that can predispose an individual to a lifetime of such change. Over the long term, mental illnesses such as depression, anxiety disorders, and somatization disorders occur (Resnick, Kilpatrick, Dansky, Saunders, & Best, 1993). Furthermore, other enduring patterns of behaviors or traits may appear inclusive of "difficulty in trusting others, irregular moods, impulsive behavior, shame, decreased self-esteem and unstable relationships" (Cohen, 2016, para. 3).

Most people who experience traumatic events recover from them, but people with PTSD continue to be severely depressed and anxious for months or even years following the event (Anxiety and Depression Association of America, 2016). One of the early areas where the connection between trauma and substance abuse was made was regarding Vietnam veterans. Many veterans who were diagnosed with PTSD were found to be utilizing substances, in all probability to deal with the symptoms of PTSD. Self-medicating is something not specific to veterans. Utilization of drug and alcohol is something found in physically, sexually, and emotionally abused individuals, including health care professionals, and is therefore not a new phenomenon. However, the effects of trauma and stress on health care professionals has not been researched sufficiently.

Fast Facts

PTSD is often associated with other psychiatric comorbidities.

The long-term impact of PTSD becomes particularly noticeable among frontline health care providers and emergency response (ER) personnel. As health care clinicians, we often just brush off our own stress and solider onward. According to Fjeldheim et al. (2016), even at the training phase of their careers, a high rate of depression (28%), alcohol abuse (23%), and chronic perceived stress (7%) and low levels of social support were found among paramedics. Furthermore, almost one out of three ER nurses met subclinical levels of anxiety, depression, and somatic complaints and 8.5% met clinical levels of PTSD (Adriaesnnens, de Gucht, & Maes, 2012). According to Veterans Affairs Canada, 30% of Royal Canadian Mounted Police disability pensioners suffered mental health conditions, such as depression and anxiety disorders. Depression is the leading cause of workplace disability and is more prevalent than PTSD in police and military organizations, although the two conditions often occur together.

PTSD often occurs with depression, substance abuse, or other anxiety disorders (Anxiety and Depression Association of American, 2015). PTSD can disrupt your whole life: your job, your relationships, your health, and your enjoyment of everyday activities (Mayo Clinic, 2016b).

According to Blore, Sim, Forbes, Creamer, and Kelsall (2015), no one is exempt from the psychiatric comorbidities that accompany PTSD, but substance abuse is particularly well recognized. "Many people with PTSD attempt to cope or 'self-medicate' with excessive amounts of alcohol and inappropriate drug use (including prescribed drugs)" (Veterans Affairs Canada, 2017, "Substance Abuse," para. 1). Individuals with PTSD are more likely than the general population to resort to substance abuse (Pietrzak, Goldstein, Southwick, & Grant, 2012). The use of alcohol, in particular, raises other issues of concern as alcohol itself is a depressant.

The presence of other mental health conditions not only makes a diagnosis increasingly difficult, but also delays treatment and/or intervention, making assessment and screening procedures increasingly difficult for the clinician. According to Dore, Mills, Murray, Teesson, and Farrugia (2012), PTSD symptoms are associated with greater trauma exposure and moderate-to-severe depressive symptoms and a history of self-harm or attempted suicide. Similarly, for women who became engaged in heroin use (Chou, Beeler-Stinn, Diamond, and Cooper-Sadlo, 2014) and in predicting the use and abuse of drugs for adolescence (Donbaek, Elkit, & Pedersen, 2014), and substance abuse by war veterans (Butler, Taylor, & Ozietta, 2015), the underlying theme of trauma seems to dominate. What is important to realize here is that drugs and alcohol are often used as a mechanism, albeit ineffective, to help individuals cope with stress.

The use of alcohol raises other issues of concern. Although people feel that they obtain much pleasure from drinking alcohol, alcohol itself is a central nervous system depressant. Although alcohol serves to provide a temporary short-term feeling of euphoria, its long-term effect slows the central nervous system. Studies consistently show that alcohol consumption increases in the first year after a disaster, whether they are manmade or natural (Keyes, Hatzenbuehler, Grant, & Hasin, 2012); thus, the growing recognition of alcohol abuse is a concerning societal trend. Furthermore, maltreatment in childhood also increases the risk for both adolescent and adult alcohol consumption (Keyes et al., 2012), and adult alcohol abuse disorders (Enoch et al., 1992), particularly when adults were in combat. According to Thomas et al. (2014), alcohol use and its associated aggressive behaviors occurred in 50% of all adults returning from combat.

As suggested by Davidson (2000), trauma has an enormous impact on both individuals and society as a whole. Recognition of the extent of this impact by the medical profession has been relatively slow but, with our growing appreciation of the prevalence of trauma exposure in civilian as well as combat populations, the true scale of trauma-related psychiatric consequences is beginning to emerge.

SOCIETAL MORBIDITIES

As people grow up from living an abused childhood, soldiers return from combat, and survivors of terrorism, natural disasters, and accidents pursue their lives, the impact of PTSD and its symptomatology remains in their families, communities, and workplaces. One of the risks rarely investigated for its impact is the health services systems that actually provide the care to these individuals. As suggested by Baker (2014), the Global War on Terror returnees are using medical services and applying for disability at higher rates than those who served in previous conflicts. Furthermore, if the costs for veterans' care peak 30 to 40 years or longer following the conflict as anticipated, it will inflict an enormous burden on services and resources. Therefore, it would be most prudent for governments, policy makers, and bureaucrats to mobilize government agencies, create public–private partnerships, and invest resources now to mitigate the approaching tsunami of veterans' health care needs, the impact on our social services, and the devastating costs to society. This is significant, given that many countries around the world are now tightening their fiscal spending allowances, declaring bankruptcy, and/or witnessing never-before-seen levels of exponential unemployment, activist uprisings, and a shrinking currency. As suggested by Davidson (2000), there is a detrimental cost to society with high financial and social consequences from the significantly elevated rates of hospitalization, suicide attempts, and alcohol abuse.

QUALITY OF LIFE

As suggested by Bravo-Mehmedbasic et al. (2010), subjects who are suffering from chronic PTSD have a lower subjective perception of their quality of life. They add, however, that combined psychopharmacological and psychotherapeutic treatment over a period of 6 months can lead to improvement in the perception of quality of life. Lončar et al. (2014) add that for those who were prisoners of war, the traumatic experience of war triggered all forms of PTSD symptomatology, hence impacting their quality of life. As added by Davidson (2000), individuals experiencing severe psychiatric stress compounded by significant comorbid illness have critical impacts on their quality of life, which result in grave functional and emotional impairment.

Fast Facts

Over the long term, quality of life and functioning at everyday activities can become compromised by PTSD.

References

Anxiety and Depression Association of America. (2016). Symptoms of PTSD. Retrieved from https://www.adaa.org/understanding-anxiety/posttraumatic-stress-disorder-ptsd/symptoms

Adriaesnnens, J., de Gucht, V., & Maes, S. (2012). The impact of traumatic events on emergency room nurses: Findings from a questionnaire survey. *International Journal of Nursing Studies*, *49*(*11*), 1411–1422.

Baker, M. S. (2014). Casualties of the Global War on Terror and their future impact on health care and society: A looming public health crisis. *Military Medicine*, *179*(4), 348–355. doi:10.7205/MILMED-D-13-00471

Blore, J. D., Sim, M. R., Forbes, A. B., Creamer, M. C., & Kelsall, H. L. (2015). Depression in Gulf War veterans: A systematic review and meta-analysis. *Psychological Medicine*, *2*, 1–16.

Bravo-Mehmedbasic, A., Kucukalic, A., Kulenovic, A. D., & Sulijc, E. (2010). Impact of chronic posttraumatic stress disorder on the quality of life of war survivors. *Psychiatrica Danubina*, *22*(3), 430–435.

Butler, R., Taylor, L., & Ozietta, D. (2015). Substance abuse and post-traumatic stress disorder in war veterans. *Journal of Human Behavior in the Social Environment*, *25*(4), 344–350.

Chen, M.-H., Pan, T.-L., Li, C.-T., Lin, W.-C., Chen, Y.-S., Lee, Y.-C., . . . Bai, Y.-M. (2015). Risk of stroke among patients with post-traumatic stress disorder: Nationwide longitudinal study. *British Journal of Psychiatry*, *206*(4), 302–307.

Chou, J. L., Beeler-Stinn, S., Diamond, R. M., & Cooper-Sadlo, S. (2014). Heroin and post-traumatic stress disorder in a women's treatment facility: An exploratory study. *Journal of Feminist Family Therapy*. *26*(3), 138–162.

Cohen, H. (2016). Associated conditions of PTSD. Retrieved from https://psychcentral.com/lib/associated-conditions-of-ptsd

Davidson, J. R. (2000). Trauma: The impact of post-traumatic stress disorder. *Journal of Psychopharmacology*, *14*(2 Suppl. 1), S5–S12.

Davis, S., Lind, B. K., & Sorensen, C. (2013). A comparison of burnout among oncology nurses working in adult and pediatric inpatient and outpatient settings. *Oncology Nursing Forum*, *40*(4), E303–E311. doi:10.1188/13.ONF.E303-E311

Donbaek, D. F., Elkit, A., & Uffe Pederson, M. (2014). Post-traumatic stress disorder symptom clusters predicting substance abuse in adolescents. *Mental Health and Substance Use*, *7*(4), 299–314.

Dore, G., Mills, K., Murray, R., Teesson, M., & Farrugia, P. (2012). Post-traumatic stress disorder, depression and suicidality in inpatients with substance use disorders. *Drug and Alcohol Review*, *31*(3), 294–303.

Enoch, M. A., Hodgkinson, C. A., Yuan, Q., Shen, P. H., Goldman, D., & Roy, A. (1992). The influence of GABRA2, childhood trauma, and their interaction on alcohol, heroin, and cocaine dependence. *Biological Psychiatry*, *67*(1), 20–27.

Fjeldheim, C. B., Nöthling, J., Pretorius, K., Basson, M., Ganasen, K., Heneke, R., . . . Seedat, S. (2016). Trauma exposure, posttraumatic stress disorder and the effect of explanatory variables in paramedic trainees. *BMC Emergency Medicine*, *14*(1), 1–14. doi:10.1186/1471-227X-14-11

Geiger-Brown, J., & Lipscomb, J. (2010). The health care work environment and adverse health and safety consequences for nurses. *Annual Review of Nursing Research*, *28*, 191–231.

Hoge, C. W., Terhakopian, A., Castro, C. A., Messer, S. C., & Engel, C. C. (2007). Association of posttraumatic stress disorder with somatic symptoms, health care visits, and absenteeism among Iraq war veterans. *American Journal of Psychiatry*, *164*(1), 150–153.

Jakupcak, M., Luterek, J., Hunt, S., Conybeare, D., & McFall, M. (2008). Posttraumatic stress and its relationship to physical health functioning in a sample of Iraq and Afghanistan war veterans seeking postdeployment VA health care. *The Journal of Nervous and Mental Disease*, *196*(5), 425–428.

Keyes, K. M., Hatzenbuehler, M. L., Grant, B. F., & Hasin, D. S. (2012). Stress and alcohol: Epidemiologic evidence. *Alcohol Research*, *34*(4), 391–400.

Loganovsky, K. N., & Zdanevich, N. A. (2013). Cerebral basis of posttraumatic stress disorder following the Chernobyl disaster. *CNS Spectrums*, *18*(2), 95–102.

Lončar, M., Plašć, I. D., Bunjevac, T., Hrabac, P., Jakšić, N., Kozina, S., . . . Marčinko, D. (2014). Predicting symptom clusters of posttraumatic stress disorder (PTSD) in Croatian war veterans: The role of socio-demographics, war experiences and subjective quality of life. *Psychiatria Danubina*, *26*(3), 231–238.

Mayo Clinic. (2016a). Post-traumatic stress disorder (PTSD)—Symptoms. Retrieved from http://www.mayoclinic.org/diseases-conditions/post-traumatic-stress-disorder/basics/symptoms/con-20022540

Mayo Clinic. (2016b). Post-traumatic stress disorder (PTSD)—Complications. Retrieved from http://www.mayoclinic.org/diseases-conditions/post-trau matic-stress-disorder/basics/complications/con-20022540

National Institute for Occupational Safety and Health. (2008). What are the potential adverse health effects of occupational stress? Retrieved from http://www.cdc.gov/niosh/docs/2008-136/pdfs/2008-136.pdf)

Poole, N. (2014). Introduction to trauma informed practice. Retrieved from http://www.sken.ca/wp-content/uploads/2014/11/TIP-Presentation _SK.pdf

Pietrzak, R. H., Goldstein, R. B., Southwick, S. M., & Grant, B. F. (2012). Psychiatric comorbidity of full and partial posttraumatic stress disorder among older adults in the United States: Results from wave 2 of the National Epidemiologic Survey on Alcohol and Related Conditions. *American Journal of Geriatric Psychiatry, 20*(5), 380–390.

Resnick, H. S., Kilpatrick, D. G., Dansky, B. S., Saunders, B. E., & Best, C. L. (1993). Prevalence of civilian trauma and posttraumatic stress disorder in a representative national sample of women. *Journal of Consulting Clinical Psychology, 61*(6), 984–991.

Sareen, J. (2014). Posttraumatic stress disorder in adults: Impact, comorbidity, risk factors and treatment. *Canadian Journal of Psychiatry, 59*(9), 460–467.

Scott, K. M., Koenen, K. C., Aguilar-Gaxiola, S., Alonso, J., Angermeyer, M. C., Benjet, C., . . . Kessler, R. C. (2013). Associations between lifetime traumatic events and subsequent chronic physical conditions: A cross-national, cross-sectional study. *PLOS ONE, 8*(11), e80573. doi:10.1371/journal .pone.0080573

Terr, L. (1991). Childhood traumas: An outline and overview. *American Journal of Psychiatry, 148*, 10–20.

Toledo, C. (2012). Life after traumatic injury: How the body responds. Retrieved from https://publications.nigms.nih.gov/insidelifescience/life -after-traumatic-injury.html

Thomas, J. L., Wilk, J. E., Riviere, L. A., McGurk, D., Castro, C. A., & Hoge, C. W. (2010). Prevalence of mental health problems and functional impairment among active component and National Guard soldiers 3 and 12 months following combat in Iraq. *Archives of General Psychiatry, 67*(6), 614–623.

Vasterling, J. J., Schumm, J., Proctor, S. P., Gentry, E., King, D. W., & King, L. A. (2008). Posttraumatic stress disorder and health functioning in a non-treatment-seeking sample of Iraq war veterans: A prospective analysis. *Journal of Rehabilitation Research and Development, 45*(3), 347–358.

Veterans Affairs Canada. (2017). Post-traumatic stress disorder (PTSD) and war-related stress. Retrieved from http://www.veterans.gc.ca/eng/services/ health/mental-health/publications/ptsd-warstress

Xiao, W. Mindrinos, M. N., Seok, J., Cuschieri, J., Cuenca, A. G., Gao, H., . . . Tompkins, R. G. (2011). A genomic storm: Refining the immune, inflammatory paradigm in trauma. *Journal of Experimental Emergency Medicine, 208*(13), doi:10.1084/jem.20111354

III

The Intricacies
of PTSD

7

Prevention of PTSD

The old adage of an ounce of prevention is worth a pound of cure still holds true when dealing with posttraumatic stress disorder (PTSD). However, the biggest challenge is that many times trauma cannot be anticipated or predicted. There are, however, many factors for health care clinicians to be cognizant of when caring for individuals with PTSD that can provide a protective or preventive effect.

The prevention of PTSD is easier said than done. It is such a complicated mental illness that can often be delayed, recurring years later before it is even recognized in an individual suffering from it. Furthermore, given that many mental illnesses already go unassessed, undiagnosed, and hence untreated (Chen et al., 2007), the same holds true for PTSD. In fact, its existence sometimes goes unnoticed until something terrible happens, such as Fort Lauderdale airport shootings in Florida in late 2016 by an individual believed to be suffering from PTSD. As astute clinicians we strive to learn the very early signs of PTSD. Although primary prevention is an ideal and preferred goal to provide early intervention, it is not always possible to carry it out. Hence, secondary and tertiary preventions also have very important roles for individuals with PTSD.

In this chapter, you will learn:

- The different classifications of prevention used for PTSD
- What strategies can be employed to help prevent PTSD at all levels
- Some general coping skills and strategies for dealing with stress

FACTORS INFLUENCING PTSD

Many factors can influence the degree to which PTSD exerts an effect on an individual subjected to trauma and/or how he or she responds to trauma. These factors have been identified in current literature and research and include the following:

- Being directly involved in the trauma, especially as a victim
- Severe and/or prolonged exposure to the event
- Personal history of prior trauma
- Family or personal history of mental illness and severe behavioral problems
- Limited social support; lack of caring family and friends
- Ongoing life stressors such as moving to a new home, or new school, divorce, job change, or financial troubles (National Institute of Mental Health [NIMH], 2014)

Furthermore, resilience, sense of coherence, and having previously undergone emergency responsiveness training were negatively correlated with PTSD symptoms (Streb, Haller, & Michael, 2014).

PRIMARY PREVENTION

Primary prevention is defined as strategies and efforts to prevent the onset of specific diseases via risk reduction by altering behaviors or exposures that can lead to disease or by enhancing resistance to the effects of exposure to a disease agent. It reduces the incidence of disease by addressing disease risk factors or by enhancing resistance. The aim is to prevent the onset and development of the disorder before it occurs.

PTSD can present with a range of symptoms, which in most adults are most commonly in the form of very vivid, distressing memories of an event or flashbacks (otherwise known as intrusive or reexperiencing symptoms); such symptoms can be easily monitored for. However, at times the most prominent symptoms may be avoidance of trauma-related situations or general social contacts. It is important when recognizing and identifying PTSD to ask specific questions in a sensitive manner about both the symptoms and traumatic experiences. A number of problems such as depression are often comorbid with PTSD. Often, these problems will improve with the treatment of the PTSD. But where this does not happen or the comorbid disorder impedes the effective treatment of the PTSD, it may be appropriate to consider providing specific treatment for that disorder (National Institute for Health and Care Excellence [NICE], 2005, p. 124). Questions used in determining the presence of such symptoms need to be asked in a highly sensitive manner, even if the individual is not physically manifesting such symptoms and regardless of the time the traumatic event occurred. Providing examples of traumatic events may trigger a memory of something that had happened months or even years previously. For children, particularly younger children, consideration should be given to asking the child and/or the parents about sleep disturbance or significant changes in sleeping patterns. Hence, focusing on the symptoms and their possible presence as outlined previously is key in this stage of prevention.

SECONDARY PREVENTION

Secondary prevention of PTSD includes procedures that detect and treat preclinical pathological changes and thereby control disease progression. Screening procedures are often the first step, leading to early interventions that are more cost-effective than intervening once symptoms appear and preventing the establishment or progression of a disease once a person has been exposed to it. In the case of PTSD, if the symptomatology of the disease is beginning to show, is screened for, and strongly suspected and even diagnosed as being present, health care providers and family/friends should work with the individual so that the disease does not progress any further. Therefore, efforts are aimed at early detection via screening procedures that detect disease at an early stage when intervention may be more cost-effective. The main goal is to halt or slow the progress of disease (if possible) in its earliest stages; goals for PTSD would include limiting long-term disability and preventing reinjury. For example:

- Telling people to regularly practice stress-reducing techniques when feeling anxious
- Recommending regular exams and screening tests in people with known risk factors for illness
- Providing suitably modified work for injured workers (Institute for Work and Health, 2006)

Given there is much societal stigma and historical taboo associated with mental illness, individuals with PTSD will often seek medical services for other physical ailments, not necessarily for the PTSD itself. Hence, many people attending medical services in a general hospital setting may have experienced traumatic events. This may be particularly so in emergency departments and in orthopedic and plastic surgery clinics. Therefore, for some people with PTSD, this may be the main point of contact with the health care system and present the opportunity for the recognition and identification of PTSD (NICE, 2005, p. 124). Again, health care providers should be well aware of the symptomatology that accompanies PTSD and use a great deal of sensitivity when asking questions about the possibility of traumatic events persons may have experienced in the recent or distant past.

TERTIARY PREVENTION

Once a disease has developed and has been treated in its acute clinical phase, tertiary prevention seeks to soften the impact caused by the disease on the patient's function, longevity, and quality of life. Examples include practicing effective coping skills such as establishing a strong social support network and seeking out support during difficult times and hardship, maintaining a medication regimen if prescribed, regularly seeking medical care if and when needed, and practicing cognitive behavioral therapy to alter the approach to episodic reminders and environmental stimuli that may trigger a PTSD exacerbation. Tertiary prevention can also include modifying risk factors, such as avoiding loud, noisy settings, situations that may make the person feel uncomfortable, and participating in PTSD- or anxiety-based support groups in the community. Where the condition is not reversible, as often happens with PTSD, tertiary prevention focuses on rehabilitation, and assisting the patient to accommodate to his or her disability with the key goal being to manage complicated long-term health problems, enhance quality of life, and prevent further mental deterioration (Institute for Work and Health, 2006). One intervention that can be done for individuals with PTSD at this stage is for the medical profession to offer regular follow-ups (e.g., every 2 to 4 weeks), which may be done in person at the clinic, by phone, or through a community health worker for the purposes of reassessing the individual for any improvement. At this point in time, it is also critical to observe for any psychiatric comorbidities that the individual may have, such as depression or anxiety. For example, using the appropriate screening tools for these disorders such as those to be identified in a later section will help determine the presence of depression.

Different forms of prevention can help ameliorate some of the impacts of trauma.

STRESS MANAGEMENT

There are many different interventions that can be shared with individuals who suffer from PTSD for relatively immediate relief. Some of these include breathing exercises, physical exercises, and progressive muscle relaxation or cultural equivalents, such as mediation, prayer, and so forth.

Breathing Exercises

This technique involves explaining that anxiety is associated with rapid, shallow chest breathing and that focusing on slow, regular, abdominal breathing reduces anxiety. The technique involves training the person to breathe from diaphragm (World Health Organization and United Nations High Commissioner for Refugees, 2013).

Physical Exercise

Physical exercise is effective for any age cohort in dealing with and/or preparing the body and mind to deal with stress.

Progressive Muscle Relaxation

This technique involves explaining that anxiety is associated with tense muscles and that systematically relaxing one's muscles reduces anxiety. The technique involves training the person to systematically tense and relax key muscle groups, usually working up from the feet to the top of the body. An example of a progressive muscle relaxation protocol can be found as an annex of WHO, War Trauma Foundation, World Vision International's (2013) manual: *Psychological First Aid: Facilitator's Manual for Orienting Field Workers.*

Coping skills of individuals for dealing with stress are critical in the prevention of mental illness and PTSD.

STRENGTHENING OF POSITIVE COPING METHODS AND SOCIAL SUPPORTS

- Build on individuals' *strengths and abilities*. Ask them what is going well. How do they keep going? How have they previously coped with hardship?
- Ask individuals to *identify people who give emotional support*. Ask them to identify other people they trust. These may be selected family members, friends, or people in the community. Encourage them to spend time with and talk to trusted people about their difficulties. Even among nurses as a professional group at risk for PTSD, social support from colleagues and supervisors has a protective effect on the occurrence of PTSD symptoms (Adriaesnnens, de Gucht, & Maes, 2012).
- Encourage *resumption of social activities and normal routines* as far as possible (e.g., school attendance, family gatherings, visiting neighbors, social activities at work, sports, community activities, outings with friends).
- *Alert the person* to the fact that alcohol and drugs do not help recovery, and that heavy use of alcohol and drugs—including medicines bought without prescription at pharmacies—can lead to new health and social problems.

Fast Facts

As a significant precipitator of PTSD, stress can be alleviated in many ways to prevent one's mental health from deteriorating.

References

Adriaesnnens, J., de Gucht, V., & Maes, S. (2012). The impact of traumatic events on emergency room nurses: Findings from a questionnaire survey. *International Journal of Nursing Studies*, 49(11), 1411–1422.

Chen, P., Kales, H. C., Weintraub, D., Blow, F. C., Jiang, L., Ignacio, R. V., & Mellow, A. M. (2007). Depression in veterans with Parkinson's disease: Frequency, co-morbidity and healthcare utilization. *International Journal of Geriatric Psychiatry*, 22, 543–548.

Institute for Work and Health. (2006). *At work*, 43(Winter 2006). Toronto, ON, Canada: Author.

National Institute for Health and Care Excellence. (2005). Post-traumatic stress disorder: The management of PTSD in adults and children in primary and secondary care. Retrieved from https://www.nice.org.uk/guidance/cg26/evidence/full-guideline-including-appendices-113-pdf-193442221

Streb, M., Haller, P., & Michael, T. (2014). PTSD in paramedics: Resilience and sense of coherence. *Behavioral and Cognitive Psychotherapy, 42*(4), 452–463.

World Health Organization and United Nations High Commissioner for Refugees. (2013). Assessment and management of conditions specifically related to stress: mhGAP intervention guide module (version 1.0). Retrieved from http://apps.who.int/iris/bitstream/10665/85623/1/9789241505932_eng.pdf

8

Clinical Interventions

Posttraumatic stress disorder (PTSD) is a complex disorder in most people, and rarely is a simple, uncomplicated presentation to a clinician. It impacts everyone differently and hence may manifest its symptomatology quite differently. Hence, the approach taken in the treatment of PTSD is an individualized one. A good mental health professional will help the person understand what symptoms are related to the PTSD, why the symptoms are occurring, what other symptoms may be associated with the development of another disorder, and how the symptoms and disorder can be addressed. The key is for the health care clinician to provide the best treatment, tailored to each individual's unique symptoms, so successful achievement of the goals can be attained (Cohen, 2016). Understanding trauma-informed care is critical to clinicians to ensure that treatment measures are effective and optimal outcomes can be achieved for patients with PTSD.

In this chapter, you will learn:

- Various clinical approaches that can be used when caring for individuals with PTSD
- Why the principles of trauma-informed care are critical for the clinician to know when caring for someone with PTSD
- What can be provided or done for an individual immediately following the trauma and as a delayed response to the trauma

TRAUMA-INFORMED CARE

When providing care for individuals with PTSD, there are various guidelines and concepts that clinicians need to be cognizant of and share with colleagues so that they provide the best care in terms of quality, safety, and competency.

The principles of a trauma-informed approach and trauma-specific interventions are designed to address the consequences of trauma in the individual and to facilitate healing (Substance Abuse and Mental Health Services Administration [SAMHSA], 2016). Some trauma-informed components, such as preparing for practice and engagement, are consistent across contexts and roles and are ongoing processes in all interactions. Other components, such as asking about trauma, making links with trauma, and skill building, vary depending on individual needs and resources, scope of role and service, purpose and goal of intervention, program policies, and so on. For some practitioners and programs, it may be enough to increase awareness and purposefulness of trauma-informed practice in terms of self-reflection and overall engagement processes. Others may be required to screen for experiences of trauma, in formal or informal ways, and may be able to offer additional support, such as a psychoeducation or skill building. The goal is to build on what is already working for individuals, practitioners, and programs. It is not about replacing existing good practices; rather it is about refining and being knowledgeable about trauma-informed approaches (Taylor, 2007).

Preparing for Trauma-Informed Practice

Trauma-informed practice means integrating an understanding of trauma into all levels of care and avoiding retraumatization or minimizing the individual's experiences of trauma. For practitioners, there is a heightened awareness and deliberation to the work: Questions are asked on a need-to-know basis in the best interest of the individual being supported; attention is paid to the individual's spoken and unspoken responses; and approaches are adapted to respond to the individual's needs. Trauma-informed practice is an overall way of working, rather than a specific set of techniques or strategies. Such preparation is a continuous process—foundational to all interactions and conversations with patients.

There is no formula. Providing trauma-informed care means recognizing that some people will need more support and different types of support than others (e.g., the driver of a vehicle who injures a pedestrian; a family who has fled war in their home country; a young mother who has experienced various forms of interpersonal violence throughout her life; a child or youth who has experienced abuse or witnessed domestic violence). It is also important to remember that human beings are resilient and resourceful, and the majority of healings happen outside of formal treatment services. Health care professionals working in trauma-informed care guide their practice by the following:

- Realize the widespread impact of trauma and understand potential paths for recovery
- Recognize the signs and symptoms of trauma in patients, families, clinicians, and others involved
- Respond by fully integrating knowledge about trauma into policies, procedures, and practices
- Seek to actively resist retraumatization (SAMHSA, 2016)

Fast Facts

Trauma-informed care reflects the basic fundamentals of care needed for clinicians to be effective.

WHAT TRAUMA THERAPY LOOKS LIKE

There is a three-phase treatment protocol that is recommended by expert bodies on trauma (Staggs, 2016):

Phase 1: Achieving patient safety, reducing symptoms, and increasing competencies. This is the skill-building phase and clinicians can use any evidence-based therapy that has outcomes of improving emotion regulation, increasing distress tolerance, mindfulness, interpersonal effectiveness, cognitive restructuring, behavioral changes, and relaxation. This phase can also help move someone out of crisis to prepare for the next phase (Staggs, 2016).

Phase 2: Review and reappraisal of trauma memories. There are different techniques for doing this, and they are described later, but the success of this phase depends on someone's ability to tolerate the discomfort of reviewing the memories. People with single incident trauma may be ready to withstand exposure with minimal distress tolerance training, whereas people with complex trauma may need months of skill-building support in order to be ready to process their trauma (Staggs, 2016).

Phase 3: Consolidating the gains. In this phase, the therapist helps the patient apply new skills and adaptive understanding of themselves and the trauma experience. This phase can also include "booster" sessions to reinforce skills, increase professional and informal support systems, and create an ongoing care plan (Staggs, 2016).

ASKING ABOUT TRAUMA

It is important to remember that it is not necessary for someone to disclose trauma in order to receive trauma-informed care. There are varying perspectives on how to discuss trauma, and how much information should be gathered about trauma histories. Depending on the service and population served, the approach may be more formal or informal. This section provides some guidelines, skills, and strategies to support the conversation as it relates to current functioning. It also offers ideas for responding to disclosure and making referrals in a trauma-informed way (Taylor, 2007).

MAKING THE LINK WITH TRAUMA

Trauma-informed practice may also involve helping people make the link between their past experiences and present health and reframe their responses as attempts to cope with what they have been through. Although not everyone involved in trauma-informed practice will provide trauma-specific information, all information can be provided in a trauma-informed way. This section outlines guidelines for sharing information, key messages related to trauma, and additional skills and strategies for information exchange (Taylor, 2007).

PRINCIPLES OF TRAUMA-INFORMED CARE

Trauma-informed care is an organizational structure and treatment framework that involves understanding, recognizing, and responding to the effects of all types of trauma. Trauma-informed care also emphasizes physical, psychological, and emotional safety for both consumers and providers, and helps survivors rebuild a sense of control and empowerment (National Institute for Health and Care Excellence

[NICE], 2005). There are several principles recognized in the delivery of trauma-informed care. These principles may be generalizable across multiple types of settings, although terminology and application may be setting or sector specific, and include trauma awareness, safety, trustworthiness, transparency, and collaboration and mutuality (SAMHSA, 2016; Taylor, 2007).

TRAUMA AWARENESS

A trauma-informed approach begins with building awareness among clinicians and patients of the commonness of trauma experiences; how the impact of trauma can be central to one's development; the wide range of adaptations people make to cope and survive after trauma; and the relationship of trauma with substance use, physical health, and mental health concerns. This knowledge is the foundation of an organizational culture of trauma-informed care (Hopper, Bassuk, & Olivet, 2010).

SAFETY AND TRUSTWORTHINESS

Depending on the type of trauma experienced, individuals may feel unsafe in new environments and have difficulty trusting others and their intentions. People seek out health care services with a whole host of life experiences that shape how they feel, what they think, and how they respond to interacting with practitioners and services.

Recognizing this is powerful, both for the practitioner and for the individual accessing services. The practitioner recognizes that an individual's reactions are not necessarily personal or about the practitioner's skills. Instead they may be influenced by what has come before, or perhaps expectations of what is to come.

For the individual accessing services, it gives permission to have reactions without feeling as if they are disrespecting a system or an individual practitioner. For those who have experienced interpersonal trauma or other forms of oppression and violence, boundary violations and abuses of power may have been present in past interactions. Some of the individuals accessing services may even be currently living in unsafe circumstances such as violent relationships. However, this should never be assumed as many who have experienced trauma have supportive families and social networks, and may not even identify the language of "trauma." Harris and Fallot (2001) note that, "trust and safety, rather than being assumed from the beginning, must be earned and demonstrated over time" (p. 20). There are a number of ways practitioners make physical and emotional safety and trustworthiness explicit:

- *Consider all barriers* (visible/invisible, concrete/perceived) to engagement:
    - Using a social-determinants-of-health lens can help practitioners broaden their understanding of the realities of many individuals' lives and the various influences that impact an individual's or family's ability to access services (poverty, homelessness, gender, and so on).
    - There may be barriers that result from current policies and rules, such as immigration law (no health coverage for someone who does not have legal status) or fear of losing children, housing, or employment if concerns or trauma is disclosed.
    - There may also be very real invisible barriers that are directly or indirectly related to prior experiences with institutions and authority; for example, individuals from cultures that have experienced intergenerational oppression or refugees distrusting of governmental organizations.
- *Attend to immediate needs:*
    - Food, clothing, medical concerns, immediate safety, housing, transportation, and child care must all be addressed. If the mandate of the practitioner's organization does not include addressing immediate needs, provide a referral to organizations that can help. Wherever possible, support the individual to make contact by phone, online, or in person. Address signs of intoxication. It is not safe nor is it possible for either party to have a helpful conversation if the individual is intoxicated. The practitioner's only agenda is then to plan how to support safety and to convey willingness to talk when the individual is no longer impaired.
    - Similarly, if someone is acutely psychotic or suicidal, the necessary steps to ensure safety should be taken, including accessing emergency services and carrying out crisis intervention measures.
- *Be as transparent, consistent, and predictable as possible:*
    - Offer translation services, or allow an interpreter to be present if required or possible.

- Allow a support person to be present if the individual thinks that would be helpful.
- Explain why before doing something.
- If a promise is made (to make a referral, make a follow-up phone call), follow through in a timely manner.
- Acknowledge and take responsibility for miscommunication.
- Ensure that self-disclosure is used only in the best interest of the individual.

- *Respect healthy boundaries and expectations by clarifying the practitioner's role:*
  - Outline the parameters of what can and cannot be done.
  - Maintain focus on patient information that is relevant to the type of work agreed to. Ask for trauma details only when it is necessary for trauma-specific interventions.
  - Use a professional tone that also conveys genuine care and concern.
  - Start and finish appointments on time; discuss backup plans when the practitioner will be away (both planned and unplanned).
  - Explain how and when to contact the practitioner.
  - Be aware of dual roles. For example, offer support to parents, keeping in mind legal responsibility to report child welfare concerns and make referrals as needed.

- *Clearly outline program/treatment expectations:*
  - The rights of those accessing services.
  - Content and format of treatment.
  - Attendance and participation.
  - The guidelines around substance use and/or other medications.
  - Specific rules of the program—be clear and consistent in explanation and enforcement.

- *Obtain informed consent; explain how information will be shared and the limits to confidentiality:*
  - Respond to verbal and nonverbal communication.
  - Use plain language without jargon. Offer a print copy of the consent form.
  - Ask for the individual's understanding; work to mitigate any concerns the individual may have about the limits to confidentiality.
  - When working with children and youth, outline what will and will not be shared with parents and in what

circumstances (discussing with both parents and youth as appropriate).

- *Collaboratively develop some grounding strategies:*
  - Ask what physical and emotional safety means to the individual.
  - Use open questions to develop a plan together: "What have you found helpful to calm down and get focused when you're feeling anxious? What makes it worse? What is helpful from my side to offer you the best support when you are upset?"

COLLABORATION, CHOICE, AND CONNECTION

Experiences of trauma often leave individuals feeling powerless, with little choice or control over what has happened to them (interpersonal violence, natural disaster, and so on), and possibly, what they have done (war, political violence, motor vehicle accident [MVA], and so on). It is imperative in trauma-informed practice that every effort is made to empower individuals (when working with children and youth, strategies for empowerment should be consistent with developmental stage). Collaboration involves sharing expertise and power. Individuals actively participate and chart their own course of action, guided by the practitioner's knowledge, experience, and access to resources. The relationship and engagement build as the practitioner elicits the individual's ideas, resources, beliefs, and strengths. By engaging with the individual as an active participant in his or her own treatment (along with the child/youth's family/caretakers where needed), the practitioner can tailor assistance specific to unique needs. Offering choice, whenever possible, gives control and responsibility back to individuals. Choice can relate to all aspects of service, for example, how individuals will be contacted; who will be involved in their care; and what the priorities and goals of treatment will be. Having a sense of personal control in interactions with practitioners who have more power is crucial to engagement and establishing and maintaining safety.

Trauma-informed services create safe environments that foster a sense of efficacy, self-determination, dignity, and personal control for those receiving care. Practitioners try to communicate openly, equalize power imbalances in relationships, allow the expression of feelings without fear of judgment, provide choices as to treatment preferences, and work collaboratively with patients. In addition, having the opportunity to establish safe connections—with treatment providers, families, peers, and the wider community—is reparative for those with early/ongoing experiences of trauma. This experience of choice, collaboration, and connection is often extended to inviting individual involvement in evaluating the treatment services, and forming service user advisory councils that provide advice on service design as well as service users' rights and grievances. Although engagement is an ongoing process in providing care, it too warrants focused attention for its crucial role in trauma-informed practice in mental health and addictions services (Taylor, 2007).

Some strategies practitioners can use to support collaboration and choice include:

- Working through the details together:
  - How an individual is contacted—by phone, in person, at home, or office
  - Time of day of appointments or meetings
  - The preferred gender of the practitioner the individual would like to work with
  - How and whether messages can be left
- Exploring and problem solving barriers to participation and attendance (child care, transportation, non-support at home, language):
  - What, if any, obstacles do practitioners foresee in getting to the program/service or connecting in the community/at home
  - Brainstorm ideas together to remove or reduce barriers
- Eliciting the individuals' priorities and hopes for treatment:
  - Find out what is most pressing for them
  - What are their hopes, expectations, concerns, and so on
  - Clarify their understanding of why they are speaking with the practitioner and how they got there (e.g., self-referred, mandated, family member request, school-based referral)
- Inquiring about others who may be helpful to include in some aspect of their care (a support person, another professional, and so forth):
  - Clearly outline how they would like the other person involved; review confidentiality with all those involved
  - Before the meeting, speak with them alone to confirm their decision to include others
  - Be sure to communicate directly with the individuals receiving care (including minors). This is especially important

when speaking through an interpreter or with someone who has cognitive challenges (Taylor, 2007)

- Using statements that make collaboration and choice explicit:
  - "I'd like to understand your perspective."
  - "Let's look at this together."
  - "Let's figure out the plan that will work best for you."
  - "What is most important for you that we should start with?"
  - "It is important to have your feedback every step of the way."
  - "This may or may not work for you. You know yourself best."
    - "Please let me know at any time if you would like a break or if something feels uncomfortable for you. You can choose to pass on any question."
  - Use appropriate metaphors: "You are the expert or the driver. I can offer to be your GPS or map to help guide you to available resources."
- Working in a feedback-informed way:
  - Purposefully elicit from individuals and families their perspective of the overall experience (e.g., "What was it like for you to get here today?" or "How was it for you to talk about this?")
  - Continuously check in throughout the course of your work with someone

STRENGTHS BASED AND SKILL BUILDING

Patients in trauma-informed services are assisted to identify their strengths and to (further) develop resiliency and coping skills. Practitioners emphasize teaching and modeling skills for recognizing triggers, calming, centering, and staying present. Again, a parallel attention must be paid to practitioner competencies and learning these skills and values. For nurses as a professional group, problem-focused coping is related to a decrease in psychological distress and perceived fatigue (Adriaenssens, de Gucht, & Maes, 2012).

At any point in the conversation, a trauma response may be triggered. In that moment, it is essential to provide safety through grounding and containment skills. This section offers a stepped approach to assist individuals in managing an in-the-moment trauma response through a range of grounding and self-care skills and practices that aim to proactively preserve safety and strengthen resiliency (Taylor, 2007).

ADDRESSING CURRENT PSYCHOSOCIAL STRESSORS

Ask about current psychosocial stressors. As far as possible, use problem-solving techniques to help the person reduce major psychosocial stressors or relationship difficulties. Involve community services and resources, as appropriate (e.g., with the person's consent).

Assess and manage any situation of abuse (e.g., domestic violence) and neglect (e.g., of children or older people). Such assessment requires a private, confidential space. If necessary, contact legal and community resources (e.g., social services, community protection networks) to report any abuse (e.g., with the person's consent). As appropriate, identify supportive family and/or friends and involve them as much as possible.

TIMING OF INTERVENTION/TREATMENT

The timing of interventions is a very important consideration for the health care clinician when interacting with patients suspected of having or showing symptomatology of PTSD. Specifically, there are immediate interventions that are deemed appropriate and those that would be inappropriate to try immediately following trauma.

The same applies for long-term effects. There are many interventions that can be used most appropriately in the later emergence of PTSD symptomatology.

Regardless of the timing of the intervention, the goal of PTSD treatment remains the same: To reduce the emotional and physical symptoms, to improve daily functioning, and to help the person better cope with the event that triggered the disorder (WebMD, 2017).

Fast Facts

Elements of safety, respect, trust, and collaboration are all integral when caring for someone with PTSD.

Immediately Post-Event

All health care clinicians should be aware of the psychological impact of traumatic incidents in their immediate postincident care of survivors and offer practical, social, and emotional support to those involved.

For individuals who have experienced a traumatic event, the systematic provision to that individual alone of brief, single-session interventions (often referred to as debriefing) that focus on the traumatic incident should *not* be routine practice when delivering services.

Clinicians "should keep in mind that it is important to prevent panic, to help provide structure in a chaotic environment, and to assist in ensuring safety of survivors. This is important in response to any disaster, whether an act of terrorism, a natural or manmade disaster, or possible future acts of nuclear or biological terrorism. Large, established organizations such as the American Red Cross and the Federal Emergency Management Agency (FEMA) have an excellent track record in providing structure for assisting disaster victims. It is important to coordinate with local health and mental health departments, professional health and mental health groups (the American Psychiatric Association, the American Medical Association, the American Psychological Association, the National Organization for Victims Assistance [NOVA], and others) mental health consumer groups (National Alliance for the Mentally Ill, the local branch of the Mental Health Association), and faith-based groups. The media can be used constructively to help victims find loved ones; to educate the public calmly about what has happened, what to expect, when and where to seek help; and to prevent panic" (American Psychiatric Association, 2004, p. 21).

It is important "not to pathologize all emotional responses to disaster. A direct victim's initial response may represent what has been called 'a normal response to an abnormal situation.' That is, s(he) may experience temporary symptoms of altered sleep, anxiety or sadness, irritability, difficulty concentrating, fatigue, appetite changes, loss of interest, memory problems, or changes in usual behavior patterns. These are often time-limited and do not generally impair functioning for long periods. Supportive interventions include reassurance; ensuring adequate rest, with temporary use of sleeping aids indicated for severe insomnia; maximizing positive coping techniques (discussed later); and returning to the workplace or prior level of functioning as soon as possible" (American Psychiatric Association, 2004, p. 21).

Most people will have some PTSD symptoms in the first few weeks after events like these. This is a normal and expected response to serious trauma, and for most people, symptoms generally lessen with time. Both direct and indirect victims may benefit from the following interventions in the immediate aftermath of disaster:

A hierarchy of basic needs should be addressed, including:

- Ensuring safety and security, both immediately and for possible ongoing threats
- Providing food and shelter
- Linking survivors to support services
- Helping disaster victims to obtain information, especially information about loved ones
- Helping survivors access normal social support networks (family, friends, community)

Screening and triage should focus on highly symptomatic or "at-risk" individuals within the first week postdisaster and beyond. Who is "at risk?" Experts agree that this group includes individuals:

- With preexisting psychiatric conditions or substance abuse problems
- Who are bereaved
- Who are children or elderly
- Who are injured
- Who are intensely exposed to the disaster (through proximity or long duration of exposure)
- Who have acute stress disorder or are clinically symptomatic as a result of the disaster. After 2 months postdisaster, if symptoms have not occurred, follow-up should occur only if specifically requested by an individual. If PTSD symptoms are present and persist, cognitive behavioral therapy should begin within the first month.

Outreach and dissemination of information:

- Outreach involves informal support and assistance to survivors wherever they may group, such as the disaster scene, shelters, assistance centers, food banks, first aid stations, and so forth. Survivors often do not seek mental health assistance because they may be preoccupied with their immediate surroundings, they may fear interventions due to stigmatization, or they may just want to avoid painful memories and feelings
- Information in the form of pamphlets, brief news releases, Internet websites, and training manuals for survivors and their caregivers can educate about symptoms that are expected,

symptoms that suggest that professional help is needed, and where to go for help. (American Psychiatric Association, 2004, pp. 22–23)

In spite of what many believe and feel, people do not often get better on their own. A study of Hurricane Katrina survivors found that, over time, more people were having problems with PTSD, depression, and related mental disorders. This pattern is unlike the recovery from other natural disasters, where the number of people who have mental health problems gradually lessens. As communities try to rebuild after a mass trauma, people may experience ongoing stress from loss of jobs and schools, and trouble paying bills, finding housing, and getting health care. This delay in community recovery may in turn delay recovery from PTSD.

Non–trauma-focused interventions such as relaxation or nondirective therapy, which do not address traumatic memories, should not routinely be offered to people who present with PTSD symptoms within 3 months of a traumatic event (NICE, 2005, p. 92).

Drug treatment may also be considered in the acute phase of PTSD for the management of sleep disturbance. In this case, hypnotic medication may be appropriate for short-term use; but if long-term drug treatment is required, consideration should also be given to the use of suitable antidepressants at an early stage in order to reduce the later risk of dependence (NICE, 2005, p. 92).

For individuals at high risk of developing PTSD following a major disaster, consideration should be given (by those responsible for coordination of the disaster plan) to the routine use of a brief screening instrument for PTSD at 1 month after the disaster, as previously eluded to. For program refugees and asylum seekers at high risk of developing PTSD, consideration should be given (by those responsible for management of the refugee program) to the routine use of a brief screening instrument for PTSD as part of the initial refugee health care assessment. This should be a part of any comprehensive physical and mental health screen (NICE, 2005, p. 103).

Fast Facts

Timing is everything if a clinician wants to be effective with the information obtained and/or the interventions provided to the person suffering with PTSD.

References

Adriaenssens, J., de Gucht, V., & Maes, S. (2012). The impact of traumatic events on emergency room nurses: Findings from a questionnaire survey. *International Journal of Nursing Studies*, *49*(11), 1411–1422. doi:10.1016/j.ijnurstu.2012.07.003

American Psychiatric Association. (2004). Disaster psychiatry handbook. Retrieved from https://psychiatry.org/File%20Library/Psychiatrists/Practice/Professional-Topics/Disaster-Psychiatry/disaster-psychiatry-handbook.pdf?_ga=1.40565286.523978515.1483453788

B. C. Ministry of Health. (2016). Post-traumatic stress disorder. Retrieved from https://www.healthlinkbc.ca/health-topics/hw184188

Cohen, H. (2016). Associated conditions of PTSD. Retrieved from https://psychcentral.com/lib/associated-conditions-of-ptsd

Harris, M., & Fallot, R. D. (2001). *Using trauma theory to design service systems*. San Francisco, CA: Jossey-Bass.

Hopper, E. K., Bassuk, E. L., & Olivet, J. (2010). Shelter from the storm: Trauma-informed care in homelessness services settings. *The Open Health Services and Policy Journal*, *3*, 80–100.

National Institute for Health and Care Excellence. (2006). Post-traumatic stress disorder: The management of PTSD in adults and children in primary and secondary care. Retrieved from https://www.nice.org.uk/guidance/cg26/evidence/full-guideline-including-appendices-113-pdf-193442221

Staggs, S. (2016). Psychotherapy treatment for PTSD. Retrieved from https://psychcentral.com/lib/treatment-of-ptsd

Substance Abuse and Mental Health Services Administration. (2016). Trauma-informed approach and trauma-specific interventions. Retrieved from https://www.samhsa.gov/nctic

Taylor, S. (2007). Choosing the treatment that is right for you. *Visions Journal*, *3*(3), 23–24.

WebMD. (2017). Posttraumatic stress disorder. Retrieved from http://www.webmd.com/mental-health/post-traumatic-stress-disorder?page=2

9

Treatment Interventions

It is not unusual for people who have experienced traumatic events to have flashbacks, nightmares, or an intrusive memory when something terrible happens, such as the explosions at the Boston Marathon. Be tolerant of your nervous system: It is having a normal reaction. Try not to get hooked on news reports, which may seem particularly compelling. Spend time with loved ones in favorite activities or outside in nature, and avoid alcohol and use of benzodiazepines (Anxiety and Depression Association of America, 2016).

The main treatments for people with posttraumatic stress disorder (PTSD) are psychotherapy (talk therapy or cognitive behavioral therapy [CBT]) medications, or both. Everyone is different, so a treatment that works for one person may not work for another (Anxiety and Depression Association of America, 2016). It is ideal for anyone with PTSD to be treated by a health care clinician who is familiar with PTSD, but realistically we know it is not always possible. People with PTSD need to try different treatments to find what works for their symptoms (National Institute of Mental Health [NIMH], 2015). Therefore, consistency of the health care clinician is an important variable. If someone with PTSD is going through an ongoing trauma, such as being in an abusive relationship, both of the problems need to be assessed and hence addressed. Remember, other ongoing simultaneous problems can include panic disorder, depression, substance abuse, and feeling suicidal (NIMH, 2015).

In this chapter, you will learn:

- The various treatment approaches and methodologies employed in the care of individuals with PTSD
- How talking and involving the patient in every aspect of care is important
- How pharmacological treatment and psychotherapy go hand in hand as a standard treatment regimen for someone suffering from PTSD

PSYCHOEDUCATION

When PTSD is first diagnosed, it is important to provide the individual with some basic information about PTSD; psychoeducation is a good first step. Educating individuals and families on the course and development of PTSD is important to enhance their understanding of the disease and knowing what to expect and when. The following guidance on psychoeducation is written for people with PTSD and their caregivers.

Explain the Course of Symptoms

In the first few days to weeks following an extremely threatening or horrific event, most people will have some stress-related reactions, such as feeling tearful, frightened, angry, or guilty. There may be physical reactions, jumpiness or difficulty sleeping, frightening dreams, or continual replaying of the event in one's mind. Most people recover from these reactions naturally.

When these reactions last more than a month, become a continuing problem, and cause difficulties in the person's daily functioning, this may indicate PTSD.

Many people recover from PTSD over time without treatment. However, treatment will speed up the process of recovery.

Explain the Nature of PTSD

People with PTSD frequently feel that they are still in danger and consequently can be very tense. They may be easily startled (jumpy) or may be constantly on the watch for danger.

- People with PTSD experience unwanted recollections of the traumatic event. When reminded of the event, they may experience emotions such as fear and horror, similar to the feelings they experienced when the event was actually happening. Sometimes, they may feel that the event is happening again. They may also have frightening dreams.
- Such intrusive thoughts and memories of the traumatic event are extremely disturbing. Consequently, people with PTSD naturally try to avoid any reminders of the event. Unfortunately, such avoidance can cause problems in their lives. For example, if a man with PTSD avoids going to work because he was assaulted there, then this will affect his livelihood.
- Paradoxically, trying to avoid thinking about something usually results in thinking about it more. Ask the person to try this thought experiment: "Try not to think about a white elephant for one minute. How successful were you? You probably found that white elephant impossible to keep out of your head. The same is true for traumatic memories when you have PTSD: The more you try to avoid thinking about them, the more you think about them."
- Explain, as applicable to the person, that people with PTSD may sometimes have concurrent problems, such as aches and pains in the body, low energy, fatigue, irritability, and depressed mood.

Explain That Effective Treatment Is Possible

Effective treatment exists. The following points are important to make clear to the individual and family members:

- It is likely to take several weeks of treatment before the person feels any reduction in PTSD symptoms
- Continue normal daily routines as far as possible
- Talk to trusted people about how they feel or what happened when they are ready to do so
- Engage in relaxing activities to reduce anxiety and tension
- Discuss culturally appropriate forms of relaxation
- Do regular physical exercise
- Try to maintain a regular sleep cycle (i.e., go to bed at the same time every night, try to sleep as much as before, avoid sleeping too much)
- Avoid using alcohol or drugs to cope with PTSD symptoms
- Recognize thoughts of suicide and come back for help when these occur (World Health Organization [WHO] & United Nations High Commissioner for Refugees [UNHCR], 2013, p. 9)

COGNITIVE BEHAVIORAL THERAPY

Trauma-focused CBT should be offered to those with severe post-traumatic symptoms or with severe PTSD in the first month after the traumatic event or in at least 3 months post-event. These treatments should normally be provided on an individual outpatient basis. The duration of the trauma-focused CBT should normally be 8 to 12 sessions; but if the treatment starts in the first month after the event, fewer sessions (about five) may be sufficient. When the trauma is discussed in the treatment session, longer sessions (90 minutes) are usually necessary. Treatment should be regular and continuous (usually at least once a week) and should be delivered by the same person. Sometimes, other treatments are used, but their effectiveness is not known.

One helpful therapy is called CBT. Cognitive behavioral interventions during the acute aftermath of trauma exposure have yielded the most consistently positive results in terms of preventing subsequent posttraumatic psychopathology (Gibson, 2014).

"Individual or group cognitive behavioral therapy with a trauma focus (CBT-T) is based on the idea that people with PTSD have unhelpful thoughts and beliefs related to a traumatic event and its consequences" (WHO & UNHCR, 2013, p. 10). CBT is based on the idea that certain ways of thinking can trigger or fuel certain mental health problems, such as PTSD. The therapist helps you understand your current thought patterns, in particular, to identify any harmful, unhelpful, and false ideas or thoughts. The aim is then to change your ways of thinking in order to avoid these ideas, and also to help your thought patterns be more realistic and helpful. It may help especially to counter recurring distressing thoughts and avoidance behavior. Therapy is usually done in weekly sessions of about 50 minutes each, for several weeks. You have to take an active part and are given homework for between sessions (Knott, 2013). These thoughts and beliefs result in unhelpful avoidance of reminders of the event(s) and maintain a sense of current threat. CBT-F usually include (imaginal and/or in vivo) exposure treatment and/or direct challenging of unhelpful trauma-related thoughts and beliefs (WHO & UNHCR, 2013, p. 10).

There are several parts to CBT. These are exposure therapy, cognitive restructuring, and stress inoculation training.

Exposure therapy

This therapy helps people face and control their fear. It exposes them to the trauma they experienced in a safe way. It uses mental imagery, writing, or visits to the place where the event happened; hence, they are facing their feared event head on. In the case of PTSD, the memories are the feared situation and/or event. The therapist uses these tools to help people with PTSD cope with their feelings (Anxiety and Depression Association of America, 2016).

It is based on the premise that anxiety often prompts people to avoid a frightening situation. Although it is a normal response for people to want to avoid painful or distressing events, this reaction can be detrimental to their recovery. Exposure therapy aims to show that this is not the case by helping the person confront the feared situation. This is done in a very controlled and gradual fashion, overseen by therapists who are experienced with the procedure, so that discomfort is kept to a minimum. By building upon repeated successes in facing these feared situations, the person is eventually able to confront them without anxiety and they are no longer avoided. This approach is much like that used in treating individuals with phobias and takes a desensitization approach to surpass the fearful emotion, slowly and step by step and working through a hierarchy of fearful events, one at a time (Veterans Affairs Canada, 2015). This process is repeated until the event or situation no longer elicits that fear or anxiety (Staggs, 2016). This phase of CBT is now advancing with technology where, in a shortage of resources and manpower, some are investigating taking a "virtual reality" approach (NIMH, 2015). Using the phone and Internet, NIMH scientists suggest that after an initial virtual meeting of identifying symptomatology triggers and learning of basic stress reduction techniques, individuals are then directed to access a website to log their symptoms and practice coping skills that ultimately reduces their PTSD symptoms over time. The treatment entails exposing the person with PTSD to a virtual environment that contains the feared situation, instead of taking the patient into the actual environment or having the patient imagine the traumatic situation (Anxiety and Depression Association of America, 2016). Again, it is important to keep in mind that this therapeutic approach may not be for everyone; therefore, a tailored assessment is needed first.

Cognitive restructuring

Following a traumatic experience, people may be left with a range of negative interpretations or beliefs about what happened, as well as about themselves and the world. For example, they may think that they are bad or evil for acting in the way they did; they may think that what happened was their fault; they may see themselves as weak or inadequate; they may think that the world has become a dangerous place and that other people are nasty, cruel, and out to take advantage. This therapy helps people make sense of the bad memories. Sometimes, people remember the event differently than how it happened. They may feel guilt or shame about what is not their fault. The therapist helps people with PTSD look at what happened in a realistic way (Anxiety and Depression Association of America, 2016). This kind of thinking leads to all sorts of unpleasant emotions, such as depression and guilt, anxiety, fear, and anger. Sometimes, therapy will be aimed at helping the person identify maladaptive thoughts, challenge them, and replace them with a more realistic view of themselves and the world (Veterans Affairs Canada, 2015). In essence, it takes one's interpretation of the fearful event/situation and identifies and highlights the mistaken perception. Erroneous thought patterns/cognitions are then replaced with more positive, realistic, and flexible beliefs and attitudes so that the individual is able to reevaluate the situation in a more positive and less fearful manner.

Stress inoculation training

This therapy tries to reduce PTSD symptoms by teaching a person how to reduce anxiety. Like cognitive restructuring, this treatment helps people look at their memories in a healthy way (NIMH, 2015). It teaches individuals the required coping skills so that they may find new ways to deal with PTSD symptoms (Gibson, 2014). For 3 months of weekly 60- to 90-minute sessions, individuals will talk about their usual ways of coping with PTSD symptoms, learn how to keep track of their stress level, and learn and practice new problem-solving strategies and coping skills that can help relax the body and breathing, stop upsetting thoughts, and stay in the moment. Overall, this therapy occurs in three interlocking and overlapping phases: (1) a conceptual educational phase; (2) a skills acquisition and skills consolidation phase; and (3) an application and follow-through phase (Meichenbaum, 2007).

Trauma-focused CBT delivered between 1 month and 6 months after the incident is also more effective for people at risk of developing chronic PTSD compared with being on a waiting list or receiving non–trauma-focused interventions, such as self-help booklets, relaxation, or general supportive counseling. Although trauma-focused

CBT is effective for people at risk of developing chronic PTSD, there is great variation in the dimensions of delivery. The variable response rates in different studies are unexplained and may be due to differences in the PTSD sufferer's intake variables (e.g., symptomatic PTSD criteria versus diagnoses of acute stress disorder), number of treatment sessions, the expertise of therapists, or the length of individual therapy sessions.

MOTIVATIONAL INTERVIEWING

Motivational interviewing is a technique in which you become a helper in the change process and express acceptance of your patient. It ultimately helps people talk themselves into changing, and changing for the good. In essence, you come to learn and believe in what you hear yourself saying out loud. In many respects, it is very person-centered and goal-oriented to prompt change and growth from the traumatic experience. You give the reins to the patient such that autonomy, independence, self-esteem, and confidence are built up and/or strengthened. Following experiences of trauma, many find it challenging to become motivated to complete even the simplest of activities of daily living. For individuals with high-level emotions of fear and anxiety, the tendency is to avoid rather than engage and seek help. However, motivational interviewing can help boost their motivation to seek help and engage.

The growth of motivational interviewing is becoming increasingly evident on the research scene. Being used for many health issues inclusive of drug use (Aharonovich et al., 2017), anxiety (Horikawa, Udaka, Crow, Takayama, & Stein, 2017), and partner violence intervention (Crane & Easton, 2017), motivational interviewing is producing a resounding impact.

Avoidance of trauma-related memories, feelings, thoughts, and situations is a natural response to painful experiences. However, avoidance can prevent processing and integration of the trauma and ultimately perpetuates symptoms and interferes with natural recovery. Chronic avoidance also leaves people stuck in the feelings and perceptions formed at the time of the trauma. Motivational interviewing involves a style of communicating with individuals that specifically resolves ambivalence and/or resistance and builds motivation for change. Because telling their story is so important to progress and recovery, motivational interviewing can help people become stabilized before getting into their stories.

As suggested by its founders Miller and Rollnick (1991), it is a way to interact with individuals suffering from PTSD, not merely as an adjunct to other therapeutic approaches, and a style of counseling that can help resolve the ambivalence that prevents patients from realizing personal goals. It involves a style of communicating with patients that specifically resolves ambivalence and/or resistance and builds motivation for change.

The clinician practices motivational interviewing with five general principles in mind:

1. Express empathy through reflective listening
2. Develop discrepancy between patients' goals or values and their current behavior
3. Avoid argument and direct confrontation
4. Adjust to patient resistance rather than opposing it directly
5. Support self-efficacy and optimism (Rockville, 1999)

PSYCHOTHERAPY

Psychotherapy is "talk" therapy. It involves talking with a mental health professional to treat a mental illness. Psychotherapy can occur one-on-one or in a group. For most people who experience some form of traumatic event, talk therapy is good practice. Talk therapy treatment for PTSD usually lasts 6 to 12 weeks, but can take more time. Research shows that support from family and friends can be an important part of the therapy (NIMH, 2015).

As with any therapy, finding a therapist one feels comfortable with and can trust is the most important thing in psychotherapy. The therapist should be clear with the client about what the treatment plan is, and should address any concerns that the client has about the symptoms and recovery. The client should be able to work with the therapist on trauma, and the therapist in turn should be flexible enough to shift the treatment plan if required. The client should talk with the therapist about the treatment approaches the therapist will use for trauma, and should seek a referral if the client feels that the therapist or the treatment model is not the right fit (Staggs, 2016).

There are many types of psychotherapy that can help people with PTSD. Some of them target the symptoms of PTSD directly and others focus on social, family, or job-related problems. The doctor or therapist may combine different therapies depending on each person's needs (NIMH, 2015). In essence, psychotherapy strategies include group psychotherapy, CBT, eye movement desensitization and reprocessing (EMDR), and hypnotherapy (Cohen, 2016). The Substance Abuse and Mental Health Services Administration (SAMHSA, 2016) endorses no therapeutic intervention over another as a separate individual assessment, plan, and intervention are needed for each intervention. As Staggs (2016) points out, however, many of these interventions do have common ground in which they each aim to achieve goals such as new coping mechanisms, emotion regulation, cognitive restructuring, relaxation and mindfulness techniques and psychoeducation about symptoms, and issues related to the type of trauma individuals experience. Furthermore, many of these interventions require an individual to revisit the event in order to heal—repeatedly retelling the story, reprocessing in a new way, or allowing the body to discharge any held energy in an effort to promote stability, safety, and/or some sense of security.

SOMATIC THERAPY

Somatic therapies are one of the newest, cutting-edge therapies being used for PTSD; hence, evidence-informed practices from research remain scarce. This therapy is based on the theory of Peter Levine about how animals typically recover from trauma (Staggs, 2016) and emphasizes the mind–body connection. This approach attempts to use the person's own body to process and work through the traumatic event. As Levine (Yalom & Yalom, 2010) points out in an interview, it is not exposing an individual to the trauma again, it is an approach that helps to restore the body's responses that were overwhelmed as a result of the trauma through the releasing of negative energy.

The premise of somatic therapy is that restoring the body's normal responses and equilibrium enables an individual to overcome the risk of developing PTSD symptomatology. It is believed that past traumas may manifest physical symptoms, such as pain, digestive issues, hormonal imbalances, sexual dysfunction and immune system dysfunction, medical issues, depression, anxiety, and addiction. As pointed out by Khan (2016), the main goal is the "recognition and release of physical tension that may remain in the body in the aftermath of a traumatic event. The therapy sessions typically involve the patient tracking his or her experience of sensations throughout the body. Depending on the form of somatic psychology used, sessions may include awareness of bodily sensations, dance, breathing techniques, voice work, physical exercise, movement and healing touch" ("How

It Works," para. 1). The focus is on restoring and rebalancing the autonomic nervous system in particular to help restore homeostasis. Through its benefits of reframing and transforming current and past negative trauma experiences, it boosts a greater sense of self, value, confidence, resilience, and hope by reducing discomfort, strain, and stress while developing a heightened ability to concentrate and focus.

GROUP THERAPY

Group therapy can be helpful for many people who have experienced trauma, since simply having experienced such an event can produce trauma symptoms that can be isolating. Knowing and realizing that you are not alone and that other people experience very similar symptoms as do you can be very reassuring to the patient with PTSD, and sharing of such information in a group setting can pose as a buffer zone or safety net in which to open up and share even more. Hence, "group members can help normalize a lot of the reactions and feelings that someone has" (Staggs, 2016, "Somatic Therapies" para. 2).

HOW TALK THERAPIES HELP PEOPLE OVERCOME PTSD

In order to heal from trauma, people need to remember to tell the story over again in a safe and validating environment in order to work it through and begin the healing process. Talking through the trauma helps individuals get "unstuck," gain more control of their thoughts and feelings about the trauma, make sense of it, and integrate it into their experience so that it does not continue to haunt them. This process of integration allows the trauma to become a part of normal memory rather than something to be perpetually feared and avoided, interfering with normal life. Revisiting the traumatic event(s) is hard at first, but many feel better over time and notice reduced symptoms as well as feeling more empowered, more connected to themselves and others, and regaining a sense of meaning in life (Toronto Psychology Centre, 2016).

THREE-STEP APPROACH

One of the most important interventions to do immediately and within 1 week post-trauma is a three-step approach. These three steps address the trauma at various stages of progression: defusing, debriefing, and individual follow-up.

Defusing

A defusing is done the day of the incident before the person(s) has a chance to sleep. The defusing is designed to assure the person/people involved that their feelings are normal, tells them what symptoms to watch for over the short term, and offer them a lifeline in the form of a telephone number where they can reach someone who they can talk to. Defusings are limited only to individuals directly involved in the incident and are often done informally, sometimes at the scene. They assist individuals in coping in the short term and address immediate needs.

Debriefing

Debriefings are usually the second level of intervention for those directly affected by the incident and often the first for those not directly involved. Debriefing is a complex process led by specially trained personnel and typically occurs 2 to 14 days (preferably within 72 hours) after the event. The team will consider other time frames. Debriefing takes approximately 2 to 3 hours. This peer-driven process focuses on psychological and emotional aspects of the event. It is not an operational critique or group therapy (Pulley, 2005). The debriefing of the incident gives the individual or group the opportunity to talk about the experience, how it has affected them, brainstorm coping mechanisms, identify individuals at risk, and inform the individual/group about services available to them in their community. The final step is to follow up with the individuals the day after the debriefing to ensure that they are safe and coping well or to refer them for professional counseling.

Although many have co-opted the debriefing process for use with other groups, the primary focus in the field of critical incident stress management (CISM) is to support clinicians, members of organizations, or members of communities that have experienced a traumatic event. The debriefing process (defined by the International Critical Incident Stress Foundation [ICISF]) has seven steps:

1. Introduction of intervenor and establishment of guidelines and inviting participants to introduce themselves (while attendance at a debriefing may be mandatory, participation is not)
2. Details of the event given from individual perspectives
3. Emotional responses given subjectively
4. Personal reaction and actions
5. Followed again by a discussion of symptoms exhibited since the event

6. Instruction phase where the team discusses the symptoms and assures participants that any symptoms (if they have any at all) are a normal reaction to an abnormal event and "generally" these symptoms will diminish with time and self-care
7. Following a brief period of shared informal discussion (generally over a beverage and treat) resumption of duty where individuals are returned to their normal tasks. The intervenor is always watching for individuals who are not coping well and additional assistance is offered at the conclusion of the process

Follow-Up

The important final step is follow-up. This is generally done within the week following the debriefing by team members as a check-in. An important aspect of peer involvement is that team members are selected to complement the group being debriefed. Examples of this include paramedics or nurses. In this way, the group can discuss their feelings with people who have shared similar experiences. Through the process, the individuals traverse the cognitive realm to the emotional realm and then return to the cognitive. The room has a circle of chairs with team members evenly dispersed. Discussion progresses around the circle of attendees. This is a voluntary process. From the CISM team's perspective, attendance is voluntary and active participation (actual talking) is voluntary (Pulley, 2005).

Fast Facts

Various different treatment modalities exist for clinicians to use for individuals suffering from PTSD.

DELAYED POST-EVENT

The onset and/or identification of PTSD can be delayed. This results in a delay of treatment. Even in the weeks posttrauma, clinical interventions should be provided for individuals whose increased symptomatology impairs, or is thought to impair, functioning or causes significant distress (NIMH, 2016).

Delayed PTSD is a common form of PTSD. It is associated with a lag of time before its symptomatology surface:

Doctors can officially identify this subtype of post-traumatic stress disorder in people who meet the criteria for a PTSD diagnosis only half a year or longer following a traumatic event. However, this does not mean that an affected person has no PTSD symptoms prior to six months. It merely means that he or she does not have enough symptoms to qualify for a diagnosis. Still, some people with delayed PTSD truly don't experience any of the disorder's symptoms in the months following trauma. Roughly one out of four people diagnosed with post-traumatic stress disorder has delayed PTSD. (The Ranch, 2014)

Delays in the expression of PTSD are not uncommon. Among war veterans, a delay of more than 6 months after the trauma has been found (Freuh, Grubaugh, Yeager, & Magruder, 2009). Hence, symptoms may come on soon after the trauma or 50 years later. That is what is meant by the *post* in PTSD. It is normal too for symptoms to come up again when faced with further trauma and in very stressful times. It is normal to be affected by trauma (American Academy of Experts in Traumatic Stress, 2014).

The presence of the delayed form of PTSD is quite real, with proven results:

> In the study published in *JAMA Psychiatry*, researchers from several Australian institutions used an examination of 1,084 people with traumatic physical injuries to identify the factors that could potentially contribute to the chances for developing delayed PTSD. Specific factors under consideration included a prior history of mental illness, the presence of a mild traumatic brain injury (MTBI), the severity of PTSD-associated symptoms, exposure to significant stress after the originating traumatic event and the amount of hospital time needed to heal the patients' physical injuries. Assessments were made three months, one year and two years after the traumatic injuries occurred.
>
> After reviewing their assessments, the researchers found that 44 percent of the study participants who had diagnosable cases of PTSD two years after a traumatic event did not have any PTSD symptoms three months after trauma exposure. (In other words, these participants eventually developed delayed PTSD.) The remaining 66 percent of the affected participants had either diagnosable PTSD or isolated PTSD symptoms after the same three-month time period.

After examining the potential contributing factors, the researchers concluded that people diagnosed with delayed PTSD tend to experience some form of mild traumatic brain injury during the events that trigger their posttraumatic stress. They also concluded that the experience of additional high-stress situations in the aftermath of a traumatic event can increase the impact of posttraumatic stress enough to push a person over the line into diagnosable delayed PTSD. The experience of additional high-stress situations can also potentially worsen the severity of symptoms found in people who receive a delayed PTSD diagnosis. Other factors that can worsen the impact of delayed PTSD include a lengthy hospital stay for the treatment of physical trauma and the development of intense, isolated symptoms prior to an official diagnosis. (The Ranch, 2014)

PHARMACOLOGICAL INTERVENTIONS

Increasingly in health care delivery, a combination of both pharmacological and nonpharmacological therapy is deemed optimal for the treatment of PTSD (Cohen, 2016). Although medications can help with controlling or alleviating the symptomatology associated with PTSD, they are not beneficial in helping with the recurring flashbacks or the emotions associated with seeing or witnessing the original trauma.

It is also important to note that if one is receiving a medication from a general practitioner or doctor, he or she should nearly always seek a psychotherapy referral in addition to the prescription (Cohen, 2016). "Drug treatments for PTSD should not be used as a routine first-line treatment for adults (in general use or by specialist mental health professionals) in preference to a trauma-focused psychological therapy" (National Institute of Clinical Excellence [NICE], 2005, p. 123).

Furthermore, some advocate that medication for PTSD should be prescribed by a psychiatrist (Cohen, 2016). For many, this may be an unrealistic expectation as waiting lists for psychiatrists can be lengthy and an individual needs immediate help, so help may be more efficiently obtained through one's general or nurse practitioner. If and when medications are used, they are always used in synchrony with some form(s) of nonpharmacological therapy.

Much research is still ongoing for the pharmacological treatment of PTSD. Thus far, the selective serotonin reuptake inhibitors (SSRIs) and serotonin–norepinephrine reuptake inhibitors (SNRIs) have been proved most effective (Friedman & Bernardy, 2016). "Drug treatments (paroxetine or mirtazapine for general use, and amitriptyline or phenelzine for initiation only by mental health specialists) should be considered for the treatment of PTSD in adults who express a preference not to engage in trauma-focused psychological treatment" (NICE, 2006, p. 123), or in the event that no progress or signs of recovery are observed with other nonpharmacological interventions. Furthermore, "for sufferers who are acutely distressed, and may in particular be experiencing significant sleep problems, consideration may be given to the use of medication" (NICE, 2005, p. 89). Cohen (2016) adds that although psychotherapy may treat some of the symptoms commonly associated with the disorder, it will not relieve a person of the flashbacks or feelings associated with the original trauma; this is why medications are important adjunctive therapies (Cohen, 2016).

The Food and Drug Administration (FDA) has approved two medications for treating adults with PTSD, sertraline (Zoloft) and paroxetine (Paxil), both of which are SSRIs. Both of these medications are antidepressants, which are also used to treat depression. They may help control PTSD symptoms, such as sadness, worry, anger, and feeling numb inside. Taking these medications may make it easier to go through psychotherapy.

Like all medications, these drugs do have side effects; however, most may dissipate over time. Furthermore, sometimes, the presence of side effects simply indicates that the medication dose needs to be reduced or the time of day it is taken needs to be adjusted to help lessen these side effects. The NICE (2005) adds that, like sertraline and paroxetine, the antidepressants fluoxetine (Prozac) and citalopram (Celexa) can help people with PTSD feel less tense or sad. Cohen (2016) supports the use of these medications and adds that these groups of medicines tend to decrease anxiety, depression, and panic associated with PTSD, as well as aggression, impulsivity, and suicidal thoughts that can occur in people with PTSD (Cohen, 2016). Furthermore, a "relapse of posttraumatic stress disorder is less likely if antidepressants are prescribed for at least a year" (Cohen, 2016).

SSRIs are the medications most commonly used for PTSD. There are various types and brands of SSRI. Paroxetine has been found to be particularly useful for general use. SSRIs most commonly help address or reduce aggression, impulsivity, and suicidal thoughts that can occur in people with PTSD.

Non-SSRI medicines are also sometimes used by specialists; these can include mirtazapine and phenelzine (Knott, 2013). These are commonly used to treat depression but have been found to help reduce the main symptoms of PTSD even if a person is not depressed.

They work by interfering with brain chemicals (neurotransmitters) such as serotonin that may be involved in causing symptoms (Knott, 2013). Antidepressants take 2 to 4 weeks before their effect begins to build up but some can take up to 3 months to take effect. A common problem is that some people stop the medicine after a week or so as they feel that it is of no value to them. If one medication does help, it is usual to stay on the medication for 6 to 12 months, sometimes longer (Knott, 2013). For people with PTSD who also have other anxiety disorders or depression, antidepressants may be useful in reducing symptoms of these co-occurring illnesses (NICE, 2005, p. 5).

Finally, the NIMH (2016) adds that benzodiazepines may be given to help people relax and sleep and give quick relief from anxiety and agitation. However, much caution should be exercised when prescribing or recommending benzodiazepines. As a clinician I would not recommend the use of benzodiazepines. People who take benzodiazepines often develop memory problems, drowsiness, and become dependent on them. Furthermore, they lose their effect if taken more than a few weeks, and can actually exacerbate PTSD (Cohen, 2016). A short course of up to 2 to 3 weeks may be prescribed now and then if people have a particularly bad spell of anxiety symptoms (Knott, 2013).

Other medications such as beta-blockers, mood stabilizers, and anticonvulsants are also being studied for their possible effectiveness for PTSD. Although lamotrigine (Lamictal) and divalproex sodium (Depakote) can help stabilize one's mood, clonidine (Catapres) and propranolol can decrease the physical symptoms associated with PTSD. It is important to realize, however, that a combination of treatments such as CBT and an SSRI antidepressant is still the most recommended approach (Knott, 2013).

As a another option, atypical antipsychotics are an alternative that some opt to prescribe for PTSD. These include risperidone (Risperdal), olanzapine (Zyprexa), and quetiapine (Seroquel). For symptomatic relief of agitation, dissociation, hypervigilence, paranoia, and brief psychotic breaks, these drugs are highly recommended by many (Cohen, 2016).

As research continues to unfold, in recent years, prophylactic measures emerged to prevent the development of PTSD. Although the surfacing of PTSD symptoms is highly unpredictable as is the time lag in which they may occur, the use of prophylactic measures may incur much debate and scrutiny. Hence, the magnitude, source, and duration of the trauma would be important components to assess beforehand. The idea is that immediately following an acute severe traumatic event, cortisol injections have been proved beneficial to help prevent the development of PTSD (Amos, Stein, & Ipser, 2014; Yehuda et al., 1990). Research on the immediate use of opioids post-acute trauma has also uncovered some positive findings in the prevention of PTSD (Holbrook, Galarneau, Dye, Quinn, & Dougherty, 2010). Holbrook et al. found that giving opioids to injured American soldiers in Iraq 1 to 3 hours immediately post-acute trauma resulted in them exhibiting significantly lower rates of PTSD compared to those injured combat soldiers who did not receive the opioids immediately post trauma.

Fast Facts

Pharmacological and psychotherapy interventions work very well together with much success researched and documented.

SELF-HELP

Joining a group in which members have similar symptoms can be useful. This does not appeal to everyone, but books and leaflets on understanding PTSD and how to combat it may help (Knott, 2013). Discussing, networking, and even just conversing openly with individuals provide a therapeutic medium through which to obtain social support, sharing of feelings and experiences, and an atmosphere of trust and honesty.

EYE MOVEMENT DESENSITIZATION

EMDR therapy is based on the idea that negative thoughts, feelings, and behaviors are the result of unprocessed memories. EMDR is the only known intervention that enables an individual to reprocess memories and events experienced. Staggs (2016) suggests that "reprocessing means that an individual accesses the relevant memory and uses dual awareness with bilateral stimulation and images, thoughts, emotions and body sensations to move through the traumatic experiences that aren't resolved" ("Reprocessing," para. 1). She compares the putting away of groceries to the storage of memories. For example, "a traumatic event was stored by shoving a bunch of stuff in a cabinet and then any time it gets opened all the stuff falls on your head" ("Reprocessing," para. 1). As a result, "EMDR allows you to pull everything out in a controlled manner and then put it away in the organized way that non-traumatic memories are stored" (Staggs, 2016, "Reprocessing" para. 1).

The EMDR treatment itself involves standardized procedures that include focusing simultaneously on (a) spontaneous associations of traumatic images, thoughts, emotions, and bodily sensations; and (b) bilateral stimulation that is most commonly in the form of repeated eye movements. Like CBT-T, EMDR aims to reduce subjective distress and strengthen adaptive beliefs related to the traumatic event. "Unlike CBT-T, EMDR does not involve (a) detailed descriptions of the event, (b) direct challenging of beliefs, (c) extended exposure, or (d) homework" (WHO & UNHCR, 2013, p. 10). EMDR has proved particularly beneficial for individuals who have developmental, complex trauma, and single incident trauma.

EMDR occurs in eight phases; the first three of these phases do not involve any bilateral stimulation and focus primarily on skill building and resourcing in preparation for the processing phases. These phases are:

- History and treatment planning
- Preparation
- Assessment
- Desensitization
- Installation
- Body scan
- Closure
- Reinstallation (EMDR, 2016)

THE SEVEN PHASES OF DEBRIEFING

There are a total of seven phases of debriefing which are important to know and understand as a clinician working with individuals with PTSD:

1. *Initial Meeting Stage:* This stage reflects the initial meeting between patient/s and clinicians/emergency response workers. Introduction with purpose of meeting is clearly communicated. It is during this first meeting that a plan is developed, decisions are made, rules are established, and the roll out of the plan is orchestrated. Emergency response personnel inform patients/individuals present that confidentiality is enforced.

2. *Gathering of Facts Stage:* This stage reflects a gathering of more information and specific details to better tailor the debriefing sessions so that individual goals can be achieved. This is often done within a group format where individuals can add to and build upon each other's statements so a clear picture is obtained and needs are identified.

3. *Cognitive Stage:* During this stage emotions can run high from the individuals. Individuals are asked emotionally charged questions to draw out exactly what they saw or witnessed and at what point they felt they were being influenced by the negative event/s more than they realized. Individuals open up and talk about their experiences and similar themes begin to emerge from the group. Recollections involve many sensations, such as visual, auditory, and other perceptual stimuli.

4. *Response Stage:* During this stage, individuals are given the opportunity to react to what they experienced as they recollect events out loud in the presence of others. No one is forced to talk about their experiences; it is an open forum, so to speak. However, emotions continue to run high in this stage as everyone listens. People begin to realize here that they were not alone in feeling or experiencing what they did. It is important to remember here that people respond differently to different levels of stress. Group support and unity become visible here as individuals reach out to help each other.

5. *Emergence of Symptoms Stage:* The experience of a critical or traumatic event elicits a variety of signs and symptoms. These are normally experienced feelings and emotions. Again, a commonality of feelings and emotions among individuals is reinforced in knowing that what they were experiencing is typical and normal for those who have experienced what they have experienced.

6. *Education Stage:* This is perhaps the most active or greatest working stage of the entire debriefing process. A great deal of information is shared at this point in time, inclusive of processes, emotions, theoretical underpinnings, physiological/behavioral reactions, and coping skills. These are all highlighted to bring some sense of normality for the individuals and to arm individuals with tools they can use to help alleviate or address their differing stress levels. Demonstrations and role playing can be done in this stage to illustrate such concepts and approaches presented.

7. *Reflection Stage:* This stage allows the group session to wrap up, first recapping individuals' feelings, emotions, and lessons learned from the group session. All individuals are given the opportunity to ask questions. Clarification, verification and/or elaboration are typical of this phase, as questions can be posed and addressed, and facts, concepts, and processes clarified. By the time this phase has been reached, individuals' emotions are not as highly charged and some consolation is found by them as a result of their participation in the debriefing session/s. It is hoped that individuals feel some sense of relief and comfort. At departure from the meeting, the coordinator's/personnel contact information is provided to individuals for possible follow-up appointments/meetings.

WHAT NOT TO DO IN THE CARE OF PTSD PATIENTS

As a health care clinician, it is important to keep current with best practices and what the most recent research recommends. Care of individuals with PTSD is a highly sensitive area of care, so it is particularly important to do and say the right things and employ the most effective and appropriate treatment. The same applies to what ought not to be done in practice.

There are a number of things that should be avoided at all costs when you know someone has experienced a traumatic event. These are as follows (NIMH, 2015):

Don't:
- Force people to tell their stories
- Probe for personal details
- Say things like "everything will be okay," or "at least you survived"
- Say what you think people should feel or how people should have acted
- Say people suffered because they deserved it
- Be negative about available help
- Make promises that you cannot keep such as "you will go home soon"

PTSD may be a challenging disorder to treat, particularly when the symptoms do not arise until later in the course of one's life. However, there are many therapies available and different approaches to be

Fast Facts

Better success can be achieved by including the individual and his or her family in the treatment modalities used.

used. What to do and what not to do for a person suffering from PTSD is highly individualized, and even the smallest improvements can amount to big gains in recovery for the person suffering from PTSD.

References

Aharonovich, E., Sarvet, A., Stohl, M., DesJarlais, D., Tross, S., Hurst, T., ... & Hasin, D. (2017). Reducing non-injection drug use in HIV primary care: A randomized trial of brief motivational interviewing, with and without HealthCall, a technology-based enhancement. *Journal of Substance Abuse Treatment, 74*, 71–79. doi:10.1016/j.jsat.2016.12.009

American Academy of Experts in Traumatic Stress. (2014). Post traumatic stress disorder in rape survivors. Retrieved from http://www.aaets.org/article178.htm

Amos, T., Stein, D. J., & Ipser, J. C. (2014). Pharmacological interventions for preventing post-traumatic stress disorder (PTSD). *Cochrane Database Systematic Review, July 8*(7), The Cochrane Library.

Anxiety and Depression Association of America. (2016). Symptoms of PTSD. Retrieved from https://www.adaa.org/understanding-anxiety/posttraumatic-stress-disorder-ptsd/symptoms

Cohen, H. (2016). Associated conditions of PTSD. Retrieved from https://psychcentral.com/lib/associated-conditions-of-ptsd

Crane, C. A., & Easton, C. J. (2017). Integrated treatment options for male perpetrators of intimate partner violence. *Drug and Alcohol Review, 36*(1), 24–33.

Eye Movement Desensitization and Reprocessing. (2016). What is the actual EMDR session like? Retrieved from http://www.emdria.org/?120

Freuh, B. C., Grubaugh, B. C., Yeager, D. E., & Magruder, K. M. (2009). Delayed-onset post-traumatic stress disorder among war veterans in primary care clinics. *British Journal of Psychiatry, 194*(6), 515–520.

Friedman, M. J., & Bernardy, N. C. (2016). Considering future pharmacotherapy for PTSD. *Neuroscience Letters, S0304-3940*(16), 30900-4. doi:10.1016/j.neulet.2016.11.048

Gibson, L. E. (2014). Acute stress disorder. Retrieved from http://www.ptsd.va.gov/professional/treatment/early/acute-stress-disorder.asp

Holbrook, T. L., Galarneau, M. R., Dye, K., Quinn, A., & Dougherty, A. L. (2010). Morphine use after combat injury in Iraq and post-traumatic stress disorder. *New England Journal of Medicine, 362*, 110–117.

Horikawa, Y. T., Udaka, T. Y., Crow, J. K., Takayama, J. I., & Stein, M. T. (2017). Anxiety associated with asthma exacerbations and overuse of medication: The role of cultural competency. *Journal of Developmental and Behavioral Pediatrics*, *38*(Suppl. 1), S56–S59. doi:10.1097/DBP.00000 00000000029

Khan, K. (2016). How somatic therapy can help patients suffering from psychological trauma. Retrieved from https://psychcentral.com/blog/arch ives/2014/09/12/how-somatic-therapy-can-help-patients-suffering-from -psychological-trauma.

Knott, L. (2013). Post-traumatic stress disorder. Retrieved from http://www .patient.co.uk/health/post-traumatic-stress-disorder-leaflet

Meichenbaum, D. (2007). Stress inoculation training: A preventative and treatment approach. In P. M. Lehrer, R. L. Woolfolk, & W. S. Sime (Eds.), *Principles and practice of stress management* (3rd ed., pp. 120–139). New York, NY: Guilford Press.

Miller, W. R., & Rollnick, S. (1991). *Motivational interviewing: Preparing people to change addictive behavior.* New York, NY: Guilford Press.

National Institute for Clinical Excellence (2005). Post-traumatic stress disorder: The management of PTSD in adults and children in primary and secondary care. Retrieved from https://www.nice.org.uk/guidance/cg26/ evidence/full-guideline-including-appendices-113-pdf-193442221

National Institute of Mental Health. (2015). How can adults help children and adolescents who experienced trauma? Retrieved from http://www.nimh .nih.gov/health/publications/helping-children-and-adolescents-cope -with-violence-and-disasters-community-members/index.shtml#pub5

National Institute of Mental Health. (2016). Post-traumatic stress disorder. Retrieved from https://www.nimh.nih.gov/health/topics/post-traumatic -stress-disorder-ptsd/index.shtml

Pulley, S. A. (2005). Critical incident stress management. Retrieved from https://web.archive.org/web/20060811232118/http:/www.emedicine.com/ emerg/topic826.htm

Staggs, S. (2016). Psychotherapy treatment for PTSD. Retrieved from https:// psychcentral.com/lib/treatment-of-ptsd.

Substance Abuse and Mental Health Services Administration. (1999). *Treatment improvement protocol (TIP; series no. 35).* Rockville, MD: Author.

Substance Abuse and Mental Health Services Administration. (2016). Trauma-informed approach and trauma-specific interventions. Retrieved from https://www.samhsa.gov/nctic

The Ranch. (2014). Why do some people develop delayed PTSD? Retrieved from https://www.recoveryranch.com/articles/mental-health-articles/why -do-some-people-develop-delayed-ptsd.

Toronto Psychology Centre. (2016). Trauma and abuse. Retrieved from http:// torontopsychologycentre.com/areas-of-focus/trauma-and-abuse

Veterans Affairs Canada. (2015). Post-traumatic stress disorder (PTSD) and war-related stress. Retrieved from http://www.veterans.gc.ca/eng/services/ health/mental-health/publications/ptsd-warstress

World Health Organization and United Nations High Commissioner for Refugees. (2013). Assessment and management of conditions specifically related to stress: mhGAP intervention guide module (version 1.0). Retrieved from http://apps.who.int/iris/bitstream/10665/85623/1/97892415 05932_eng.pdf

Yalom, V., & Yalom, M. H. (2010). Peter Levine on somatic experiencing. Retrieved from https://www.psychotherapy.net/interview/interview-peter -levine

Yehuda, J. R., Southwick, S. M., Nussbaum, G., Wahby, V., Giller, E. L. Jr., & Mason, J. W. (1990). Low urinary cortisol excretion in patients with post-traumatic stress disorder. *Journal of Nervous and Mental Disorders, 178* (1990), 366–369.

10

Coping With PTSD

The way people respond to trauma significantly influences whether or not they will develop posttraumatic stress disorder (PTSD). People have different coping mechanisms that they find effective; an effective coping strategy for one person may be significantly different from those for others. We have discussed stress, different sources of stress, and the impact stress has on our bodies and minds. Now we focus on how individuals can help identify, deal with, and learn from stressful events, all of which help strengthen their mental health and enhance how they can respond successfully to other increasingly stressful events. However, as indicated before, people perceive, experience, and respond to stress in very different ways, so what works for one may not necessarily work for another. Knowing one's own body and recognizing the stressors that impact it is half the battle for how individuals with PTSD can respond productively to stress. For example, knowing the triggers of one's stress can help prepare a person to better respond to stress once it does occur.

People are usually surprised that reactions to trauma can last longer than they expected. It may take weeks, months, and, in some cases, many years to fully regain equilibrium. Many people will get through this period with the help and support of family and friends. But sometimes friends and family may push people to "get over it" before they are ready. Let them know that such responses are not helpful for you right now, though you appreciate that they are trying to help. Many people find that individual, group, or family counseling is helpful, and in particular, eye movement desensitization and reprocessing (EMDR) is a phenomenally rapid and wonderful therapeutic method. Another superior therapeutic method is internal family systems (IFS). Either way, the key word is *connection*—ask for help, support, understanding, and opportunities to talk (Levin, 2011).

Also, personality and cognitive factors, such as optimism and the tendency to view challenges in a positive or negative way (National Institute of Mental Health [NIMH], 2015), as do social factors, such as the availability and use of social support, appear to influence how people adjust to trauma. More research may show what combinations of these or perhaps other factors could be used to predict who will develop PTSD following a traumatic event (NIMH, 2015).

In this chapter, you will learn:

- Everyone has different coping styles and strategies; there is no standard strategy that works any better than another
- Coping is an individualized and critical component for dealing with stressors and illnesses such as PTSD
- The impact of PTSD may precipitate individuals to resort to less effective coping strategies
- Courage and resilience are two key components for coping with stress

COPING STRATEGIES

When confronted with acute stressors and the potential development of PTSD, coping strategies are critical to help individuals maintain good mental health and also in the extent to which PTSD will become manifested. Coping with stress can be very difficult; however, it remains very important for individuals to learn to deal with stress to decrease or alleviate the negative impact that stress can create.

For years, research has explored the value of coping with stress and doing so effectively. As people respond to and cope with stress in very individualized ways, there should be various options available to choose from, as what works for one person may not work for another. Moreover, people usually draw upon coping strategies that they have found to be effective in the past. Some of the most common coping strategies that seem to work when dealing with stress are presented in Box 10.1.

BOX 10.1 SUGGESTED STRATEGIES TO HELP COPE WITH STRESS

- Mobilize a support system—reach out and connect with others, especially those who may have shared the stressful event; talk about the traumatic experience with empathic listeners
- Cry hard
- Do exercises such as jogging, aerobics, bicycling, walking and relaxation exercises such as yoga, stretching, massage; and add humor, prayer, and/or meditation
- Listen to relaxing guided imagery
- Exercise progressive deep muscle relaxation
- Take hot baths
- Listen to music and engage in art
- Maintain a balanced diet and sleep cycle as much as possible
- Avoid overusing stimulants such as caffeine, sugar, or nicotine and commit to something personally meaningful and important every day
- Hug those you love, pets included
- Eat warm turkey, boiled onions, baked potatoes, cream-based soups—these are tryptophan activators, which help you feel tired but good
- Respond proactively toward personal and community safety
- Organize or do something socially active
- Write about your experience in detail, just for yourself or to share with others

Source: Levin (2011).

Positive coping strategies would include things such as exercising, eating better, and so forth. The actual coping strategies used may very well be making the situation more stressful and worse for you than it is already (Smith, Segal, & Segal, 2013). Positive coping strategies such as relaxation techniques, visualization or imagery, and exercise all serve to relieve stress, improve sleep, promote positivism, and boost self-esteem and confidence. Keeping a positive attitude will help you forget what you do not want and save your energy to focus on what you want (Koffman, 2006); thus, you achieve success by committing yourself and staying motivated. Success is what gives you pleasure, but integrity in getting there is what will give you happiness. Even meditation, acupuncture, massage therapy, eating spicy food, or breathing deeply cause your body to produce endorphins naturally—the body's physiological brain-enhancing chemicals that promote positive mental health, elevated mood, and less anxiety (Rattue, 2012).

However, *negative coping strategies* can include such things as overeating, smoking, drinking alcohol, and using drugs. Furthermore, as suggested by Johansen (2014), avoidant conflict management style is used to resolve conflicting priorities because emergency response (ER) nurses feel that there is not enough time to address conflict even though it may affect work stress and patient care. If your methods of coping with stress are not contributing to your greater emotional and physical health, it is time to find healthier ones. Whichever option you choose, the four As will assist you in this process (Smith et al., 2013):

- *Avoid* unnecessary stressors and address the ones you absolutely need right here and now; do not waste your energy and brain power on stress you cannot control. Learning how to say "no" can help you with this, so know your limits and stick to them. Surround yourself with calm, positive, and happy people as anxiousness can be contagious, take control of your environment, avoid controversial topics such as religion or politics, and prioritize what you need to do between the "shoulds" and the "musts."

- *Alter* the stressor/situation if you cannot avoid it. Figure out what you can do to change things so the problem does not reappear in the future, express your feelings instead of bottling them up to avoid resentment, compromise and deal with problems head on, take a break to recharge your mind and body, go ahead and book that much-needed vacation.

- *Adapt* to the stressor and change yourself, values, or attitudes if you cannot change the stressor. Since you still have some sense of control, review your problems through a positive lens, pause and regroup your thoughts, and look at the big picture to know whether you really need to worry. Adjusting your standards may be required because no one is perfect, not even you.

- *Accept* the stressor if you cannot control any part of it, for example, the death of a loved one. Acceptance may be difficult, but look at what you can learn from it, share your feelings and learn to forgive.

Managing your emotions such as anger, fear, frustration, and so forth is an important step as you try to cope with daily stressors.

Identify those stress triggers: Writing them down to decrease their power over you, pay attention to what works so you keep on the right track, talk to a friend, take a break and go for a walk, find a quiet place to sit or otherwise relax and refocus. Do not work through breaks and lunch when you are stressed; and of course don't forget to breathe, so the brain oxygen supplies remain adequate. As suggested by Ward (2011), the way nurses manage their stress is often intrinsically linked to their job satisfaction. Setting realistic goals, enjoying yourself and having fun, maintaining a healthy lifestyle, and talking also help to address stress in a healthy way (Mental Health Foundation, 2013). Finally, you need to accept who you are, or else you will never be happy or content with who you are and what you do.

WHEN TO SEE A DOCTOR

If you have disturbing thoughts and feelings about a traumatic event for more than a month, if they are severe, or if you feel you are having trouble getting your life back under control, talk to your health care professional. Get treatment as soon as possible to help prevent PTSD symptoms from getting worse (Mayo Clinic, 2015).

Fast Facts

Coping can sometimes only get an individual so far in the fight against stress and PTSD, at which point he or she may resort to more ineffective measures to cope.

COURAGE

Courage is important in coping with overwhelming stressors and the experience of PTSD. It is vital to help overcome stress and can even be instrumental in transforming stress into something productive. The definition of courage varies according to sources, but one thing is for certain, it "is something that everybody wants—an attribute of good character that makes us worthy of respect" (Greenberg, 2012, para. 1). Nelson Mandela, for example, suggested that courage represents triumph over fear.

Isolating a definition of courage is a challenge. Many definitions of courage are presented in Box 10.2.

BOX 10.2 COURAGE . . .

- Trying to do better in all you do
- Recognizing your mistakes and/or limitations and being able to say "I am sorry"
- Asking for help when you need it
- Knowing when you have had enough
- Knowing when to stop
- Knowing when to say yes and going for it
- Aspiring to new heights and learnings
- Grasping every opportunity for growth within yourself
- Knowing your own vulnerabilities and weaknesses
- Reaching out to help others in need
- Choosing the positive over the negative
- Loving instead of hating
- Trusting in others as they have trusted in you
- Standing up for what you believe in
- Pursuing your dreams and wishes
- Learning how to walk away when you feel you need to
- Learning you cannot be everything to everyone
- Giving of yourself, instead of expecting to receive
- Crying and feeling your emotions so your body can rejuvenate itself
- Exploring new territory for new lessons and experiences in life
- Taking a break when you feel you need to
- Embracing the vulnerable and sharing your strength with them
- Helping the sick and weak instead of turning the other way

There are six recognized attributes of courage and it is these attributes that can help an individual surpass the fear initiated by trauma. These categories of courage developed by Greenberg (2012) are as follows:

1. *Feeling fear yet choosing to act:* Taking little steps is important. Making the choice to take action is one small step toward moving past the fear. It is being able to do or try to do what you are afraid to do.

2. *Following your heart:* Everyone has passion and it is through passion we strive to achieve our goals. Passion puts us on the road toward achieving courage and stepping outside of our comfort zone, one step at a time, toward doing what we want or would like to do.

3. *Persevering in the face of adversity:* Adversity challenges us to keep going and succeed. We are able to overcome the small setbacks, recognize the delays, but keep our focus on moving forward. The delays and adversity gently remind us that we always have tomorrow or next week to try again.

4. *Standing up for what is right:* It helps us in recognizing and adhering to our beliefs and values. We know what is right and wrong and what is moral or immoral, and thus we let our values and beliefs guide us in those decisions. Standing up, confronting, and voicing against what is wrong makes us a stronger individual and builds our confidence, esteem, and individuality.

5. *Expand your horizons and let go of the comfortable or familiar:* Living and existing in the status quo does not provide the opportunity to learn and grow. Sometimes, we need to move outside of our comfort zone into new and unchartered territory to enhance our growth, expand our knowledge, and live the existential life.

6. *Face suffering with dignity or faith:* Take the good from the bad and replace suffering with something positive. We all have weaknesses, but we all have strengths as well. It is okay to cry and be ashamed, but our faith, dignity, and integrity will shine through our strengths.

RESILIENCE

Many factors play a part in whether a person will get PTSD. As discussed earlier, some of these are risk factors that can increase an individual's predisposition to developing PTSD. However, many people can be subjected to the exact same crisis or event but yet react differently and differ in the extent, if any, to which they will develop PTSD. These mitigating factors are called resilience factors. These factors help reduce the risk and/or impact of PTSD. Some of these resilience factors are present before the trauma and others become important during and after a traumatic event.

Resilience is defined as "that ineffable quality that allows some people to be knocked down by life and come back stronger than ever. Rather than letting failure overcome them and drain their resolve, they find a way to rise from the ashes" ("Resilience," 2017). The American Psychological Association (2017) adds that "resilience is the process of adapting well in the face of adversity, trauma, tragedy, threats, or significant sources of stress" ("What is Resilience," para. 1). Although the concept of resilience is elusive and fleeting for many veterans of war, remarkably most service members exposed to horrific war trauma are not incapacitated by the experience (Litz, 2014).

Some of the factors that make an individual resilient are positive attitude, optimism, the ability to regulate emotions, and the ability to see failure as a form of helpful feedback. "Even after misfortune, resilient people are blessed with such an outlook that they are able to change course and soldier on" ("Resilience," 2017).

Resilience Factors

Resilience factors play a significant role in the extent to which one experiences traumatic events and/or the development of PTSD. As such, they are critical in educating individuals and families on how to alleviate the impact of traumatic events, as well as health care professionals, such as nurses, when assessing patients for the impact of trauma. Many studies show that the primary factor in resilience is having caring and supportive relationships within and outside the family.

Resilience and coping factors play a significant role in making primary prevention successful. Some such examples as they apply to PTSD are:

- Education about PTSD and how to cope with stressful events
- Education on how good nutrition and the importance of regular exercise can be in dealing with stress
- The dangers of alcohol and other drugs that can be used as a coping mechanism
- Regular exams and screening tests to monitor risk factors for illness
- Very early monitoring of the individual immediately after the traumatic event
- Controlling potential hazards and other crisis events at home and in the workplace (Institute for Work and Health, 2006).

"Relationships that create love and trust, provide role models, and offer encouragement and reassurance help bolster a person's resilience" (American Psychological Association, 2017, "Resilience Factors & Strategies," para. 1). Some other factors are described in Box 10.3 (American Psychological Association, 2017; NIMH, 2009, 2015):

BOX 10.3 RESILIENCE

- Seeking out support from other people, such as friends and family
- Finding a support group after a traumatic event
- Feeling good about one's own actions in the face of danger
- Having a coping strategy, or a way of getting through the bad event and learning from it
- Being able to act and respond effectively despite feeling fear
- The capacity to make realistic plans and take steps to carry them out
- A positive view of yourself and confidence in your strengths and abilities
- Skills in communication and problem solving
- The capacity to manage strong feelings and impulses

Developing resilience is a personal experience and differs for everyone. People do not all react the same to traumatic and stressful life events. An approach to building resilience that works for one person might not work for another. People use varying strategies. The American Psychological Association (2017) has identified many strategies to help develop one's resilience. Some of these ways to build resilience and develop your own personal strategy include the following:

- *Make connections:* Good relationships with close family members, friends, or others are important. Accepting help and support from those who care about you and will listen to you strengthens resilience. Some people find that being active in civic groups, faith-based organizations, or other local groups provides social support and can help with reclaiming hope. Assisting others in their time of need can also benefit the helper.
- *Avoid seeing crises as insurmountable problems:* You cannot change the fact that highly stressful events happen, but you can change how you interpret and respond to these events. Try looking beyond the present to how future circumstances may be a little better. Note any subtle ways in which you might already feel somewhat better as you deal with difficult situations.

- *Accept that change is a part of living:* Certain goals may no longer be attainable as a result of adverse situations. Accepting circumstances that cannot be changed can help you focus on circumstances that you can alter.

- *Move toward your goals:* Develop some realistic goals. Do something regularly—even if it seems like a small accomplishment—that enables you to move toward your goals. Instead of focusing on tasks that seem unachievable, ask yourself, "What's one thing I know I can accomplish today that helps me move in the direction I want to go?"

- *Take decisive actions:* Act on adverse situations as much as you can. Take decisive actions, rather than detaching completely from problems and stresses and wishing they would just go away.

- *Look for opportunities for self-discovery:* People often learn something about themselves and may find that they have grown in some respect as a result of their struggle with loss. Many people who have experienced tragedies and hardship have reported better relationships, greater sense of strength even while feeling vulnerable, increased sense of self-worth, a more developed spirituality, and heightened appreciation for life.

- *Nurture a positive view of yourself:* Developing confidence in your ability to solve problems and trusting your instincts helps build resilience.

- *Keep things in perspective:* Even when facing very painful events, try to consider the stressful situation in a broader context and keep a long-term perspective. Avoid blowing the event out of proportion.

- *Maintain a hopeful outlook:* An optimistic outlook enables you to expect that good things will happen in your life. Try visualizing what you want, rather than worrying about what you fear.

- *Take care of yourself:* Pay attention to your own needs and feelings. Engage in activities that you enjoy and find relaxing. Exercise regularly. Taking care of yourself helps to keep your mind and body primed to deal with situations that require resilience.

There are other ways of increasing resilience. For example, some people write about their deepest thoughts and feelings related to trauma or other stressful events in their life. Meditation and spiritual practices help some people build connections and restore hope. The key is to identify ways that are likely to work well for you as part of your own personal strategy for fostering resilience.

FOR THE FAMILY MEMBER AND/OR FRIEND LOOKING TO HELP

If you know someone who has PTSD, it affects you too. The first and most important thing you can do to help a friend or relative is to help that person get the right diagnosis and treatment. You may need to make an appointment for your friend or relative and go with him or her to see the doctor. Encourage your friend or relative to stay in treatment, or to seek different treatment if symptoms do not get better after 6 to 8 weeks.

To help a friend or relative, you can:

- Offer emotional support, understanding, patience, and encouragement
- Learn about PTSD so you can understand what your friend or relative is experiencing
- Talk to your friend or relative, and listen carefully
- Listen to feelings your friend or relative expresses and understand situations that may trigger PTSD symptoms
- Invite your friend or relative out for positive distractions, such as walks, outings, and other activities
- Remind your friend or relative that, with time and treatment, he or she can get better
- Never ignore comments from your friend or relative about self-harm and report such comments to your friend's or relative's therapist or doctor (Substance Abuse and Mental Health Services Administration [SAMHSA], 2016)

COPING WITH THE FALLOUT

Prevention and coping go hand in hand as an individual strives to maintain homeostasis and everyday functioning. Because PTSD has such an impact, there are various positive coping strategies and approaches that an individual can implement to prevent some of the negative fallout from PTSD that often lead to poor or inappropriate coping measures. Some examples are provided here.

Substance Abuse

As previously highlighted, substance abuse is a common occurrence for individuals dealing with traumatic events and/or PTSD. In an effort to prevent it or recognize it before it becomes too severe, the following are suggested:

- Education about the use and effect of the substance
- Decisions regarding total abstinence versus controlled use of the drug
- Recording "danger" times and identifying patterns of use
- Developing coping strategies for high-risk times
- Assertiveness training when others are applying peer pressure
- Planning and scheduling activities not associated with the substance
- Response prevention—methods of resisting the "urge" (Veterans Affairs Canada, 2017)

Anxiety Management

Techniques aimed at reducing levels of anxiety and arousal are an important part of treatment (Veterans Affairs Canada, 2017). These techniques are as follows:

- Relaxation training to reduce overall levels of anxiety
- Breathing techniques to reduce panic-like symptoms
- Thought-interruption methods to break the tendency to "ruminate" or think excessively about the past
- Rational self-talk to help manage high-anxiety situations and depressing thoughts
- Techniques to help you organize your time effectively, scheduling enjoyable and productive activities, and providing some structure to your days

Anger Management

Techniques to reduce levels of anger and irritability with others are important. Strategies that are commonly used include the following:

- Education to understand the nature and purpose of anger
- Methods of identifying early warning signs of stress and irritability

- Methods of identifying high-risk situations and how to prepare for them
- Methods of realistically reevaluating the situation, keeping it in perspective
- Strategies to reduce arousal and stay calm in difficult situations
- Effective communication methods (verbal and nonverbal)
- Differentiating assertive from aggressive behavior
- Problem-solving strategies to effectively deal with disagreements
- Distraction and removal techniques to avoid "flare-ups"
- Practice in imagined and real-life situations (Veterans Affairs Canada, 2017)

Sleep Disturbances

Sleep disturbances are a common symptom as a result of PTSD. Individuals frequently complain about difficulty falling to sleep, waking up several times throughout the night, nightmares, night terrors, and waking early in the morning. Techniques to help promote adequate sleep are:

- Drink warm milk, and avoid alcohol, caffeine, smoking, and heavy meals at night
- Stick to a sleep schedule
- Maintain a relaxing bedtime ritual each night, for example, avoiding bright lights
- Avoid naps during the day and avoid sleeping during the morning
- Exercise or engage in some form of activity daily, but not in the evening
- Unwind at the end of your day—relaxing and calming your body down after a long day will help promote a restful state, and reading is a great activity to help in this regard
- Make sure your bed, pillow, and number of blankets are adequate for your comfort
- Evaluate the comfort, noise level, lighting, and temperature of your bedroom, and best to take television, radio, and computer out of the bedroom
- Use bright light during the daytime to keep your circadian rhythm on tract
- As a last resort, see your physician or nurse practitioner for a medication that will help you sleep (National Sleep Foundation, 2017)

Dealing With Stress in General

- *Think positively:* Try to avoid negative thinking and overanalyzing others, as these can distort your perception and increase your stress levels

- *Develop new skills:* Read about assertiveness training, communication skills, or conflict resolution. Practice the art of politely but firmly saying "no" and learn how to confront a difficult person or situation

- *Learn relaxation techniques:* Practicing deep breathing, meditation, or a simple stress-busting exercise can help your body relax and improve your well-being

- *Remember to laugh:* Humor is an excellent medicine to help alleviate stress. Share a joke with a colleague, curl up at home with a comedy on TV, and look for the humor in every challenging situation

- *Make lifestyle changes:* Exercising regularly reduces tension, helps you sleep better, and improves self-esteem. Eating healthy foods instead of junk food on the run or at your desk is better for you and can help you feel better

- *Take a break:* Include regular breaks, from 10-minute walks at lunch time, to a day off to do something you enjoy, to an annual or semiannual vacation

- *Talk to your employer:* If you are dealing with a stressful workplace situation, ask for help to improve it. For example, if your environment is excessively noisy or dangerous or if a colleague is behaving inappropriately, talk to your boss, manager, or your human resources department about steps you can take

- *Seek help:* Take advantage of an employee assistance program if your employer offers one or ask your health care provider to refer you to someone who can help

Fast Facts

Your astute clinical assessment should include how an individual often copes with stress.

References

American Psychological Association. (2017). The road to resilience. Retrieved from http://www.apa.org/helpcenter/road-resilience.aspx

Greenberg, M. (2012). The six attributes of courage. Retrieved from https://www.psychologytoday.com/blog/the-mindful-self-express/201208/the-six-attributes-courage

Institute for Work and Health. (2006). At work, 43(Winter 2006). Toronto, ON, Canada: Author. Retrieved from http://www.iwh.on.ca/system/files/at-work/at_work_43.pdf

Johansen, M. L. (2014). Conflicting priorities: Emergency nurses' perceived disconnect between patient satisfaction and the delivery of quality patient care. Journal of Emergency Nursing, 40(1), 13–19.

Koffman, F. (2006). Conscious business: How to build values through values. Boulder, CO: Sounds True.

Levin, P. (2011). Common responses to trauma and coping strategies. Retrieved from http://www.trauma-pages.com/s/t-facts.php

Litz, B. T. (2014). Resilience in the aftermath of war trauma: A critical review and commentary. Interface Focus, 4(5), doi:10.1098/rsfs.2014.0008

Mayo Clinic. (2015). Post traumatic stress disorder (PTSD): Symptoms. Retrieved from http://www.mayoclinic.org/diseases-conditions/post-traumatic-stress-disorder/basics/symptoms/con-20022540

Mental Health Foundation. (2013). How to look after your mental health. Retrieved from https://www.mentalhealth.org.uk/publications/how-to-mental-health

National Institute of Mental Health. (2015). Post-traumatic stress disorder. Retrieved from https://www.nimh.nih.gov/health/publications/post-traumatic-stress-disorder-basics/index.shtml

Rattue, P. (2012). Exercise affects the brain. Medical News Today. Retrieved from http://www.medicalnewstoday.com/articles/245751.php

"Resilience." (2017). Retrieved from https://www.psychologytoday.com/basics/resilience

Substance Abuse and Mental Health Services Administration. (2016). Trauma-informed approach and trauma-specific interventions. Retrieved from https://www.samhsa.gov/nctic/trauma-interventions

Smith, M., Segal, J., & Segal, R. (2013). Preventing burnout. Retrieved from http://www.helpguide.org/mental/burnout_signs_symptoms.htm

Veterans Affairs Canada. (2017). Post-traumatic stress disorder (PTSD) and war-related stress. Retrieved from http://www.veterans.gc.ca/eng/services/health/mental-health/publications/ptsd-warstress#Item3-2

Ward, L. (2011). Mental health nursing and stress: Maintaining balance. International Journal of Mental Health Nursing, 20(2), 77–85. doi:10.1111/j.1447-0349.2010.00715.x

11

Community Involvement

The effects of posttraumatic stress disorder (PTSD) sometimes spread beyond work and home. Traumatic events can affect a community as a whole, whether directly or indirectly; the experience can have lasting and profound impacts for many. As was seen in recent happenings such as the January 2017 Fort Lauderdale airport shooting, society quickly became impacted as individuals lost their loved ones and/or became injured themselves. A similar incident occurred in Cleveland, Ohio, in August 2016, when a 26-year-old Marine Corps male shot and killed a woman following a car crash. Natural disasters like Hurricanes Katrina and Sandy have destroyed many people's homes and lives. It is through these horrific stories that we see the impact of PTSD in our communities. But exactly what can communities and/or societies do to help address such concerns?

In this chapter, you will learn:

- The value for how community and society at large can help address individuals and the manifestations of PTSD
- How stigma is counterproductive in the care and treatment of individuals with PTSD
- How schools and workplaces and many other public places can assist in the understanding and effects of PTSD
- Why support groups, governments, and public prevention programs can promote an atmosphere and awareness conducive to those suffering in silence

PTSD IN THE COMMUNITY

The impact of PTSD can be found anywhere and everywhere. As a united front, communities and societies at large can work together to help address the effects of PTSD. This chapter highlights the presence of PTSD in communities and what role communities can play in helping to ameliorate some of the effects of PTSD. Although much of the resources are directed toward individuals returning from combat, the same principles apply to noncombat PTSD.

STIGMA

Stigma is perhaps one of the most significant barriers to helping people and communities experiencing PTSD recover and normalize to some degree. Stigma can be defined as a perceived negative attribute that causes someone to devalue or think less of the whole person (Gluck, 2016). It often arises as a result of not knowing the difference or being uneducated to just plain ignorance. It is much like the overwhelming degree of stigma today that causes a general tendency to ostracize individuals suffering from various mental illnesses (Byrne, 2000).

Because of the stigma people may have about PTSD, others may look down on you because of your condition. People may believe things about PTSD that are not true, which can cause them to treat you and your family differently.

Some people may have good intentions but still feel uncomfortable when they find out you have PTSD. This can make it difficult to find a job or a place to live.

Stigma occurs when others:

- Do not understand PTSD
- Do not realize that PTSD is an illness that can be treated
- Think that mental illness is "your own fault" or that you can "get over it"
- Are afraid they might catch what you have
- Think PTSD makes you dangerous

The presence of stigma, however, can further exacerbate the negative effects already felt as a result of PTSD.

Trauma in Your Community

The presence and effects of trauma in any community are becoming commonplace. But there are many community resources that can help people become educated and better understand PTSD as well as identify its presence and deal with the fallout of PTSD. Outlets and resources that already exist in many communities can help buffer the impact of PTSD.

Media

Media can play a significant role in how PTSD at a community level can be portrayed. Unfortunately, often we only hear about the negative. However, in the same manner, media can be used as a tool to help with the effects of trauma and PTSD in communities. Through media stories, education can be promoted and resources can be advertised.

Work

Because most people spend roughly about 30% of their lives at work, this environment can prove instrumental in helping to buffer the impact of PTSD. It is important to realize that your colleague and/or employee may be fighting a silent battle all their own with PTSD that no one knows about.

Strategies to Employ in the Workplace   There are many simple strategies we can use in the workplace as a buffer against the effects of PTSD. Although many of them seem like common sense, they are nonetheless important to practice and could potentially go a long way in helping others deal with the fallout of their PTSD.

1. *Maintain open communication with the individual:* If individuals with PTSD sense any stigma whatsoever, this will prevent them from seeking help. Let them know you are there to help them if needed.
2. *Listen empathetically:* Give them your undivided attention with good eye contact. Sometimes, they may be reluctant to talk, so just let them know you are there to listen to them when they are ready to seek help. Be comfortable with periods of silence, and once they begin to talk, don't interrupt them to express your thoughts.
3. *Meet their needs.* Accommodating employees in the workplace conveys concern, interest in the individual, and respect. If they

are experiencing memory difficulties as a result of PTSD, provide for them a list of tasks. If they are having problems concentrating, place them in a quiet office away from noises. During times of stress, let them take frequent breaks to get away.

4. *Deal with any issues promptly:* Patience is a virtue. If they are struggling with a task, ask them about it and what you can do to offer help. Be firm but yet constructive and kind.

5. *Educate and train all staff:* To help overcome any stigma present among other staff, sometimes people need to be educated. Educating staff should promote understanding, support, patience, and empathy.

6. *Enforce respectful workplace policies:* It is important for workplaces to develop and enforce respectful workplace policies so that all staff are treated fairly and anyone breaching that policy will be reprimanded.

7. *Employee assistance program:* Most workplaces now have an employee assistance program to help their staff with health and social issues. Whenever needed, refer individuals to this program or at least let them know it is there for them if they feel they need help.

School

If hurt by violence, in addition to having to cope with physical or medical problems, a child may also have mental health problems such as PTSD. Many think that young children are not harmed by community violence because they are too young to understand or remember. However, studies have found signs of PTSD in babies and young children (National Center for PTSD, 2017). Teachers need to understand that children may have new problem behaviors as a result of the trauma. These behaviors need patience and understanding. Ask for help from friends, family, and medical and mental health experts for the child.

For students, a traumatic experience may cause ongoing feelings of concern for their own safety and the safety of others. These students may become preoccupied with thoughts about their actions during the event, oftentimes experiencing guilt or shame over what they did or did not do at the time. They might engage in constant retelling of the traumatic event, or may describe being overwhelmed by their feelings of fear or sadness (The National Child Traumatic Stress Network, 2017).

Similar to adults' commitment to work, children, too, spend approximately 30% of their young lives attending school. Unlike adults, children often do not know about PTSD or understand what it means. When a child is perceived as behaving oddly in a peer pressure environment such as school, bullying and other condescending remarks and behaviors can occur. This will leave the child who is already suffering from PTSD even more traumatized. There are many simple things that schools and the accompanying administration can employ to prevent such occurrences from happening.

Fast Facts

Communities have a significant role to play in the treatment and recovery of individuals with PTSD.

PTSD SIGNS IN SCHOOL SETTINGS

Teachers spend a great deal of time on a daily basis with children. Hence, they are in very strategic positions to identify learning and behavior changes in children. PTSD symptoms for school teachers to know and be able to identify are given in Box 11.1.

BOX 11.1 SIGNS OF PTSD TEACHERS CAN WATCH FOR IN THE CLASSROOM SETTING

- Anxiety, fear, and worry about safety of self and others (more clingy with teacher or parent)
- Worry about recurrence of violence
- Increased distress (unusually whiny, irritable, moody)
- Increase in activity level
- Decreased attention and/or concentration
- Withdrawal from others or activities
- Angry outbursts and/or aggression
- Absenteeism
- Distrust of others, affecting how children interact with both adults and peers

(continued)

BOX 11.1   SIGNS OF PTSD TEACHERS CAN WATCH FOR IN THE CLASSROOM SETTING (*CONTINUED*)

- A change in ability to interpret and respond appropriately to social cues
- Increased somatic complaints (e.g., headaches, stomach-aches, overreaction to minor bumps and bruises)
- Difficulty with authority, redirection, or criticism
- Reexperiencing the trauma (e.g., nightmares or disturbing memories during the day)
- Hyperarousal (e.g., sleep disturbance, tendency to be easily startled)
- Avoidance behaviors (e.g., resisting going to places that remind them of the event)
- Emotional numbing (e.g., seeming to have no feeling about the event)

SCHOOL STRATEGIES

Although most children recover fine on their own over a period of months from trauma and PTSD, some do not, particularly if there is no intervention or treatment given. Children can be helped. The best thing for a child is a caring adult. If a child is touched by violence, spend time with the child. Be sure the child understands that you are there to listen. Help the child talk about the trauma, but do not make him or her talk. Answer questions honestly using words that the child understands.

- Openly communicate with the parents and/or family of the child to find out if there is a health concern for the child. This is often done through the guidance counselor or community nurse or social worker assigned to the school.
- Train teachers on what to look for in children who have suffered from trauma.
- Help children and caregivers reestablish a sense of safety.
- Use techniques for dealing with overwhelming emotional reactions.
- Take an opportunity to talk about and make sense of the traumatic experience in a safe, accepting environment.
- Become involved, when possible, with primary caregivers in the healing process.

- Provide support to child and family. Providing support and/or advising of supportive agencies and sources can be very helpful to individuals who are very new to a PTSD illness.
- Ask teachers to notice the changes in the child and contact social or welfare services for the child/family so they may seek help.
- Provide tutoring if the student is experiencing a great deal of difficulty concentrating on his or her work; the teacher can help by providing additional tutoring or after-school academic support.
- Liaison for the child and/or family who are dealing with PTSD. A teacher would have many established connections in the community and help the child and/or family transition to getting help.
- Monitor treatment of the child in school settings. Because children often do not understand different behaviors that can occur as a result of PTSD, they are likely to be tormented. Teachers can be a valuable resource to address unacceptable treatment from others toward the child. A zero-tolerance policy should be adopted in schools for those who are bullied or tormented; for example, disciplining children who torment and often tease the child who has PTSD.

OUR RETURNING VETERANS

Our veterans who are returning home from combat are having a particularly difficult time integrating back into society. Given the level of fighting and unrest in the Middle Eastern world today and the advanced technology and weaponry used, returning veterans are noticeably impacted by the trauma they lived during these wars. This holds true for whether they are peacekeepers or frontline defense personnel. Given that there are 22 U.S. war veterans committing suicide per day (Shane & Kime, 2016), increased community efforts need to focus on our war veterans in particular.

At present, PTSD treatment for veterans is orchestrated through the U.S. Department of Veterans Affairs. However, because there are many obstacles being encountered (Guin, 2016), the role of the clinician in helping this population is critical. As explained by Guin (2016), miscommunication and poor coordination have resulted in "increased failed relationships, troubles with reintegration into community and employment opportunities. This shows evidence of the severity given the extensiveness of the vast amount of veterans and the individual VA's functioning" ("Abstract," para. 1).

With a great deal of work already completed by the National Center for PTSD (2017) and the New York State Office of Mental Health (2017), the following should be reinforced as psychological first aid:

- *Contact and engagement:* Respond to contacts initiated by affected persons, or initiate contacts in a nonintrusive, compassionate, and helpful manner
- *Safety and comfort:* Enhance immediate and ongoing safety, and provide physical and emotional comfort
- *Stabilization (if needed):* Calm and orient emotionally overwhelmed or distraught survivors
- *Information gathering*: Identify immediate needs and concerns, gather additional information, and tailor psychological first aid interventions
- *Practical assistance:* Offer practical help to the survivor in addressing immediate needs and concerns
- *Connection with social supports:* Help establish opportunities for brief or ongoing contacts with primary support persons or other sources of support, including family members, friends, and community helping resources
- *Information on coping:* Provide information (about stress reactions and coping) to reduce distress and promote adaptive functioning
- *Linkage to collaborative services:* Link survivors with needed services and inform them about available services that may be needed in the future

Fast Facts

Government sectors such as Veterans Affairs can often miss the mark in helping war veterans returning from combat. War veterans are a particularly high-risk group for struggling with PTSD in the community and trying to meet the basics of shelter, employment, and survival.

Finding Work or Housing

PTSD can change individuals' relationships with their community as well as their family. Because of stigma and fear, many may shy away from those individuals because of PTSD. Hence, getting work or finding a place to live may be challenging. Individuals need to be told that they are in control of this perception through their actions and how they treat others, which can ultimately influence people's view about PTSD.

For returning veterans in particular, it can become increasingly difficult to find gainful employment once they return home. Existing stigma about PTSD, in particular, can make it hard to find work, and even finding housing can be a problem. But many cities have a local job service, employment office, or state health and welfare office. These organizations can help them get work or find a place to live. They can also find information about these services on the Internet. As a clinician, you should become familiar with the resources in your community that can help veterans find work and/or housing. Even a local church can be a valuable resource. As a clinician, you can also refer these individuals to a social worker or case manager who can help them find a place to live. Assisted living centers are a mainstay in many communities in today's society; at a reasonable cost, they may service these individuals quite well in integrating back into society.

Work in particular serves many purposes for individuals. It gives them identity, makes them feel like a valued member of society, provides them a social forum to build relationships, and helps them make friends and obtain support and an income to live, survive, and enjoy life. It is often through our work that we grow and develop as individuals. As clinicians, it is important to remind our patients/families that most communities have resources, such as a local job service, which can help them find a job. Community services include (National Center for PTSD, 2017):

- *Job skills training:* This covers getting ready for interviews, preparing resumes, and other skills needed to find work.
- *On-the-job training placement:* This helps you get work experience.
- *Nonpaid work experience placement:* This may be volunteer work that can help you make connections and get experience.
- *Special employer incentive placement:* This makes it easier for employers to hire you.

HEALTH CARE CLINICIANS

As clinicians we are in the business of providing help and care during an individual's time of need. As clinicians are often the first point of contact for individuals suffering from PTSD or the effects of trauma, they are strategically positioned to help. Clinicians have valuable networking contacts as well as access to resources and referral bases that individuals can resort to for dealing with PTSD. Here are some simple ways and approaches you can offer individuals with PTSD to help others better understand PTSD:

- Let others know that PTSD is a medical condition that can be treated.
- Talk about your recovery. This will help others understand the challenges you face.
- Show them your strengths and talents. Do not let PTSD keep you from going after things you want to do.
- Remember that "you are the message." You can show how you want to be treated by the way you act. Treating yourself with respect can set an example for everyone.
- Accept that you may need breaks during activities. Your symptoms may make it harder to focus on things for a long time.
- Work with your family and doctor to set manageable goals. Let them know what changes you want to make in your life.

PREVENTION PROGRAMS

Prevention programs are also important to keep community violence, crime, and other dangers from happening. These programs can help children and teens at risk for violence learn how to peacefully solve problems, how to assertively say "No" to drug use, and how to walk away from dangerous or threatening people. Such programs and lessons are often better retained if they are taught at home or in schools; however, public forums where parents accompany children are highly meaningful as well. Programs should also try to prevent high-risk behaviors, such as alcohol and drug use and carrying weapons. Clinicians serve a key role in educating young children and/or adults about the dangers of certain events/people in society.

The Centers for Disease Control and Prevention (2016) is a significant proponent of increasing awareness of violence prevention in the community. CDC recognizes that violence is a serious public health problem and it affects people in all stages of life. While recognizing that more and more people survive violence and suffer physical, mental, and or emotional health problems throughout the rest of their lives, it is important to do what we can as a community to prevent violence from occurring.

POLICY DEVELOPMENT

Governments should have the knowledge, skill set, funding, opportunity, and approval to make policies conducive to violence prevention and to assist societies and individuals to deal with the impact of PTSD. For example, as Guin (2016) states, "implementing policy change would make an immense difference among the stigma that surrounds veterans with PTSD. Changing the word 'disorder' or omitting it completely to PTS, could eradicate the stigma of having a mental disorder; something that is not seen after coming home from war. Innovating change for mental health assessments would be an obstacle worth looking into. The stages of change would enhance veterans to gain control over their recovery by advancing a pathway into becoming civilian individualists" ("Action Plan," para. 2).

At the state and municipal levels of government, press releases, public awareness campaigns, media events around all forms of violence and trauma and the impact they have on communities are great starting points. Developing an action or strategic plan would also be quite valuable.

ACTION PLAN

A successful comprehensive plan to battle against the stigma and effects of PTSD in our communities should be a top priority. Again, with an emphasis on veterans, although the same principles apply to everyone, the following components can be included:

- Include changing policy before discharge
- Change the negative connotation of "disorder" into something more empowering
- Allow the PTSD veteran to debrief and receive treatment prior to beginning work

- Provide family members with respective treatment to address the many issues they must navigate
- Individualize the treatment for the veteran, to include dialectical behavior therapy (DBT)
- Establish individualized diagnoses
- Transition the veteran into an appropriate community environment (e.g., housing and employment)

SUPPORT GROUPS

Support groups are perhaps one of the greatest benefits communities can offer to individuals suffering from PTSD and other effects of trauma, and have increasingly shown many positive effects on those with PTSD (Sloan, Bovin, & Schnurr, 2012). Support groups provide an atmosphere conducive to feeling safe and secure and the feeling and knowledge that you are not alone in this battle. It provides the opportunity to engage with others who are fighting the same struggles as you are as a result of some form of trauma they experienced. Although support groups are not a substitute for therapy/treatment, they can certainly help achieve many positive and valuable lessons and goals. Support groups can help individuals simply feel better about themselves, feel more comfortable in opening up and talking with others, feel more connected with others and society, enhance their coping abilities/skills, reduce PTSD symptoms, and help them deal with those emotions of guilt, fear, anger, and so forth.

Here are some ideas to help one find a peer support group that can help deal with PTSD or a traumatic experience:

- Do an online search for "PTSD support groups" or for a group that relates to the specific trauma you experienced, like "disaster support groups."
- Anxiety and Depression Association of America offers a list of support groups across the country for a number of different mental health conditions, including PTSD.
- Sidran Institute Help Desk locates support groups for people who have experienced trauma. Sidran does not offer clinical care or counseling services, but can help you locate care or support.
- National Alliance on Mental Illness (NAMI) provides support, referral, and information on mental illness care. You may also find family support groups in an NAMI state or local affiliate online or by calling 1(800)950-NAMI (6264).

- We also have information on our Helping a Family Member Who Has PTSD (enEspañol) webpage for anyone providing care to a loved one with PTSD.
(National Center for PTSD, 2017).

The Colorado Springs PTSD Support Group is one such group. As a support group, it also has on its team professionals who provide PTSD therapy and PTSD treatment. They include PTSD psychologists, PTSD psychotherapists, and PTSD counselors. I provide additional resources in the following:

PTSD United.   PTSD United's community outreach coordinators promote the mission of PTSD United in their communities. Coordinators are expected to engage in various outreach activities and community education. Possibilities include organizing social support meet-ups, tabling at events, neighborhood awareness campaigns, school-based programs, and special events, and educate the community about PTSD United's resources, services, and volunteer program. Their vision is: A loving and compassionate world where everyone is accepted and nobody is suffering because of their past or current circumstances.

PTSD Foundation of America: National Outreach.   The scope of veterans suffering from PTSD is not localized to any one region, but certainly has its affects nationwide. The PTSD Foundation of America recognizes the current and growing need to assist veterans and families of all branches of service throughout the country. Currently, there are multiple ways one can contact the foundation for support outside of its local program areas. As its resources and support groups continue to expand nationwide, individuals can coordinate with the foundation for information and assistance regarding their own or a loved one's PTSD and for assistance linking with support in their area (ongoing) by visiting their website (www.ptsdusa.org/get-help/national -outreach).

The goals of PTSD Foundation of America (2017) are to combat posttraumatic stress by:

1. *Bringing healing* to the military community (active duty, reserves and national guard, veterans, and their families) through pastoral counseling, and peer mentoring, both on an individual basis and in group settings

2. *Raising awareness* of the increasing needs of the military community through public events, media outlets, social media, service organizations, and churches
3. *Networking* government agencies, service organizations, churches, and private sector businesses into a united "Corps of Compassion," to bring their combined resources together to meet the needs of the military community on a personal and individual/family level

HealthyPlace. Yet another recognized support group for PTSD is HealthyPlace (www.healthyplace.com). It is one of the largest consumer mental health sites, providing comprehensive, trusted information on psychological disorders and psychiatric medications from both a consumer and expert point of view. It has an active mental health social network for support, online psychological tests, breaking mental health news, mental health videos, a live mental health TV and radio show, unique tools such as "mood journal," and more. It offers face-to-face and online support groups where a groups exists for every kind of mental illness known.

WHAT CAN COMMUNITY MEMBERS DO FOLLOWING A TRAUMATIC EVENT?

Community members play important roles by helping people who experience violence or disaster. They also help children cope with trauma and protect them from further trauma exposure (National Institute of Mental Health, 2015).

It is important to remember:

- Children should be allowed to express their feelings and discuss the event, but not be forced.
- Community members should identify and address their own feelings; this may allow them to help others more effectively.
- Community members can also use their buildings and institutions as gathering places to promote support.
- Community members can help people identify resources and emphasize community strengths and resources that sustain hope.
- Children's reactions to trauma are strongly influenced by adults' responses to trauma

- People from different cultures may have their own ways of reacting to trauma

Community members need to be sensitive to:

- Difficult behavior
- Strong emotions
- Different cultural responses

Fast Facts

Help from support groups, governments, schools, workplaces, and health care clinicians alike provides a united and supportive environment when individuals are suffering from PTSD.

References

Byrne, P. (2000). Stigma of mental illness and ways of diminishing it. *Advances in Psychiatric Treatment, 6*(1), 65–72. doi:10.1192/apt.6.1.65

Centers for Disease Control and Prevention. (2106). Violence prevention. Retrieved from https://www.cdc.gov/ViolencePrevention/index.html

Gluck, S. (2016). What is stigma? Retrieved from http://www.healthyplace.com/stigma/stand-up-for-mental-health/what-is-stigma

Guin, A. (2016). Bridging PTSD veterans with community: An underestimated problem. Retrieved from http://www.myusvet.org/bridging-ptsd-veterans-with-community-an-underestimated-problem

National Center for PTSD. (2017). Peer support groups. Retrieved from http://www.ptsd.va.gov/public/treatment/cope/peer_support_groups.asp

National Child Traumatic Stress Network. (2017). The effects of trauma on schools and learning. Retrieved from http://www.nctsn.org/resources/audiences/school-personnel/effects-of-trauma

National Institute of Mental Health. (2015). Post-traumatic stress disorder (PTSD). Retrieved from https://www.nimh.nih.gov/health/publications/helping-children-and-adolescents-cope-with-violence-and-disasters-community-members/index.shtml

New York State Office of Mental Health. (2017). Psychological first aid field operations guide. Retrieved from https://www.omh.ny.gov/omhweb/disaster_resources/pandemic_influenza/doctors_nurses/physchological_first_aid_manual.html

PTSD Foundation of America. (2017). PTSD: Get involved. Retrieved from http://ptsdusa.org

Shane, L., & Kime, P. (2016). New VA study finds 20 veterans commit suicide each day. Retrieved from http://www.militarytimes.com/story/veterans/2016/07/07/va-suicide-20-daily-research/86788332

Sloan, D. M., Bovin, M. J., & Schnurr, P. P. (2012). Review of group treatment for PTSD. *Journal of Rehabilitative Research Development, 49*(5), 689–702. doi:10.1682/JRRD.2011.07.0123

12

Cultural Implications

Beliefs and attitudes about posttraumatic stress disorder (PTSD) and mental illness vary across cultures, countries, and ethnicities. A person's culture might have an impact on how he or she communicates feelings and deals with adversity—for example, whether and how a person connects with significant others, including extended family members and community resources. With growing cultural diversity, people have greater access to a number of different approaches to building resilience (American Psychological Association, 2015).

In this chapter, you will learn:

- To better appreciate the differing views of mental illness, and therefore how an illness like PTSD may often go unrecognized, and hence not discussed
- Some basic standards of practice clinicians use in the provision of culturally competent care
- How everyone does not respond to the call for help when individuals are at their lowest
- Culturally competent care is a necessity for all suffering from PTSD, regardless of the cause

CULTURES AND TRAUMA

As people from different cultures may have their own ways of reacting to trauma (National Institute of Mental Health, 2015), it is critical for the health care provider/clinician to assess for and recognize any cultural innuendos relating to trauma or mental illness first. As stigma is still very much present in other cultures, it can actually prevent mentally ill individuals from seeking treatment, adhering to treatment regimens, finding employment, and living successfully in community settings. Therefore, understanding individual and cultural beliefs about mental illness is essential for the implementation of effective approaches to mental health care.

From a research perspective, many cultural differences for how mental illness is perceived have been identified. For instance, although some American Indian tribes do not stigmatize mental illness, others stigmatize only some mental illnesses, and other tribes stigmatize all mental illnesses. In Asia, where many cultures value "conformity to norms, emotional self-control, [and] family recognition through achievement," mental illnesses are often stigmatized and seen as a source of shame (Abdullah & Brown, 2011).

The stigmatization of mental illness can also be influenced by other factors, such as the perceived cause of the illness. In a 2003 study (WonPat-Borja, Yang, Link, & Phelan, 2012), Chinese Americans and European Americans were presented with a vignette in which an individual was diagnosed with schizophrenia or a major depressive disorder. Participants were then told that experts had concluded that the individual's illness was "genetic," "partly genetic," or "not genetic" in origin, and participants were asked to rate how they would feel if one of their children dated, married, or reproduced with the subject of the vignette. Genetic attribution of mental illness significantly reduced unwillingness to marry and reproduce among Chinese Americans, but it increased the same measures among European Americans, supporting previous findings of cultural variations in patterns of mental illness stigmatization (WonPat-Borja et al., 2012). Further differences were highlighted in the study by Carpenter-Song et al. (2010) where European Americans frequently sought care from mental health professionals and tended to express beliefs about mental illness that were aligned with biomedical perspectives on disease, which was unlike that of African Americans and Latinos who were more likely to emphasize "non-biomedical interpretations" of mental illness symptoms.

A country that has undergone continuous war and turmoil in recent years is Ukraine. Within Ukraine, as in other parts of the world, there are some notable cultural differences to remain cognizant of when providing care to individuals with mental illness such as PTSD. For example, Targum, Chaban, and Mykhnyak (2013) state that the word "insane" sounds like "free of God" in Ukranian and means that the person has lost God. Hence, the term "insane" describes the attitude of many people toward the mentally ill: Those with mental illness might be considered as requiring more compassion and help to return to the faith.

Like any other country, Ukraine is not exempt from the stigma around mental illness. Hence, there is a big need to overcome prejudices and promote the integration of mental illness patients into the community. As suggested by Targum et al. (2013), "the general attitude on mental disorders in the Ukraine depends, in part, on the peculiarities of the region of the country. For instance, in the more industrial eastern regions, mental disorders are associated with more load or pressure on the personality and a lack of spirituality, which is believed to provoke anxiety or even aggression in some people. On the other hand, there is more tolerance of those with mental disorders in the western regions of the country due to more religiousness and a more sincere and merciful attitude among the people" (p. 42). Currently, the physicians in Ukraine share the same point of view as European psychiatrists in their concept of the biological and social–psychological dichotomy that may be present in any mental disorder.

Fast Facts

PTSD as a form of mental illness is perceived and treated differently by the various cultures that exist in our world today.

Many Ukrainians, including soldiers with PTSD associated with a yearlong war in which more than 6,000 people were killed, are leery of going to psychologists. There is still a large stigma attached to seeking psychological care. Some of the practitioners there see a connection to the legacy of Soviet medicine, which focused on treating external ailments, while psychology was frequently tied to political questions. A current fear among many soldiers is that psychologists will prevent them from serving in the army (Tomkiw, 2015). It is only now that in this deeply religious country, psychologists are teaming up with unlikely allies: priests of the Ukrainian Greek Catholic Church, the Ukrainian Orthodox Church under the Moscow patriarchate, the Ukrainian Orthodox Church under the Kiev patriarchate, and the Ukrainian Autocephalous Orthodox Church.

For the health care clinician, the provision of culturally sensitive care is important to ensure that the individual's physical and mental health needs are met effectively and with much quality and safety for optimal health and well-being. Guidelines and some standards that should help clinicians provide culturally competent and sensitive care follow.

Fast Facts

Recognizing one's own values and beliefs about mental illness is important in providing care to individuals suffering from it.

STANDARDS OF PRACTICE AND GUIDELINES FOR CULTURALLY COMPETENT CARE

Guidelines

All mental health and addictions clinicians should be respectful, non-judgmental, culturally sensitive, and nonbiased in the care they provide to individuals with mental health and/or addiction concerns.

Standards

All mental health and addictions clinicians working with patients who have mental health and/or addictions concerns should adhere to the following standards of cultural competence:

- All mental health and addictions clinicians working with patients who have a mental health disorder shall practice cultural competency and demonstrate the ability to interact comfortably, and communicate effectively with people from a wide range of ethnic/cultural and linguistic backgrounds in a manner that is respectful of the beliefs, values, customs, and traditions (Saldaña, 2001).
- Core concepts of cultural competency include (Nova Scotia Department of Health, 2005):
  - Awareness of one's own cultural worldview, values, and attitude
  - Knowledge of different cultural practices and worldviews
  - Appropriate attitude and respect toward cultural differences
  - Knowledge and demonstration of cross-cultural skills
  - A defined set of values and principles that demonstrate how behaviors, attitudes, policies, and structures enable

one to understand, communicate, and effectively interact cross-culturally

- Recognize racism and the institutions or behaviors that breed racism
- Engage in activities that help reframe one's thinking, allowing him or her to hear and understand others' experiences and perspectives
- Familiarize oneself when needed with core cultural elements of the communities served, including physical and biological variations, concepts of time, space and physical contact, styles and patterns of communication, physical and social expectations, social structures, and gender roles
- Engage patients to share how their reality is similar to, or different from, what they have learned about their core cultural elements. Unique experiences and histories will result in differences in behaviors, values, and needs
- Learn how different cultures define, name, and understand disease and treatment. Engage patients to share how they define, name, and understand their ailments
- Develop a relationship of trust with patients and coworkers by interacting with openness, understanding, and a willingness to hear different perceptions
- When and where necessary, mental health and addiction publications should be made available in a population's most common and appropriate languages
- Create a welcoming environment that reflects the diverse communities served

■ All mental health and addictions clinicians shall be cognizant and respectful of the view that cultural competency is a process that includes correcting one's own false beliefs, assumptions, and stereotypes, tuning in to different world views than one's own, and adapting skills and interventions accordingly (Nova Scotia Department of Health, 2005).

■ All mental health and addictions clinicians should be encouraged to use language translators, if and when the need arises.

Fast Facts

The provision of culturally competent care is a requirement for the care of individuals diagnosed with PTSD.

References

Abdullah, T., & Brown, T. L. (2011). Mental illness stigma and ethnocultural beliefs, values, and norms: An integrative review. *Clinical Psychology Review, 31*, 934–948.

American Psychological Association. (2015). The road to resilience. Retrieved from http://www.apa.org/helpcenter/road-resilience.aspx

Carpenter-Song, E., Chu, E., Drake, R. E., Ritsema, M., Smith, B., & Alverson, H. (2010). Ethno-cultural variations in the experience and meaning of mental illness and treatment: Implications for access and utilization. *Transcultural Psychiatry, 47*(2), 224–251.

National Institute of Mental Health. (2015). Post-traumatic stress disorder (PTSD). Retrieved from https://www.nimh.nih.gov/health/publications/helping-children-and-adolescents-cope-with-violence-and-disasters-community-members/index.shtml

Nova Scotia Department of Health. (2005). A cultural competence guide for primary health care professionals in Nova Scotia. Retrieved from http://www.healthteamnovascotia.ca/cultural_competence/Cultural_Competence_guide_for_Primary_Health_Care_Professionals.pdf

Saldaña, D. (2001). Cultural competency: A practice guide for mental health providers. Retrieved from http://www.psyrehab.ca/files/documents/Hogg_Foundation_for_MentalHealth.pdf

Targum, S. D., Chaban, O., & Mykhnyak, S. (2013). Psychiatry in the Ukraine. *Innovations in Clinical Neuroscience, 10*(4), 41–46. Retrieved from http://www.ncbi.nlm.nih.gov/pmc/articles/PMC3659038

Tomkiw, L. (2015). Ukraine war forces a nation to talk about a taboo: Post-traumatic stress disorder. Retrieved from http://www.ibtimes.com/ukraine-war-forces-nation-talk-about-taboo-post-traumatic-stress-disorder-1869506

WonPat-Borja, A. J., Yang, L. H., Link, B. G., & Phelan, J. C. (2012). Eugenics, genetics, and mental illness stigma in Chinese Americans. *Social Psychiatry and Psychiatric Epidemiology, 47*(1), 145–156.

13

Special Population Considerations

As one would expect of any medical condition, trauma and post-traumatic stress disorder (PTSD) impact individuals of different age groups to varying degrees of severity and/or symptomatology. From a young age when the body and brain are still developing and coping mechanisms are not yet refined and/or developed, children remain highly vulnerable to the impact of trauma. For the elderly, different factors come into play. Although the brain is fully developed and coping strategies have matured over the years, the body's response to stress, particularly of a high magnitude such as accompanying trauma and disaster, may be somewhat slowed or associated with an emotional fear that one may die as a result of such trauma.

In this chapter, you will learn:

- How the treatment of PTSD differs across ages
- The delicacy and sensitivity needed particularly for children to assess for the impact of trauma
- The value of family support and understanding when working with special populations
- Why seniors are one of the most difficult populations to treat for mental illnesses such as PTSD

CHILDREN AND YOUTH

When the diagnosis of PTSD was first made in 1980 (Friedman, 2016), it was initially believed that it would not be relevant to children and young people. This was soon demonstrated to be false and it is now accepted that children and young people can develop PTSD following traumatic events (National Institute for Health and Care Excellence [NICE], 2005). In reality, children are just as susceptible to the development of PTSD as any other age cohort.

Given that the brain is still undergoing significant development during childhood, the child who experiences trauma may suffer that much more due to the impact of the trauma. Furthermore, what makes trauma so damaging to a child is that the child is often unable to cognitively comprehend what occurred and the impact it left.

Risk factors also exist for children, making them increasingly susceptible to the development of PTSD. Many of the risk factors for children are no different than they are for adults. What is critical to recognize here is that the child who is still undergoing significant brain and body development has an increased risk for the development of stress-related disorders, such as PTSD. For example, a child who consistently experiences physical and/or sexual abuse will often manifest anxiety, depression, and other mental health concerns (Allen, Tellez, Wevodau, Woods, & Percosky, 2014; Elklit, Christiansen, Palic, Karsberg, & Eriksen, 2014) and other negative lifelong mental illness symptomatology (Allen et al., 2014; Elklit et al., 2014). Furthermore, from a socioeconomic perspective, children who come from lower income families report higher levels of emotional and behavioral problems, neuroticism, and PTSD (Khamis, 2015).

Much of PTSD seen clinically in adulthood stems from such childhood events as child abuse and neglect. This area needs to be assessed. As a result, when trying to plan a treatment regime, it is important to delve into the cognitive, social, and biological consequences of childhood trauma that can prevent effective recovery from the trauma of acute first-episode psychosis resulting in postpsychotic PTSD. Treatment strategies for postpsychotic PTSD must address childhood trauma and related PTSD (Bendall, Alvarez-Jimenez, Hulbert, McGorry, & Jackson, 2012).

ASSESSMENT AND SCREENING OF THE CHILD

When assessing a child or young person for PTSD, health care professionals should ensure that they separately and directly question the child or young person about the presence of PTSD symptoms. They should not rely solely on information from the parent or guardian in any assessment.

Clinicians should also assess for maltreatment, exclusion, or bullying. Ask the child or adolescent directly about these in private. As much as possible, work with family, school, and community to ensure the child's or adolescent's safety. Furthermore, the clinician should assess for mental, neurological, and substance use disorders (particularly depression) and psychosocial stressors in caregivers of children and adolescents.

The Child PTSD Symptom Scale (CPSS) is one tool found effective to assess for PTSD symptomatology and severity in children (Foa, Johnson, Feeny, & Treadwell, 2001). It is a 26-item self-report tool and is best suited for children aged 8 to 18. It includes two event items, 17 symptom items, and seven functional impairment items. Symptom items are rated on a 4-point frequency scale (0 = "not at all" to 3 = "five or more times a week"). Functional impairment items are scored as 0 = "absent" or 1 = "present." The CPSS yields a total symptom severity scale score (ranging from 0 to 51) and a total severity-of-impairment score (ranging from 0 to 7). Scores can also be calculated for each of the three PTSD symptom clusters (i.e., B, C, and D; Foa et al., 2001).

CHILDREN AGED 7 YEARS OR YOUNGER

According to the National Institute of Mental Health (NIMH, 2015), a young child's response to trauma is quite different than that of an adult. Only recently has this category, pre-school–type PTSD, been added to the *Diagnostic and Statistical Manual of Mental Disorders*, Fifth Edition (*DSM-5*; American Psychiatric Association, 2013; Scheeringa, 2006). A child, for example, may manifest the following extreme symptomatology in response to a traumatic event:

- Bedwetting, when the child has previously learned how to use the toilet
- Forgetting how to talk or being unable to talk
- Acting out the scary event during playtime
- Being unusually clingy with a parent or other adult (NIMH, 2016)

No consensus has emerged as to how to measure PTSD symptoms in children aged 7 years or younger. In the recent past, a range of scales measuring behavioral problems have been adopted, such as the Child Behavior Checklist (CBCL) and, for children who have suffered sexual abuse, the Child Sexual Behavior Inventory (CSBI).

Structured interviews indicate the most likely adverse life events that may result in PTSD in children and young people, but they do not constitute formal measures. General practitioners, pediatricians, and child mental health workers who see a child presenting with a sudden change in sleep pattern, nightmares, and jumpiness should enquire about intrusive images and then ask whether the child has experienced any life-threatening event such as a bad accident, natural disaster, or physical or sexual abuse. Increasing attention is being paid to cognitive factors such as the way in which children attribute blame for an event or the extent to which they erroneously believe that they might have died in the accident. The effective social support that is available to the child is also likely to be a key determinant of whether the child continues to respond adversely. Standard measures of these aspects are still being developed. In addition, children with PTSD often display regressive behaviors, such as bedwetting, clinging, and temper tantrums (NIMH, 2015).

For preschool children, there are specific recommendations for the assessment and treatment of PTSD. Standardized screening and assessment instruments have been developed for caregivers of this age group, with both self-administered checklists and diagnostic interviews. For example, evidence-based treatments for PTSD, such as cognitive behavioral therapy, are effective (Deblinger, Stauffer, & Steer, 2001; Scheeringa, Weems, Cohen, Amaya-Jackson, & Guthrie, 2011). A long-term, relationally based treatment has shown effectiveness following interpersonal violence. Play therapy, eye movement desensitization and reprocessing (EMDR), and other modalities may be effective if the traumatic memories can be engaged in developmentally appropriate methods.

CHILDREN OLDER THAN 7 YEARS

More is known about screening, assessment, and diagnosis in children older than 7 years because above that age many children can read independently and can complete self-rating scales. It is much more time-consuming and expensive to conduct standardized clinical interviews with both parent and child to establish a diagnosis with large groups of children.

The response to trauma in older children and teens parallels much of what is found in adults. For example, they can begin to show very disruptive, disrespectful, and destructive behaviors compared to previous and can even have thoughts of guilt for not preventing the trauma or revenge and thoughts of retaliation (NIMH, 2015).

The most widely used self-report scales in research and clinical settings are the Children's Impact of Traumatic Events Scale, the Child Posttraumatic Stress Reaction Index, and the Child PTSD Symptom Scale (CPSS). The CPSS is a 17-item scale used both in the initial diagnosis and in monitoring progress; it contains a brief functional impairment rating. The Children's Impact of Traumatic Events Scale—Revised (CITES–R) is a measure of PTSD symptoms arising from sexual abuse and measures aspects such as social reactions to disclosure, eroticism, and abuse-related attributions in addition to nontrauma-specific PTSD symptoms.

SYMPTOMATOLOGY IN THE CHILD

The child who experiences trauma and the eventual development of PTSD exhibits many problematic behaviors. Reactions (responses) to trauma can be immediate or delayed. Reactions to trauma differ in severity and cover a wide range of behaviors and responses. Children with existing mental health problems, past trauma experiences, and/or limited family and social supports may be more reactive to trauma. Frequently experienced responses among children after trauma are loss of trust and a fear of the event happening again (NIMH, 2015).

These behaviors may consist of:

- Refusing to go places that remind them of the event
- Emotional numbness
- Behaving dangerously
- Unexplained anger/rage
- Sleep problems including nightmares

The symptoms as expressed by children vary slightly across age groups (see Boxes 13.1, 13.2, and 13.3).

POSTTRAUMATIC STRESS REACTIONS IN CHILDREN

The broad categories of PTSD symptoms (reexperiencing, avoidance/numbing, and increased arousal) are present in children as well as in adults. The requirements of *Diagnostic and Statistical Manual of Mental Disorders*, Fifth Edition (*DSM-5*; American Psychiatric Association, 2013) criteria for the diagnosis of PTSD in children are that children must exhibit at least one reexperiencing symptom, three

BOX 13.1   CHILDREN AGED 5 AND YOUNGER

- Facial expressions of fear
- Clinging to parent or caregiver
- Crying or screaming
- Whimpering or trembling
- Moving aimlessly
- Becoming immobile
- Returning to behaviors common to being younger
- Thumb sucking
- Bedwetting
- Being afraid of the dark (NICE, 2005; NIMH, 2015)

BOX 13.2   CHILDREN AGED 6 TO 11

- Isolating themselves
- Becoming quiet around friends, family, and teachers
- Having nightmares or other sleep problems
- Refusing to go to bed
- Becoming irritable or disruptive
- Having outbursts of anger
- Starting fights
- Being unable to concentrate
- Refusing to go to school
- Complaining of physical problems
- Developing unfounded fears
- Becoming depressed
- Becoming filled with guilt
- Feeling numb emotionally
- Doing poorly with school and homework
- Loss of interest in fun activities (NICE, 2005; NIMH, 2015)

BOX 13.3 ADOLESCENTS AGED 12 TO 17

- Having flashbacks to the event (flashbacks are the mind reliving the event)
- Having nightmares or other sleep problems
- Avoiding reminders of the event
- Using or abusing drugs, alcohol, or tobacco
- Being disruptive, disrespectful, or behaving destructively
- Having physical complaints
- Feeling isolated or confused
- Being depressed
- Being angry
- Loss of interest in previously enjoyable activities
- Having suicidal thoughts
- Feeling guilty for not being able to prevent injury or deaths; may have thoughts of revenge (NIMH, 2015)

avoidance/numbing symptoms, and two increased arousal symptoms. From the age of 8 to 10 years, following traumatic events, children display reactions closely similar to those manifested by adults. Below 8 years of age, and in particular below the age of 5 years, there is less agreement as to the range and severity of the reactions. Scheeringa et al. (2011) have suggested an alternative set of criteria for the diagnosis of PTSD in children, placing more emphasis on regressive behaviors and new fears, but these have yet to be fully validated.

Traumatic reactions in children have been less extensively studied than in adults, and there are few naturalistic, longitudinal studies mapping the natural history of these reactions. It has long been recognized (Eth, 2001) that it is much more difficult to elicit evidence of emotional numbing in young children. Other items indicating avoidance reactions in children simply are not relevant, thereby making it difficult for children to meet *DSM* criteria for that part of the diagnostic algorithm (although this does not apply to the *International Classification of Disease [ICD]* diagnosis). In general, it is agreed that children display a wide range of stress reactions. To some extent these vary with age, with younger children displaying more overt aggression and destructiveness. They may also show more repetitive play about the traumatic event, and this may even be reflected in repetitive drawing (NICE, 2006, p. 103).

As with other anxiety disorders, children's reactions are influenced by parental reactions. In addition to modeling on their parents' reactions (social influence), there are probably also inherited dispositions to react adversely to traumatic events (genetic influence). This has not been adequately studied in relation to PTSD in children.

What is clinically described and widely accepted is that children are very sensitive to their parents' reactions—both to the event itself and to talking about it afterward. Children often say that they choose not to discuss a traumatic event and/or their reactions to it with their parents, as they do not wish to upset the parents further. This is related to the fact that parents grossly underestimate the degree of stress reactions experienced by their children. Thus, one cannot rely solely on parental report when making diagnoses or estimating prevalence. A study by McFarlane (1987) suggested that in an Australian bush fire, the children's reactions to the event were fully accounted for by the mothers' own mental health, rather than by the exposure to the fire. However, as mothers had rated both their own adjustment and that of their children, this finding was suspect. Follow-up studies (e.g., Smith, Perrin, Yule, & Rabe-Hesketh, 2001) have found that direct exposure is usually a stronger determinant of child reaction, with maternal reactions being important modifying influences. Therefore, it is always important to consider the nature and extent of a child's exposure to a traumatic event.

Many children presenting with symptoms of PTSD may have been subjected to multiple traumas, such as childhood sexual abuse or domestic violence. The most common form of multiple traumas for children that has been studied and investigated is childhood sexual abuse, which often occurs in secret and is repeated over a long period. The traumatic reactions associated with such multiple traumas can be usefully construed as similar to those that follow from single traumas, although issues of abuse of power, loss of trust, and so on do make them different. Although there is evidence that the social circumstances and events surrounding multiple traumas for children may have consequences for their future management (Ramchandani & Jones, 2003), the evidence does not support the idea that multiple traumas are associated with significantly different outcomes or that the treatment required for PTSD is significantly different when compared with single traumas (NICE, 2005, p. 105).

Bedwetting as a Symptom of Acute Stress in Children

Obtain a history of bedwetting to confirm whether the problem started only after a stressful event. Rule out and manage possible physical causes (e.g., when the child has signs suggestive of urinary tract infection), even if the bedwetting started within 1 month of the potentially traumatic event.

- Assess for and manage caregivers' mental disorders and psychosocial stressors.
- Educate caregivers. Explain that they should not punish the child for bedwetting. Explain that bedwetting is a common reaction in children who experience stressors and that punishment adds to the child's stress. Explain to caregivers the importance of being calm and emotionally supportive. Educate caregivers not to overly focus on the symptoms and to give positive attention to the child at other times.
- Consider training parents in the use of simple behavioral interventions (e.g., rewarding avoidance of excessive fluid intake before sleep, rewarding toileting before sleep). The rewards can be extra playtime, stars on a chart, or a local equivalent.
- If the problem persists after 1 month, reassess for and treat any concurrent physical or mental disorder. If there is no concurrent mental disorder or no response to treatment of a concurrent mental disorder, consult a specialist (World Health Organization & United Nations High Commissioner for Refugees, 2013, p. 13).

DO CHILDREN REACT DIFFERENTLY THAN ADULTS?

Children and teens can have extreme reactions to trauma, but their symptoms may not be the same as those of adults. In very young children, these symptoms can include:

- Bedwetting, when they have learned how to use the toilet before
- Forgetting how to talk or being unable to talk
- Acting out the scary event during playtime
- Being unusually clingy with a parent or other adult

INTERVENTIONS FOR CHILDREN AND ADOLESCENTS

The help for a child that has experienced trauma can begin immediately, even at the scene of the event (NIMH, 2015). Although most children recover within a few weeks of traumatic experience, some may need help longer. Grief, a deep emotional response to loss, may take months to resolve. Children may experience grief over the loss of a loved one, teacher, friend, or pet. Grief may be reexperienced or worsened by news reports or the event's anniversary. Children who continue to show problematic behaviors after the event may need help from a mental health professional (NIMH, 2015). As a very early intervention as well, trauma-focused cognitive behavioral therapy (CBT) should be offered to older children with severe posttraumatic symptoms or with severe PTSD in the first month after the traumatic event (NICE, 2006, p. 115).

The support of a parent, guardian, and/or loved one is crucial for the child at this stage when symptomatology begins to develop and manifests itself. For example, the adult needs to pay close attention to the child, observe the child and watch to see what behaviors are occurring. Second, adults need to listen closely to the child and hear what he or she is saying or is not saying. Third, adults should accept what feelings the child has without any confrontation, criticism, and sarcasm. The feelings are very real to the child experiencing them and should be accepted and taken seriously; paying particular attention to any severe reactions that may become evident in the child's everyday living. Such reactions may be illustrated in sudden changes in behaviors, speech, language use, or in strong emotions. Helping the child cope with the reality of the experiences is critical, so assessing the child, openly communicating with the child, and reinforcing that sense of trust is needed (NIMH, 2015). To promote healing the adult needs to acknowledge that it will take varying lengths of time as each child responds differently to a variety of traumatic events possible.

Following the occurrence of a traumatic event for a child, it is important to keep additional stressors at a minimum as the child's body and mind is already so overwhelmed from the preexisting traumatic event. The addition of further stress will only act to compound the problem even more so, hence making it increasingly difficult for the child to recover and move forward.

Perhaps most significant above all else is what parents, loved ones, and/or guardians do to help support and just be there for the child. Loving the child, supporting the child in what he or she does and says, and being with the child whenever and wherever possible are needed to help the child toward successful recovery from the trauma experienced.

Early intervention would be attractive if it could be shown that it prevented later development of PTSD or other disorders, but, as with adult studies, there have been few properly controlled trials with children of any early intervention. For children older than 7 years who have suffered sexual abuse, treatment of the mother alone seems to be ineffective when compared with treatment of the child alone. Indeed, delivering

CBT to the mother as well as the child does not itself seem to confer much advantage over treatment of the child alone on PTSD symptoms.

The evidence base from which to draw conclusions about the treatment of children younger than 7 years suffering from PTSD is sparse. The lack of agreement on and use of a common set of measures is particularly of concern for studies of PTSD in very young children, and adds to the difficulties of interpreting an extremely limited data set. All treatments need to be adapted to accommodate young children's less mature ways of thinking about their world, and often clinicians will use play materials and drawings to help children focus on what happened to them and how they feel (NICE, 2006, p. 113).

Other interventions are also indicated for children suffering from trauma. These are as follows:

■ Changing unhealthy and wrong views that have resulted from the trauma. Children often need help to overcome such ideas as "if he did that bad thing to me it must be because I'm bad" or "children like me can never have a normal life again."

■ Involving parents. No one has more influence in a child's life than a parent. Parents can play an important role in treatment, sometimes by participating in interventions with the therapist and by helping the child "practice" new therapeutic strategies at home. Parents have key information about their child that therapists need in developing and implementing treatment. Most importantly, parents can create the stable, consistent, and caring environment in which the child can learn that a traumatic experience does not have to dominate life.

■ Teaching children stress management and relaxation skills to help them cope with unpleasant feelings and physical sensations about the trauma.

■ Using what therapists call "exposure strategies," or talking about the traumatic event and feelings about it at a speed that does not distress the child.

■ Creating a coherent "narrative" or story of what happened. It is often a difficult process for children to reach the point where they are able to tell the story of a traumatic event, but when they are ready, the telling enables them to master painful feelings about the event and to resolve the impact the event has on their lives.

■ Correcting untrue or distorted ideas about what happened and why. Children sometimes think something they did or did not do may have caused the trauma or that if only they had acted a certain way a traumatic experience might have turned out differently. This is rarely true, and getting the story right helps a child stop prolonging the traumatic stress by punishing himself or herself (National Child Traumatic Stress Network, 2003, pp. 1–2).

- Children and young people with PTSD, including those who have been sexually abused, should be offered a course of trauma-focused CBT (TF-CBT) adapted appropriately to suit their age, circumstances, and level of development.

- Where appropriate, families should be involved in the treatment of PTSD in children and young people. However, treatment programs for PTSD in children and young people that consist of parental involvement alone are unlikely to be of any benefit for PTSD symptoms.

- The duration of trauma-focused psychological treatment for children and young people with chronic PTSD should normally be 8 to 12 sessions when the PTSD results from a single event. When the trauma is discussed in the treatment session, longer sessions than usual are usually necessary (e.g., 90 minutes). Treatment should be regular and continuous (usually at least once a week) and should be delivered by the same person.

- When considering treatments for PTSD, parents and, where appropriate, children and young people should be informed that, apart from trauma-focused psychological interventions, there is at present no good evidence for the efficacy of widely used forms of treatment of PTSD, such as play therapy, art therapy, or family therapy (NICE, 2005, p. 115).

Regardless of the child's age, clinicians should include assessment of peer victimization experiences when evaluating sexually abused school-age children. Prevention initiatives in terms of peer victimization could indirectly prevent worsening of symptoms in abused children (Hebert, Langevin, & Daigneault, 2016).

Fast Facts

The impact of trauma in children varies across age brackets and is often reflective of their achieved growth and development.

COMORBIDITIES

As with adults, children can develop mental illness comorbidities as a result of exposure to trauma and the development of PTSD. For example, as suggested by Khamis (2015), 30% of the Palestinian children who were exposed to higher levels of war traumas have developed PTSD with excess risk for comorbidity with other disorders such as emotional symptoms and neuroticism.

COPING

Various coping strategies have been investigated for children who have developed PTSD. According to Khamis (2015), although emotion-focused coping was positively associated with emotional and behavioral problems, neuroticism, and PTSD, problem-focused coping that involved cognitive behavioral interventions was negatively associated with neuroticism and PTSD.

PSYCHOLOGICAL

PTSD is a common and potentially disabling condition in children as well as adults (Giaconia et al., 1995). Although up to 50% of children may develop PTSD following a traumatic event (Yule et al., 2000), many individuals recover without specific intervention; however, a significant proportion of individuals, perhaps more than 30% of victims of major disasters, go on to develop a chronic disorder with associated psychological and social handicaps (Morgan, Scourfield, Williams, Jasper, & Lewis, 2003).

Trauma-focused psychological interventions are generally effective for the treatment of PTSD in adults but only a limited evidence base exists for children and young people (Cohen, Mannarino, Berliner, & Berliner, 2000). In addition, much of the evidence is drawn from work with children who have experienced childhood sexual abuse as well as developing PTSD (Ramchandani & Jones, 2003) and therefore the evidence base for interventions for PTSD arising from other traumas is weaker. For children younger than 7 years who develop PTSD, there are virtually no formal randomized controlled trials (RCTs) of appropriate psychological interventions. A number of noncontrolled trials suggest that treatments (specifically CBT and eye movement desensitization reprocessing [EMDR]) are efficacious, but these have not been formally tested (Cohen et al., 2000).

PHARMACOLOGICAL

As was supported and practiced in the past, drug treatments should not be routinely prescribed for children and young people with PTSD (NICE, 2005, p. 116). Although drugs are prescribed less often for childhood disorders in the United Kingdom than in the United States, there is nonetheless a considerable rate of prescribing of psychotropic drugs for children by general practitioners in the United Kingdom (Montoliu & Crawford, 2002).

Given that there is too little evidence from RCTs, open-label studies, or case-control studies to recommend the use of any psychotropic medication to treat PTSD in children or young people (NICE, 2005, p. 114) and few psychotropic medicines are licensed for use with children, the use of pharmacological agents should not be recommended. However, there are exceptional times for which there is no other alternative and medications are considered. Hence, many prescriptions have to be made "off label" on a named patient basis (NICE, 2005, p. 114).

Most recently, however, there has been a slight change in practice, where the medication for children experiencing PTSD is permissible. As highlighted by Lubit and Pataki (2016), clinical experience suggests that selective serotonin reuptake inhibitors (SSRIs) are helpful for treating PTSD in children; these agents have already been proved as therapy for PTSD in adults. Additional pharmacological agents that have been used clinically to treat PTSD symptoms in children and adolescents include alpha agonists, beta-adrenergic blocking agents, mood stabilizers, and atypical antipsychotic medications. However, the use of these agents is not as well supported by evidence as the use of antidepressants and cautious observation is still highly encouraged, as the child is at risk for suicidal ideations, regardless of the pharmacological intervention being used.

COGNITIVE BEHAVIORAL THERAPY FOR CHILDREN

TF-CBT should be offered to older children with severe posttraumatic symptoms or with severe PTSD in the first month after the traumatic event. Children and young people with PTSD, including those who have been sexually abused, should be offered a course of TF-CBT adapted appropriately to suit their age, circumstances, and level of development (NICE, 2005, p. 123).

SPECIFIC RECOGNITION ISSUES FOR CHILDREN

Children, particularly those younger than 8 years, may not complain directly of PTSD symptoms, such as reexperiencing or avoidance. Instead, children may complain of sleeping problems. It is therefore vital that all opportunities for identifying PTSD in children should be taken. Questioning the children as well as parents or guardians will also improve the recognition of PTSD. PTSD is common (up to 30%) in children following attendance at emergency departments for a traumatic injury. Emergency department clinicians should inform parents or guardians of the risk of their child developing PTSD following emergency attendance for a traumatic injury and advise them on what action to take if symptoms develop.

When assessing a child or young person for PTSD, health care professionals should ensure that they separately and directly question the child or young person about the presence of PTSD symptoms. They should not rely solely on information from the parent or guardian in any assessment.

INTERVENTIONS FOR FAMILIES OF CHILDREN

Families and caregivers have a central role in supporting people with PTSD. When a family is affected by a traumatic event, more than one family member may suffer from PTSD. If this is the case, health care professionals should ensure that the treatment of all family members is effectively coordinated (NICE, 2005, p. 126). However, depending on the nature of the trauma and its consequences, many families may also need support for themselves. Health care professionals should be aware of the impact of PTSD on the whole family.

In all cases of PTSD, health care professionals should consider the impact of the traumatic event on all family members and, when appropriate, assess this impact and consider providing appropriate support. Health care professionals should ensure, where appropriate and with the consent of the PTSD sufferer where necessary, that the families of PTSD sufferers are fully informed about common reactions to traumatic events, including the symptoms of PTSD and its course and treatment. In addition to the provision of information, families and caregivers should be informed of self-help groups and support groups and encouraged to participate in such groups where they exist.

A key step in helping children with trauma is to help adults so they can provide better care for their children. The first steps include creating safe conditions, remaining calm and friendly, and connecting to others. It is also important to be sensitive to difficult people and encourage respect for adult decision making.

Some children will have prolonged problems after a traumatic event. These may include grief, depression, anxiety, and PTSD. Some trauma survivors get better with some support. Others may need prolonged care by a mental health professional. If, after a month in a safe environment, children are not able to perform their normal routines or new behavioral and emotional problems develop, then consider contacting a health professional.

Factors influencing how children may respond to the experiences and/or triggers of trauma are quite similar to adults, with some differences noted where necessary (NIMH, 2015):

- Being directly involved in the trauma, especially as a victim
- Severe and/or prolonged exposure to the event
- Personal history of prior trauma
- Family or personal history of mental illness and severe behavioral problems
- Limited social support; lack of caring family and friends
- Ongoing life stressors such as moving to a new home, or new school

Some symptoms may require immediate attention. Contact a mental health professional if these symptoms occur:

- Flashbacks
- Racing heart and sweating
- Being easily startled
- Being emotionally numb
- Being very sad or depressed
- Thoughts or actions to end life

It is also important to recognize that in the confusion or chaos after a crisis event, children and adults can be particularly vulnerable to predators. Adults caring for children must be mindful of the limitations of environments that are created for shelter or other services (NIMH, 2015).

The initial goals of treatment for children with PTSD are as follows:

- Provide a safe environment
- Provide reassurance, emotional support, nurturance
- Attend to urgent medical needs

Psychological therapy for PTSD in children involves the following:

- Helping the child gain a sense of safety
- Addressing the multiple emotional and behavioral problems that can arise

Nonpharmacological forms of therapy include the following:

- CBT, especially TF-CBT
- Dialectical behavior therapy (DBT)
- Relaxation techniques (e.g., biofeedback, yoga, deep relaxation, self-hypnosis, or meditation; efficacy unproven)
- Play therapy

In children who have persistent symptoms despite CBT or who need additional help with control of symptoms, pharmacological treatment may be considered, as follows:

- SSRIs—medications of choice for managing anxiety, depression, avoidance behavior, and intrusive recollections; however, not specifically approved by the Food and Drug Administration (FDA) for treatment of PTSD in the pediatric population
- Beta-blockers (e.g., propranolol)
- Alpha-adrenergic agonists (e.g., guanfacine and clonidine)
- Mood stabilizers (e.g., carbamazepine and valproic acid)
- Atypical antipsychotics (infrequently used; Lubit & Pataki, 2016)

SENIORS

Although older adulthood is recognized as a time of continued growth and development that provides opportunities to develop unique capacities (Fritsch et al., 2007; Penick & Fallshore, 2005), mental illnesses such as PTSD can occur at any time. Furthermore, as war veterans grow older and children grow up into adulthood and older adulthood, the effects of PTSD can continue.

As our war veterans grow older, a more astute assessment of the effects of trauma is important.

Seniors, however, are one age cohort that makes the diagnosis of a mental illness even more challenging due to the age factor alone. The presentation of mental illness in seniors often differs from that in other age cohorts (Depp & Jeste, 2005). Instead of social withdrawal, indecisiveness, and feelings of hopelessness and helplessness that typify depression in younger age cohorts (Souery et al., 2011), older adults present with anxiety, agitation, somatic complaints and complaints of physical and memory disorders (Shah, Evans, & King, 2000), loss of appetite, difficulty sleeping, constipation, and/or loneliness (American Psychiatric Association, 2003). These atypical presentations contribute to overlooking or misdiagnosing mental illness in seniors (Sternberg, Wolfson, & Baumgarten, 2000). The availability of psychogeriatric experts would facilitate a more accurate and timely diagnosis and treatment.

The presence of stigma for older adults with mental illnesses is a genuine reality. Based on the beliefs and presence of mental illness during historical times, reasons such as fear, stigma, and being ostracized by family and friends (Ballard, 2010; Wrigley, Jackson, Judd, & Komiti, 2005) have led many seniors to try to mask their psychiatric symptoms and/or be hesitant to talk openly about them. Hence, the delay and/or missed treatment not only increases morbidity, mortality, and disability of seniors, but it also increases their risk of institutionalization, hospitalization, and hospital stay (Crabb & Hunsley, 2006).

With increased age, although the body becomes increasingly challenged to actively engage in some of the activities it previously mastered, people do not necessarily become depressed, isolated, and rigid; in fact, seniors who were well adjusted and happy when they were young are likely to remain so in late life (Fritsch et al., 2007; Penick & Fallshore, 2005). Physically and mentally/cognitively, the body experiences many normal age-related changes across the life span, but none of these is clearly or definitively related to the occurrence of mental illness.

Many seniors lead happy and fulfilling lives without significant cognitive changes and/or altered mental status (Barnes et al., 2007; Fritsch et al., 2007). As a group, seniors have distinct advantages over other age groups in that they have more experiences with coping, problem solving, and crisis management merely by virtue of the years they have lived. Many of today's seniors have lived and coped with experiences of immigration, deaths of family members and friends, and epidemics. Some have fought in or had family members fight in world wars and survived the Great Depression (Kimhi, Hantman, Goroshit, Eshel, & Zysberg, 2011); experiences that offered the opportunity to develop excellent coping skills (Cloyd & Dyer, 2010). Ironically, these strengthened coping mechanisms sometimes enable seniors to cover up the early signs of mental illness because they fear being threatened by restrictions on their freedoms and living situations (Ballard, 2010). For example, as suggested by Shrira, Palgi, Ben-Ezra, and Shmotkin (2011), seniors indeed have a certain degree of resilience. When confronted by a natural disaster, American older adults are generally resilient, which is suspected to be partly related to the strength successfully extracted from previous exposure to adverse events. Hence, the diagnosing of PTSD in seniors is no different.

Particularly for seniors who are now aging war veterans, the effects of trauma do persist. According to Avidor, Benyamini, and Solomon (2014), PTSD appears to be implicated in the link between health measures and subjective age in later life, pointing to the long-term effect of captivity and war-induced traumatic distress on aging.

As children and adults become older adults, the trauma of childhood events also continues. As suggested by Ogle, Rubin, and Siegler (2013), older adults who experienced their most distressing traumatic event during childhood exhibited more severe symptoms of PTSD and lower subjective happiness compared with older adults who experienced their most distressing trauma after the transition to adulthood. Similar findings emerged for measures of social support and coping ability. Furthermore, as later expressed by Ogle et al. (2013), cumulative exposure to childhood violence and adulthood physical assaults were most strongly associated with PTSD symptom severity in older adulthood, suggesting that the cumulative impact of exposure to traumatic events throughout the life course contributes significantly to posttraumatic stress in older adulthood above and beyond other known predictors of PTSD.

EPIDEMIOLOGY OF PTSD IN SENIORS

According to the U.S. Department of Veterans Affairs, of the general population, approximately 70% to 90% of adults aged 65 and older have been exposed to at least one potentially traumatic event during their lifetimes (Norris, 1992). Gender differences exist in regard to trauma exposure. Based on a community sample of older adults, about 70% of older men reported lifetime exposure to trauma; older women reported a lower rate, around 41% (Creamer & Parslow, 2008).

There exists a dearth of studies examining trauma among geriatric populations. It is, therefore, possible that current estimates may underrepresent the prevalence of PTSD in older adults (Cook & Niederehe, 2007).

- The prevalence of current PTSD in adults older than 60 ranges from 1.5% to 4%, as reported in several community studies (Acierno et al., 2007).
- The lifetime prevalence of PTSD in the general adult population is about 8% (Kessler et al., 2005), with point estimates ranging from 2% to 17% among U.S. military samples (Richardson, Frueh, & Acierno, 2010).
- Although many older adults do not meet full criteria for a PTSD diagnosis, they may still exhibit some symptoms. The percentage of older adults with subclinical levels of PTSD symptoms ranges from 7% to 15%.

TREATMENT INTERVENTIONS FOR SENIORS

Many of the interventions used for adults in the treatment of PTSD can also be used for older adults as well. Although CBT was criticized for not being effective for older adults, Clapp and Beck (2012) found otherwise. In their case analysis, they have discovered that cognitive behavioral interventions do indeed continue to be effective in treating PTSD with this population. The trauma-informed practice approach and increased sensitivity as outlined are very much needed when assessing the impact of psychological factors arising from trauma.

Hospitalization of seniors for PTSD symptomatology is not advisable, unless, of course, actual or potential threat of harm or loss of life to oneself or others is present. Hospitalization may exert a negative influence on the development or exacerbation of mental illnesses. Hospitalization of seniors not only promotes recovery, intervention, and healing, but may also paradoxically compromise overall health physiologically (De Coster, Bruce, & Kozyrskyi, 2004) and mentally, either by initiating a mental illness (Arend & Christensen,

2009) or exacerbating an existing mental illness (Braden et al., 2008; Sayers et al., 2007).

The management of seniors in acute-care hospitals has long been a concern (Fisher, 2003). Although hospitalization is beneficial for stabilizing illnesses, it is often identified as a sentinel event for seniors (De Coster et al., 2004). A sentinel event is an unexpected occurrence involving increased risk of, or death from, serious physical or psychological injury while one is hospitalized (Joint Commission on Accreditation of Healthcare Organizations, 2011). Hospitalization and/or repeated admissions and lengthy stays symbolize a loss of independence for seniors (Kozyrskyj, Black, Chateau, & Steinbach, 2004), challenge their emotional well-being as bodily functions decline (Kozyrskyj et al., 2004), and create frustration and discouragement (Kozyrskyj et al., 2004); all of which challenge their mental health. Loss of function further increases a senior's incidence of adverse events, falls, and iatrogenic complications (Kozyrskyj et al., 2004).

Fast Facts

Hospitalizing seniors for PTSD is not advisable and can potentially do more harm than good.

References

Acierno, R., Lawyer, S. R., Rheingold, A., Kilpatrick, D. G., Resnick, H. S., & Saunders, B. E. (2007). Current psychopathology in previously assaulted older adults. *Journal of Interpersonal Violence*, *22*, 250–258.

Allen, B., Tellez, A., Wevodau, A., Woods, C. L., & Percosky, A. (2014). The impact of sexual abuse committed by a child on mental health in adulthood. *Journal of Interpersonal Violence*, *29*(12), 2257–2272.

American Psychiatric Association. (2013). *Diagnostic and statistical manual of mental disorders* (5th ed.). Arlington, VA: American Psychiatric Publishing.

Arend, E., & Christensen, M. (2009). Delirium in the intensive care unit: A review. *Nursing in Critical Care*, *14*(3), 145–154.

Avidor, S., Benyamini, Y., & Solomon, Z. (2014). Subjective age and health in later life: The role of posttraumatic symptoms. *The Journal of Gerontology: Series B, Psychological Sciences and Social Sciences*, *71*(3), 415–424.

Ballard, J. (2010). Forgetfulness and older adults: Concept analysis. *Journal of Advanced Nursing*, *66*(6), 1409–1419.

Barnes, D. E., Cauley, J. A., Lui, L. Y., Fink, H. A., McCulloch, C., Stone, K. L., & Yaffe, K. (2007). Women who maintain optimal cognitive function into old age. *Journal of the American Geriatric Society, 55*(2), 259–264.

Bendall, S., Alvarez-Jimenez, M., Hulbert, C. A., McGorry, P. D., & Jackson, H. J. (2012). Childhood trauma increases the risk of post-traumatic stress disorder in response to first-episode psychosis. *Australian and New Zealand Journal of Psychiatry, 46*(1), 35–39. doi:10.1177/0004867411430877

Braden, J. B., Zhang, L., Fan, M., Unutzer, J., Edlund, M. J., & Sullivan, M. D. (2008). Mental health service use by older adults: The role of chronic pain. *American Journal of Geriatric Psychiatry, 16*(2), 156–167.

Clappa, J. D., & Beck, J. G. (2012). Treatment of PTSD in older adults: Do cognitive-behavioral interventions remain viable? *Cognitive Behavioral Practices, 19*(1), 126–135.

Cloyd, E., & Dyer, C. B. (2010). Catastrophic events and older adults. *Critical Care Nursing Clinics of North America, 22*(4), 501–513.

Cohen, J. A., Mannarino, A. P., Berliner, L., & Berliner, E. (2000). Trauma-focused cognitive behavioural therapy for children and adolescents. *Journal of Interpersonal Violence, 15*, 1202–1223.

Cook, J. M., & Niederehe, G. (2007). Trauma in older adults. In M. J. Friedman, T. M. Keane, & P. A. Resick (Eds.), *Handbook of PTSD: Science and practice* (pp. 252–276). New York, NY: Guilford Press.

Crabb, R., & Hunsley, J. (2006). Utilization of mental health care services among older adults with depression. *Journal of Clinical Psychology, 62*(3), 299–312.

Creamer, M. C., & Parslow, R. A. (2008). Trauma exposure and posttraumatic stress disorder in the elderly: A community prevalence study. *American Journal of Geriatric Psychiatry, 16*, 853–856.

Deblinger, E., Stauffer, L., & Steer, R. (2001). Comparative efficacies of supportive and cognitive behavioral group therapies for young children who have been sexually abused and their non-offending mothers. *Child Maltreatment, 6*, 332–343.

De Coster, C., Bruce, S., & Kozyrskyi, A. (2004). Use of acute care hospitals by long-stay patients: Who, how much and why? *Canadian Journal on Aging, 24*(Supp. 1), 97–106.

Depp, C. A., & Jeste, D. V. (2009). Definitions and predictors of successful aging. *Focus, 7*, 137–150.

Elklit, S., Christiansen, D. M., Palic, S., Karsberg, S., & Eriksen, S. B. (2014). Impact of traumatic events on posttraumatic stress disorder among Danish survivors of sexual abuse in childhood. *Journal of Child Sexual Abuse, 23*(8), 918–934.

Eth, S. (2001). PTSD in children and adolescents. *Review of Psychiatry, 20*, 59–86.

Fisher, R. (2003). *The health care system and the elderly colloquium series on "Ethics and Care of the Elderly."* Toronto, ON, Canada: University of Toronto.

Foa, E. B., Johnson, K. M., Feeny, N. C., & Treadwell, K. R. H. (2001). The Child PTSD Symptom Scale: A preliminary examination of its psychometric properties. *Journal of Clinical Child Psychology, 30*, 376–384.

Friedman, M. J. (2016). PTSD history and overview. Retrieved from https://www.ptsd.va.gov/professional/ptsd-overview/ptsd-overview.asp

Fritsch, T., McClendon, M. J., Smyth, K. A., Lerner, A. J., Friedland, R. P., & Larsen, J. D. (2007). Cognitive functioning in healthy aging: The role of reserve and lifestyle factors early in life. *The Gerontologist, 47*(3), 307–322.

Giaconia, R. M., Reinherz, H. Z., Silverman, A. B., Pakiz, B., Frost, A. K., & Cohen, E. (1995). Traumas and posttraumatic stress disorder in a community population of older adolescents. *Journal of the American Academy of Child and Adolescent Psychiatry, 34*, 1369–1380.

Hebert, M., Langevin, R., & Daigneault, I. (2016). The association between peer victimization, PTSD, and dissociation in child victims of sexual abuse. *Journal of Affective Disorders, 193*, 227–232. doi:10.1016/j.jad.2015.12.080

The Joint Commission on Accreditation of Healthcare Organizations. (2011). The Joint Commission. Retrieved from http://www.jointcommission.org

Kessler, R. C., Berglund, P. A., Demler, O., Jin, R., Merikangas, K. R., & Walters, E. E. (2005). Lifetime prevalence and age-of-onset distributions of DSM-IV disorders in the National Comorbidity Survey Replication. *Archives of General Psychiatry, 62*, 593–602.

Khamis, V. (2015). Coping with war trauma and psychological distress among school-age Palestinian children. *American Journal of Orthopsychiatry, 85*(1), 72–79.

Kimhi, S., Hantman, S., Goroshit, M., Eshel, Y., & Zysberg, L. (2011). Elderly people coping with the aftermath of war: Resilience versus vulnerability. *American Journal of Geriatric Psychiatry, 20*(5), 391–401.

Kozyrskyj, A. L., Black, C., Chateau, D., & Steinbach, C. (2004). Discharge outcomes in seniors hospitalized for more than 30 days. *Canadian Journal on Aging, 24*(Suppl. 1), 107–119.

Lubit, R. H., & Pataki, C. (2016). Posttraumatic stress disorder in children. Retrieved from http://emedicine.medscape.com/article/918844-overview

McFarlane, A. C. (1987). Posttraumatic phenomena in a longitudinal study of children following a natural disaster. *Journal of the American Academy of Child and Adolescent Psychiatry, 26*, 764–769.

Montoliu, L., & Crawford, T. (2002). Prescribing practices of general practitioners for children with mental health problems. *Child and Adolescent Mental Health, 7*(3), 128–130.

Morgan, L., Scourfield, J., Williams, D., Jasper, A., & Lewis, G. (2003). The Aberfan disaster: 33-year follow-up of survivors. *British Journal of Psychiatry, 182*, 532–536.

National Child Traumatic Stress Network. (2003). Effective treatments for youth trauma. Retrieved from http://www.nctsn.org/sites/default/files/assets/pdfs/effective_treatments_youth_trauma.pdf

National Institute for Health and Care Excellence. (2005). Post-traumatic stress disorder: The management of PTSD in adults and children in primary and secondary care. Retrieved from https://www.nice.org.uk/guidance/cg26/evidence/full-guideline-including-appendices-113-pdf-193442221

National Institute of Mental Health. (2015). Post-traumatic stress disorder. Retrieved from https://www.nimh.nih.gov/health/publications/post-traumatic-stress-disorder-basics/index.shtml

Norris, F. H. (1992). Epidemiology of trauma: Frequency and impact of different potentially traumatic events on different demographic groups. *Journal of Consulting and Clinical Psychology, 60*, 409–418.

Ogle, C. M., Rubin, D. C., & Siegler, I. C. (2013). The impact of the development timing of trauma exposure on PTSD symptoms and psychosocial functioning among older adults. *Developmental Psychology, 49*(11), 2191–2200.

Penick, J. M., & Fallshore, M. (2005). Purpose and meaning in highly active seniors. Retrieved from http://www.highbeam.com/doc/1G1-132850508.html

Ramchandani, P., & Jones, D. P. (2003). Treating psychological symptoms in sexually abused children: From research findings to service provision. *British Journal of Psychiatry, 183*, 484–490.

Richardson, L., Frueh, C., & Acierno, R. (2010). Prevalence estimates of combat-related post-traumatic stress disorder: Critical review. *Australian and New Zealand Journal of Psychiatry, 44*, 4–19.

Sayers, S. L., Hanrahan, N., Kutney, A., Clarke, S. P., Reis, B. F., & Riegel, B. (2007). Psychiatric comorbidity and greater hospitalization risk, longer length of stay and higher hospitalization costs in older adults with heart failure. *Journal of the American Geriatrics Society, 55*, 1585–1591.

Scheeringa, M. S. (2006). Posttraumatic stress disorder: Clinical guidelines and research findings. In J. L. Luby (Ed.), *Handbook of preschool mental health: Development, disorders, and treatment* (pp. 165–185). New York, NY: Guilford Press.

Scheeringa, M. S., Weems, C. F., Cohen, J. A., Amaya-Jackson, L., & Guthrie, D. (2011). Trauma-focused cognitive-behavioral therapy for posttraumatic stress disorder in three through six year-old children: A randomized clinical trial. *Journal of Child Psychology and Psychiatry, 52*(8), 853–860.

Shah, D. C., Evans, M., & King, D. (2000). Prevalence of mental illness in a rehabilitation unit for older patients. *Postgraduate Medical Journal, 76*, 153–156.

Shrira, A., Palgi, Y., Ben-Ezra, M., & Shmotkin, D. (2011). Transgenerational effects of trauma in midlife: Evidence for resilience and vulnerability in offspring of Holocaust survivors. *Psychological Trauma, 4*, 394–402.

Smith, P., Perrin, S., Yule, W., & Rabe-Hesketh, S. (2001). War exposure and maternal reactions in the psychological adjustment of children from Bosnia-Hercegovina. *Journal of Child Psychology and Psychiatry, 42*, 395–404.

Souery, D., Zaninotto, L., Calati, R., Linotte, S., Mendlewicz, J., Sentissi, O., & Serretti, A. (2011). Depression across mood disorders: Review and analysis in a clinical sample. *Comprehensive Psychiatry, 15.*

Sternberg, S. A., Wolfson, C., & Baumgarten, M. (2000). Undetected dementia in community-dwelling older people: The Canadian study of health and aging. *Journal of the American Geriatric Society, 48*(11), 1430–1434.

World Health Organization and United Nations High Commissioner for Refugees. (2013). Assessment and management of conditions specifically related to stress: mhGAP intervention guide module (version 1.0). Retrieved from http://apps.who.int/iris/bitstream/10665/85623/1/9789241505932_eng.pdf

Wrigley, S., Jackson, H., Judd, F., & Komiti, A. (2005). Role of stigma and attitudes toward help-seeking from a general practitioner for mental health problems in a rural town. *Australian and New Zealand Journal of Psychiatry, 39*(6), 514–521.

Yule, W., Bolton, D., Udwin, O., Boyle, S., O'Ryan, D., & Nurrish, J. (2000). The long-term psychological effects of a disaster experienced in adolescence. I: The incidence and course of PTSD. *Journal of Child Psychology and Psychiatry, 41,* 503–511

14

Future Trends and Directions for Treating PTSD

The world remains a continuously evolving and complex place. And it will remain as such long after current generations are gone. The advent of technology puts a lot of the world's horrors and devastation right on our doorstep. Hence, even though a traumatic event is not localized within our own communities or states, we still bear witness to a great deal of it through many social media forums and the Internet highway. Given such connections we have with all other parts of the world, it is not unexpected that we would then be impacted by such events. Some noticeable trends and/or occurrences that are happening in the present are often fearful events that leave many of us with a great deal of uncertainty about the possibilities of what the human species is capable of doing to each other. Some of these trending concerns include global terror, the rising crime rates, human trafficking, government politics, as well as the changing climate that can begin to threaten our very existence.

In this chapter, you will learn:

- How significant events throughout the world can bring traumatic effects into the homes of individuals located far from the event

(continued)

- How human beings are becoming the cause of the demise of their own existence
- The issues of concern in society that promote a sense of feeling insecure, distrustful, and fearful

THE CONTINUANCE OF WAR/GLOBAL TERROR

Global Terror

The onslaught of terrorism has played a role in bringing fear, anxiety, and trauma to many in all corners of the world. As groups such as Al-Qaeda, Islamic State of Iraq and Syria (ISIS), and Boko Haram upload their videos into our immediate high-traffic information highway via the Internet and showcase their fatalistic achievements, millions around the world look on in worry and fear over what is possible at the hands of humanity and how humans endeavor to destroy each other. In what Baker (2014) calls the Global War on Terror, conflicts of Middle Eastern nations create "polytrauma" victims or victims of explosions incurring a complexity of trauma wounds, physical and mental.

What makes many of the acts of terrorism even more horrifying of an event is that many of the actions of terrorists are supposedly in the name of religion, or what many perceive as a spiritual, gentle, faithful, and holy event and/or worship that provides guidance throughout life. Baker (2014) states that the September 11, 2001, events in the United States, an orchestrated act of terrorism, has traumatically scarred both workers and citizens alike in both hidden and obvious ways. Resulting mental health comorbidities later become manifested through suicide, depression, family violence, disruptive behaviors, and even homelessness.

Through social media and technology, which literally connect one side of the world to the other, global terror continues to surround people, populations, and countries and infiltrates our homes. From the conflict in the Middle East, to the constant public reminders of North Korean's warfare capabilities, and to the despicable crimes of ISIS rebels and extremist groups such as Boko Haram and Al-Qaeda, all have instilled fear and threat into many a home and society. As beheadings, beatings, killings, and other atrocities of war and violence get live streamed through public arenas, the threat becomes very real for many of us. Unfortunately, many of the casualties of this terror often go unnoticed and are creating a looming public health crisis plagued by traumatic brain injuries, polytrauma blast victims, stress disorders, and suicides (Baker, 2014), setting the stage for what can finally become a posttraumatic stress disorder (PTSD).

The ongoing struggles and challenges of the growing drug warfare and the development of synthetic opiate drugs of the underworld fueled by various mafia and biker gangs have also wreaked havoc in the minds and lives of individuals in every corner of the world. These societal realities have exponentially increased crime, and again fear in many, as individuals illegally seek any resources possible to maintain their addiction.

It is important to be cognizant of the fact that intentional acts of interpersonal violence, in particular sexual assault, and combat are more likely to lead to PTSD than accidents or disasters (Creamer & Parslow, 2008; Kessler, Sonnega, Bromet, Hughes, & Nelson, 1995). Hence, this would include individuals subjected to such criminal acts as we have described here as they relate to terror (Ozer, Best, Lipsey, & Weiss, 2003).

Fast Facts

The worldwide events of violence and natural disasters can provoke a great deal of stress in individuals, which could possibly precipitate a crisis event and/or compromise mental health.

THE RISE IN CRIME

The onslaught of illicit drug development, the economic recession roller-coaster that many countries find themselves in, and the replacement of workers with technology that strains household finances even more, all have contributed to the rise in crime in today's world. The desperation of individuals to survive economic hardship and to feed their addiction with more and increasingly potent drugs becomes even more prominent in the world of crime. However, let us first clarify that committing of crime is not a PTSD symptom.

Although anyone can be at risk of developing PTSD, there is a compelling association between PTSD in war veterans and the committing of crimes (Hafemeister & Stockey, 2010; Orth & Wieland, 2006). Because of this observed association, Judge Robert Russell established the first Veterans Treatment Court to address this problem. These courts are based on the "drug treatment courts" and follow an agenda of addressing the problems that led to the criminal behavior. After the success of Judge Russell's court, other jurisdictions followed suit. Although many states now have veterans courts, many do not (Smith, 2014), so ongoing efforts to establish them nationwide would be advisable. However, for the purposes of this book, we are looking at crime as a cause for imposing fear in individuals, not as a result of PTSD.

Sadly, crime affects everyone. No one in today's society is exempt from being affected by crime. Victimization, or the event of being subjected to trauma/crime, is a stressful event resulting in significant levels of psychological and/or emotional stress (Hanson, Sawyer, Begel, & Hubel, 2010; The National Center for Victims of Crime, n.d.). The sad reality continues when we see that others visibly disrespect each other and feel that we have a right to take someone's property. What happens is that we become afraid of society, our community, and even our neighbors in some regard. We are afraid to go for that walk or that jog by ourselves, and we avoid certain areas of town and particular social venues—we literally become paralyzed by fear of "what if."

When a loved one or family member is taken from us as a result of crime, the psychological impact is particularly devastating. We can begin to manifest many of the symptomatology of PTSD. Our sense of security and safety is shattered and we feel invaded, angry, and hurt, not to mention vulnerable and helpless. However, another tragic psychological impact of crime and violence that can occur is becoming desensitized; we begin to view and accept crime as normal, as our way of life. But as a society, we need to guard against the tragedy of desensitization and make sure that crime and violence do not become a characteristic of our culture.

As ongoing research continues, the evidence becomes magnified for how crime impacts people, families, and communities. As found by Dustmann and Fasani (2012), crime causes considerable mental distress in residents, and interestingly these effects are mainly driven by property crime. So, the threat to one's worldly possessions becomes the main trigger. Becker and Rubinstein (2011) suggest that major criminal acts such as terrorist attacks inflict greater degrees of harm because they create fear and changes in people's behaviors and the lifestyle choice they then proceed to make.

HUMAN TRAFFICKING

At present, society is beginning to witness a worrying trend. This trend is the practice or trade of human trafficking and has now become the third largest criminal activity in the world. In accordance with the Federal Bureau of Investigation (FBI, 2017), "human trafficking is a form of human slavery which must be addressed at the interagency level. Human trafficking includes forced labor, domestic servitude, and commercial sex trafficking. It involves both U.S. citizens and foreigners alike, and has no demographic restrictions."

For those subjected to human trafficking and/or the involved families, the consequences are horrific. Hossain, Zimmerman, Abas, Light, and Watts (2010) investigated females who were trafficked. Consistent with what occurs with PTSD, females who were trafficked showed greater levels of mental disorders and PTSD, but this depended on specific variables. These variables included injuries and sexual violence during trafficking, the amount of time spent in trafficking, and very recent events of trafficking. Furthermore, Tsutsumi, Izutsu, Poudyal, Kato, and Marui (2008) add that not only is PTSD a concern, but other forms of mental illness such as anxiety and depression are also apparent in the population under study.

Fortunately, there is a victim-centered approach used by the FBI. It has a gentler, individualized focus, which means that ensuring the needs of the victims takes precedence over all other considerations. As such, "the FBI is committed to ensuring that victims receive the rights they are entitled to and the assistance they need to cope with crime. Treating victims with respect and providing them with assistance benefits victims and helps to build better cases" (FBI, 2017). The Department of Health Policy Research Programme (2015) in its report adds that "the complex needs of this vulnerable group—many of whom will be far from home, cut off from their families and disadvantaged in their access to education, social activities and physical healthcare—must be taken into consideration when assessing patient risk and planning therapeutic interventions."

GOVERNMENT POLITICS

Governments in many countries around the world hold a great deal of power and control over the people whom they govern. Overall, 68% of countries worldwide are said to have a "serious corruption problem." From the well-known corruption of Russia (Krastav, 2016) to the most corrupt countries in the world, Somalia and North Korea (Chew, 2016), people are left to death, despair, and destitution.

We have learned this repeatedly throughout history, from the times of Hitler and the Holocaust (Cowley & Parker, 1996), Stalin (History .com, 2017), to the Rwandan Genocide (Encyclopedia Britannica, 2017), and then on to perhaps the biggest mass murder in the world by Mao Zedong, leader/ruler of China (Somin, 2016). From 1958 to 1962, Mao's Great Leap Forward policy led to the deaths of up to 45 million people—all for the goal of trying to advance China past its competitors to be the best (Somin, 2016).

In the year 2017, many countries still face turmoil, upset, and discontent. For example, the United States has elected a new President, Donald Trump. A man not experienced in the political arena and who, since being elected, has made some troubling decisions for many of the people of the United States. Without going into detail on some of the decisions, such as the travel ban that was quickly overturned by the courts (Townsend, Walters, & Otten, 2017), a discrete conversation with the leader of Taiwan that angered China (Philips, 2017), and isolated arguments with the Australian Prime Minister and Mexican President (Greenwood, 2017), many citizens of the United States feel insecure, uncertain, and unsure of what may come next or how things may impact them. Although more than 50% of Americans are found to be stressed by the current political environment, of which 57% felt it was a significant source of stress (Scanlon, 2017), for many, the biggest fear is that many of the involved foreign countries may seek retaliation against the United States for the decisions made by the president (Brinkhurst-Cuff, Chulov, & Dehghan, 2017).

A PARADIGM SHIFT IN CLIMATE AND NATURAL DISASTERS

The shift in the Earth's climate is gaining momentum. Furthermore, global climate is projected to continue to change over this century and beyond. With increased technology, the evidence is becoming even more transparent.

Climate change is already having a significant impact on ecosystems, economies, and communities. Rising average temperatures do not simply mean balmier winters. Some regions will experience more extreme heat, whereas others may cool slightly. Flooding, drought, and intense summer heat could result (Suzuki, 2014; U.S. Environmental Protection Agency [EPA], 2016), not to mention increased mortality in general (Kalkstein & Valimont, 1987). Given these changes and further projected changes that impact the life we live on Earth as humans, many are beginning to realize the consequences climate change can have on their livelihood, lifestyle, and survival, all of which can represent a significant source of stress and impact their mental health. For example, such changes can impact the food supply chain and result in malnutrition, the spread of infectious diseases, and compromised mental health for obvious reasons (Berniston, 2010). As a society, we have structured our day-to-day lives around historical and current climate conditions. We are accustomed to a normal range of conditions and may be sensitive to extremes that fall outside of this range (EPA, 2016). Furthermore, those in high-risk areas such as along the coast, in the interior subject to drought, in cities with increased pollution, and at sea level that can experience increased flooding and potential tsunamis, may be particularly worried (EPA, 2016). For the harvesters of the north, many Aboriginal groups are planning now to better prepare themselves. The Inuit of Newfoundland and Labrador, Canada, for example, are trying to better understand the importance of this topic. They have united together to begin a regional assessment of the impacts of climate change on mental health and well-being, and to look at potential mental health adaptation strategies and support services to explore and examine the connections among changes in snow, ice, weather, water, animals, and plants throughout the Nunatsiavut region and the mental and emotional health and well-being of its people (Willox, 2014).

CONCLUSION

The relationship between trauma and PTSD is a critical one for all health care clinicians to understand. As trauma comes in many forms and from many sources and knows no boundaries for age, gender, and location, the extent to which it becomes manifested in individuals varies, depending on many characteristics of the trauma itself, inclusive of duration, frequency, intensity, and whether it arose intentionally or naturally. Although an individual may respond differently to the stressors and has his or her own set of coping strategies and resilience factors to help him or her through such times of crisis, it is critically important for the health care clinician to remain cognizant of the symptomatology of PTSD and how to readily assess it, identify it, and begin to incorporate many levels of prevention so as to minimize its impact on the individual and to prevent its exacerbation into a full-blown PTSD diagnosis. Intervening to help an individual experiencing PTSD is no easy task and takes minute steps toward recovery, but it is a recovery that is deemed possible provided the treatment regime is tailored to the needs and symptomatology of the individual. Working with the affected individual and providing culturally sensitive, appropriate, and evidence-based care is key to success, so that the individual is able to maintain and live a fully functioning and happy life that is of great quality and that brings him or her much physical and mental meaning in all he or she does. Looking forward, society is still dealing with health care clinicians' additional challenges potentially related to PTSD, the continuance of war and conflict, climate change, the rise in crime from the development of powerful synthetically produced drugs, and the emergence of human trafficking.

Recognizing and understanding the critical factors involved in providing culturally sensitive care, the various coping mechanisms individuals may use to deal with stress and the specific differences to remain cognizant of when dealing with specialized populations such as children, seniors, and war veterans are important for all health care professionals to embrace. The provision of care to an individual with PTSD is challenging at best; however, given the various specialized populations groups, and the many other mitigating factors that can impact one's experience in PTSD, special attention is needed so that assessment, diagnosing, and interventions are appropriate and implemented in the timeliest manner possible so as to promote optimal outcome.

Fast Facts

The unimaginable happenings such as human trafficking, corrupt governments, and the paradigm shift in the earth's climate all exude potential sources of threat that create significant perceived stress.

References

Baker, M. S. (2014). Casualties of the global war on terror and their future impact on health care and society: A looming public health crisis. *Military Medicine, 179*(4), 348–355.

Becker, G., & Rubinstein, Y. (2011). *Fear and the response to terrorism: An economic analysis* (CEP Discussion Paper No. 1079). Retrieved from http://cep.lse.ac.uk/pubs/download/dp1079.pdf

Berniston, M. (2010). Climate change and its impacts: Growing stress factors for human societies. *International Review of the Red Cross, 92*(879), 1–12. doi:10.1017/S1816383110000342

Brinkhurst-Cuff, C., Chulov, M., & Dehghan, S. K. (2017, January 29). Muslim-majority countries show anger at Trump travel ban. *The Guardian.* Retrieved from https://www.theguardian.com/us-news/2017/jan/29/muslim-majority-countries-anger-at-trump-travel-ban

Chew, J. (2016). These are the most corrupt countries in the world. Retrieved from http://fortune.com/2016/01/27/transparency-corruption-index

Cowley, R., & Parker, G. (1996). Adolf Hitler. Retrieved from http://www.history.com/topics/world-war-ii/adolf-hitler

Creamer, M. C., & Parslow, R. A. (2008). Trauma exposure and posttraumatic stress disorder in the elderly: A community prevalence study. *American Journal of Geriatric Psychiatry, 16,* 853–856.

Department of Health Policy Research Programme. (2015). New research offers first clinical evidence on the mental health toll of human trafficking. Retrieved from https://www.eurekalert.org/pub_releases/2015-10/kcl-nro101615.php

Dustmann, C., & Fasani, F. (2012). The effect of local area crime on the mental health of residents. Retrieved from http://www.ucl.ac.uk/~uctpb21/Cpapers/Crime_and_Mental_Health%20EJ.PDF

Encyclopedia Britannica. (2017). Rwanda genocide of 1994. Retrieved from https://www.britannica.com/event/Rwanda-genocide-of-1994

Federal Bureau of Investigation. (2017). Human trafficking/involuntary servitude. Retrieved from https://www.fbi.gov/investigate/civil-rights/human-trafficking

Greenwood, M. (2017, February 1). Report: Trump lashes out at Australian PM on phone call. *The Hill.* Retrieved from http://thehill.com/homenews/administration/317480-trump-fields-tense-phone-call-with-australian-pm-report

Hafemeister, T. L., & Stockey, N. A. (2010). Last stand? The criminal responsibility of war veterans returning from Iraq and Afghanistan with posttraumatic stress disorder. *Indiana Law Journal, 85,* 87–141.

Hanson, R. F., Sawyer, G. K., Begle, A. M., & Hubel, G. S. (2010). The impact of crime victimization on quality of life. *Journal of Trauma and Stress, 23*(2), 189–197.

History.com. (2017). Joseph Stalin. Retrieved from http://www.history.com/topics/joseph-stalin

Hossain, M., Zimmerman, C., Abas, M., Light, M., & Watts, C. (2010). The relationship of trauma to mental disorders among trafficked and sexually exploited girls and women. *American Journal of Public Health, 100*(12), 2442–2449. doi:10.2105/AJPH.2009.173229

Kalkstein, L. S., & Valimont, K. M. (1987). Climate effects on human health. In *Potential effects of future climate changes on forests and vegetation, agriculture, water resources, and human health.* EPA Science and Advisory Committee Monograph no. 25389, 122–52. Washington, DC: U.S. Environmental Protection Agency.

Kessler, R. C., Sonnega, A., Bromet, E., Hughes, M., & Nelson, C. B. (1995). Posttraumatic stress disorder in the National Comorbidity Survey. *Archives of General Psychiatry, 52*(12), 1048–1060.

Krastav, I. (2016, May 15). Why Putin tolerates corruption. *The New York Times*. Retrieved from https://www.nytimes.com/2016/05/16/opinion/why-putin-tolerates-corruption.html?_r=0

Orth, U., & Wieland, E. (2006). Anger, hostility, and posttraumatic stress disorder in trauma-exposed adults: A meta-analysis. *Journal of Consulting and Clinical Psychology, 74*, 698–706. doi:10.1037/0022-006X.74.4.698

Ozer, E. J., Best, S. R., Lipsey, T. L. & Weiss, D. S. (2003) Predictors of posttraumatic stress disorder and symptoms in adults: A meta-analysis. *Psychological Bulletin, 129*, 52–73.

Philips, T. (2017). China warns Trump that Taiwan policy is "non-negotiable." *The Guardian*. Retrieved from https://www.theguardian.com/us-news/2017/jan/15/china-warns-trump-that-taiwan-policy-is-non-negotiable

Scanlon, K. (2017). Poll: Most Americans are stressed out by current political climate. Retrieved from http://www.apa.org/news/press/releases/2016/10/presidential-election-stress.aspx

Smith, B. A. (2014). Posttraumatic stress disorder (PTSD) in the criminal justice system. *The Military Psychologist*. Retrieved from http://www.apadivisions.org/division-19/publications/newsletters/military/2014/04/ptsd.aspx

Somin, I. (2016, August 3). Remembering the biggest mass murder in the history of the world. *The Washington Post*. Retrieved from https://www.washingtonpost.com/news/volokh-conspiracy/wp/2016/08/03/giving-historys-greatest-mass-murderer-his-due/?utm_term=.f7ad279ebda1

Suzuki, D. (2014). Climate change. Retrieved from http://www.davidsuzuki.org/issues/climate-change

The National Center for Victims of Crime. (n.d.). Mental health consequences of crime. Retrieved from http://sdcedsv.org/media/sdcedsvfactor360com/uploads/Articles/MentalHealthConsequences.pdf

Townsend, M., Walters, J., & Otten, C. (2017). Global fury as Donald Trump's ban on migrants takes effect. *The Guardian*. Retrieved from https://www.theguardian.com/us-news/2017/jan/29/global-fury-donal-trump-us-ban-immigration-muslim-countries

Tsutsumi, A., Izutsu, T., Poudyal, A. K., Kato, S., & Marui, E. (2008). Mental health of female survivors of human trafficking in Nepal. *Social Sciences Medicine, 66*(8), 1841–1847.

Unknown. (2014). How does climate change affect human health? Retrieved from https://bigpictureeducation.com/how-does-climate-change-affect-human-health

U.S. Environmental Protection Agency. (2016). Climate impacts on society. Retrieved from https://www.epa.gov/climate-impacts/climate-impacts-society

Willox, A. C. (2014, January 10). Mental health and adaptation to climate change. *CBC News*. Retrieved from http://www.cbc.ca/news/technology/climate-change-rattles-mental-health-of-inuit-in-labrador-1.2492180

Index

CPSIA information can be obtained
at www.ICGtesting.com
Printed in the USA
LVHW031827261118
598298LV00015B/161/P

9 780826 170088